The Cg Tutorial

The Cg Tutorial

The Definitive Guide to Programmable Real-Time Graphics

Randima Fernando

Mark J. Kilgard

✦✦Addison-Wesley

Boston • San Francisco • New York • Toronto • Montreal
London • Munich • Paris • Madrid
Capetown • Sydney • Tokyo • Singapore • Mexico City

The publisher offers discounts on this book when ordered in quantity for bulk purchases and special sales. For more information, please contact:

U.S. Corporate and Government Sales
(800) 382-3419
corpsales@pearsontechgroup.com

For sales outside of the U.S., please contact:

International Sales
(317) 581-3793
international@pearsontechgroup.com

Visit Addison-Wesley on the Web: www.awprofessional.com

Library of Congress Control Number: 2002117794

ISBN 0-321-19496-9
Text printed on recycled paper
1 2 3 4 5 6 7 8 9 10—CRS—0706050403
First printing, February 2003

For my parents and my sister
—P.R.F.

For Deirdre
—M.J.K.

Cg Language Concepts

Contents

Chapter 3
Parameters, Textures, and Expressions. 61

Chapter 4
Transformations 89

Chapter 5

Chapter 6
Animation 143

Chapter 7
Environment Mapping Techniques 169

Appendix C
The CgFX File Format 291

Appendix D
Cg Keywords 299

Appendix E
Cg Standard Library Functions 301

Figures and Plates

Figures

Plates

The 31 plates listed here can be found in the color insert bound into the center of the book.

Examples

Tables

Equations

Foreword

Real-time computer graphics hardware is undergoing a major transition, from supporting a few fixed algorithms to being fully programmable. At the same time, the performance of graphics processors (GPUs) is increasing at a rapid rate—even greater than that of CPUs—because GPUs can effectively exploit the enormous parallelism available in graphics computations. These improvements in GPU flexibility and performance are likely to continue in the future, and will allow developers to write increasingly sophisticated and diverse programs that execute on the GPU.

Until recently, most GPU programs were written in assembly language, but history has shown that developers make the most creative and effective use of programmable hardware when they have the opportunity to program in a high-level language. Our goal in designing Cg was to provide developers with the same flexibility and performance available in assembly language, but with the expressiveness and ease-of-use of a high-level language. The C language has demonstrated enormous success in achieving these goals on the CPU, and so we chose C's syntax and philosophy as the starting point for defining Cg. In particular, this choice gave us confidence that the Cg language would be able to implement any GPU program, rather than restricting developers to a predefined framework designed specifically for shading computations.

Cg also builds on ideas and lessons learned from earlier work in computer graphics. My personal interest in programmable graphics hardware was inspired by the PixelFlow project at the University of North Carolina and, in particular, by the shading language compiler that Marc Olano and others built for PixelFlow. In many respects, the most direct predecessor to Cg was the real-time programmable shading system that Kekoa Proudfoot, Pat Hanrahan, I, and others built at Stanford for single-chip GPUs. The knowledge that we acquired from building the Stanford system was crucial to the design of Cg. Offline movie rendering has relied on programmable shading for much longer. The RenderMan language designed by Pat Hanrahan at Pixar served as a major source of inspiration for Cg, particularly in the choice of Cg's built-in functions.

The desire to create one GPU programming language that would be widely supported for both the OpenGL and Direct3D APIs led us to collaborate with Microsoft on the design of Cg. Microsoft's implementation of the language is called HLSL, and it is shipped as part of DirectX 9. At Microsoft, Craig Peeper and Loren McQuade were particularly influential in the design of the language. The examples in this book work equally well with HLSL and Cg.

Designing and implementing Cg in less than a year was possible only because we had a large and highly talented team of people working together. Two individuals made particularly unique contributions. Steve Glanville's extensive compiler and language expertise was crucial to the Cg design effort, and he implemented most of the front end of the first version of the Cg compiler. Kurt Akeley's experience as a system designer was invaluable throughout the project.

In this book, Randy and Mark have assembled a series of Cg tutorials that introduce Cg while simultaneously describing many of the real-time shading techniques supported by modern GPUs. By integrating these two sets of concepts within one collection of tutorials, this book enables you to experience the fun of writing and experimenting with your own GPU programs. Enjoy the journey!

Bill Mark
Cg Language Lead Designer
Assistant Professor
The University of Texas at Austin

Preface

Once upon a time, real-time computer graphics was all about vertices, triangles, and pixels. In fact, it still is. However, the level at which a programmer controls the processing and appearance of these graphics primitives has advanced considerably. Until a few years ago, programmers had to rely on the CPU to process all the transformation and rasterization algorithms needed to produce computer-generated images. Over time, hardware engineers executed these algorithms via specialized, high-performance 3D graphics hardware. Rather than implement the algorithms directly, programmers learned to access the hardware-provided graphics functionality through standard 3D programming interfaces, such as OpenGL (developed by Silicon Graphics [SGI]) and Direct3D (developed by Microsoft). At first, such costly 3D graphics hardware appeared only in high-priced UNIX workstations and flight simulators. Now, through the miracle of Moore's Law, the benefits of graphics hardware acceleration have been bestowed on low-cost PCs and game consoles.

Although the performance gained by employing dedicated graphics hardware to execute the brute-force tasks of transforming vertices, rasterizing triangles, and updating pixels far exceeded the performance possible just with CPU programming, real-time 3D programmers gave up a considerable measure of control in exchange for this speed. Developers were limited to using a fixed-function palette of graphics operations that the hardware could handle. Sometimes a skilled and dedicated programmer could coax the graphics programming interface and hardware to accomplish something beyond the ordinary, but this was usually hard, time-consuming work.

While graphics hardware engineers were advancing the real-time performance of their specialized pixel-pushing hardware, off-line computer graphics software packages such as Pixar's PhotoRealistic RenderMan were changing the look of movies and television with amazing computer-generated special effects. The pre-recorded nature of movies and most television content makes these media well suited for offline rendering. Computer-generated images for film and video are not rendered in real time but instead carefully constructed frame by frame in hours, days, or weeks using standard general-purpose CPUs. The advantage of using general-purpose CPUs is that rather than settle for hard-wired hardware algorithms, programmers and artists can use the CPU to create any effect they might imagine. What these so-called offline rendering systems lack in relative speed, they make up in rendering quality and realism.

The flexibility and generality of offline rendering systems are the key features that have been missing from preceding generations of 3D graphics hardware. In other words, what was lost was programmability.

Realizing this limitation, computer graphics architects have designed a new generation of graphics hardware that permits an unprecedented degree of programmability. Now, many of the programmable shading techniques that are employed so successfully in offline rendering can enter the realm of real-time graphics.

Developers of offline rendering systems created a type of specialized computer language known as a *shading language* to express the graphics operations required to make surfaces look the way artists intend. A shading language for programmable graphics hardware provides the same sort of functionality but in the context of real-time graphics hardware. Graphics programmers and artists benefit from such a high-level programming language in much the same way that conventional programmers do from C++ or Java. Using a high-level language for graphics hardware automates the process of translating the programmer's intent into a form that the graphics hardware can execute.

This book is about Cg, the premier language for programmable graphics hardware. NVIDIA developed Cg in close collaboration with Microsoft. Cg is the most portable and productive way for you to unleash the power within programmable graphics hardware. This book is a tutorial to teach you how to write Cg programs.

Our Intended Audience

We tried to write this book in a way that makes it valuable to both novices and advanced readers. If you're new to the world of programmable graphics, this book should give you a firm foundation on which to build. If you encounter a word or concept that is foreign to you and not sufficiently explained, consult the "Further Reading" section at the end of each chapter.

The main audience for this book is 3D game and application programmers, managers of such projects, real-time 3D artists, and computer graphics students—or anyone else interested in learning about the state of the art in real-time rendering. You do not have to be an experienced programmer to learn Cg from this book, though you should be relatively familiar with programming language concepts. If you are familiar with C or one of its derivatives, such as C++ or Java, Cg will be very approachable. Cg programs are relatively short, often less than a page, so even an artist or novice programmer can get the gist of Cg from this tutorial and learn to write interesting Cg programs.

Computer graphics programming involves math. Understanding basic algebra and trigonometry will help you appreciate several sections. You should also be familiar with the math behind basic computer graphics vertex transformation and lighting models. You do not need to know OpenGL or Direct3D, but familiarity with either programming interface is very helpful. All of the Cg examples described work with either OpenGL or Direct3D unless otherwise noted. Some examples that require advanced Cg functionality may not work on older graphics processors.

The Book's Structure

Chapter 1 introduces Cg. Each chapter that follows is a short tutorial that presents specific Cg concepts and techniques. The tutorials build upon each other, so we recommend reading the chapters in order.

- Chapter 1 lays out the foundations of Cg and real-time programmable graphics hardware.
- Chapter 2 presents the simplest Cg programs.
- Chapter 3 explains parameters, textures, and expressions.
- Chapter 4 shows how to transform vertices.
- Chapter 5 covers the implementation of lighting models with Cg.
- Chapter 6 describes how to animate and morph models with Cg vertex programs.
- Chapter 7 explains environment mapping with Cg.
- Chapter 8 shows how to implement bump mapping.
- Chapter 9 discusses a number of advanced topics: fog, cartoon shading, projected spotlights, shadow mapping, and compositing.
- Chapter 10 explains the set of currently available Cg vertex and fragment profiles, and provides advice for improving the performance of Cg programs.

This book gets you started but does not contain everything you will eventually want to know about Cg. This tutorial complements other documentation (such as the *Cg Toolkit User's Manual: A Developer's Guide to Programmable Graphics*) included with the Cg Toolkit. Please consult the user's manual and other Cg documentation for further information.

Formatting Conventions

Various elements in this book are specially formatted for easier reading. Code samples are written in the Courier font on a light reverse highlight. Variables and keywords are in **bold Courier** in the text, and key concepts are *italicized*.

In addition, we use icons to identify special topics, as shown here.

 Advanced Topic. Provides extra insight for advanced readers but can be safely glossed over without loss of continuity.

 Caution. Indicates a subtlety or concept to be wary of when writing Cg code, to avoid errors.

 CineFX. Describes algorithms or features that are available only on the NVIDIA CineFX architecture, or on architectures with similar advanced capabilities.

 Coding Tip. Gives guidelines about good coding practices.

 Performance Tip. Points out ways to use Cg to achieve optimal GPU performance.

Trying the Examples

We've designed the accompanying software framework so that you can get straight to work, even if you don't know anything about OpenGL, Direct3D, C, or C++. Our goal is to isolate the Cg language and allow you to experiment freely with it. Of course, as you move toward starting a real-world application with Cg, your project will probably require some combination of OpenGL, Direct3D, C, and C++.

The accompanying software framework allows you to try out the various Cg examples in the book without worrying about graphics APIs, C, or C++ code. The latest versions of the applications are free to download via the book's companion Web site. The software on the accompanying CD works only on the Windows platform, but versions for Linux and Macintosh systems are available online. Appendix A explains how to download the latest versions of Cg and the accompanying tutorial application.

The tutorial application makes it easy for you to tweak the book's examples, to see how changing a particular Cg example can immediately affect the rendered 3D result. If you can, have a computer that supports Cg nearby to try out the examples. With our software, you just write Cg programs without worrying about the particulars, such as loading 3D models and textures. When you want to know all the gory details, examine the source code, all of which is freely available for download, so you can see how Cg interfaces with C++ and OpenGL or Direct3D. The Cg Toolkit also comes with several simple examples that you can learn from.

The end of each chapter includes suggested exercises that you can work on to explore Cg further.

Acknowledgments

We would like to thank our many colleagues at NVIDIA who contributed to Cg and helped us with this book. Bill Mark, Steve Glanville, Mark Kilgard, and Kurt Akeley worked to define the original Cg language in 2001 and 2002. David Kirk, Jensen Huang, Dwight Diercks, Matt Papakipos, and Nick Triantos recognized the need for a high-level language for graphics processors and provided the resources necessary to make Cg a priority and a reality in just over a year's time. Geoff Berry, Michael Bunnell, Chris Dodd, Cass Everitt, Wes Hunt, Craig Kolb, Jayant Kolhe, Rev Lebaredian, Nathan Paymer, Matt Pharr, Doug Rogers, and Chris Wynn developed the Cg compiler, Standard Library, and runtime technology. Sim Dietrich, Ashu Rege, and Sébastien Dominé worked on the original CgFX technology. Chris Seitz gave us a great deal of support in all aspects of the project, helping out in ways that are too numerous to list, but without which this book would not exist. John Spitzer provided the clear foresight, as well as the essential resources, for Cg's development, and gave us the backing from his team to make this book possible. Sanford Russell's contagious motivation helped to get this book started. Cyril Zeller created the handy tutorial framework that accompanies this book and contributed the material for Appendix B. Sim Dietrich shared his knowledge of CgFX in Appendix C. Kevin Bjorke lent his insight by writing the compositing section of the advanced chapter. Teresa Saffaie, Catherine Kilkenny, and Debra Valentine reviewed our writing in an effort to make it clear. Caroline Lie, Spender Yuen, Dana Chan, Huey Nguyen, and Steve Burke lent their creativity and imagination to design and beautify the book's cover, figures, and artwork. NVIDIA's demo team (Curtis Beeson, Dan Burke, Joe Demers, Eugene d'Eon, Steve Giesler, Simon Green, Daniel Hornick, Gary King, Dean

Lupini, Hubert Nguyen, Bonnie O'Clair, Alexei Sakhartchouk, and Thant Tessman, under the direction of Mark Daly) contributed several of the color plates.

We are also grateful to Jason Allen, Geoff Berry, Michael Bunnell, Sim Dietrich, Chris Dodd, Gihani Fernando, Simon Green, Larry Gritz, Eric Haines, Wes Hunt, Gary King, Craig Kolb, Jayant Kolhe, Eric Lengyel, Cameron Lewis, Gilliard Lopes, Viet-Tam Luu, Kurt Miller, Tomas Akenine-Möller, Russell Pflughaupt, Matt Pharr, John Spitzer, Nick Triantos, Eric Werness, Matthias Wloka, Cyril Zeller, and our anonymous reviewers for their invaluable comments in the review process. Each set of comments helped to make the book clearer and more accurate.

Microsoft and NVIDIA collaborated to agree on the syntax and semantics of a standard hardware shading language. The DirectX 9 High-Level Shading Language and Cg are the same language because of this effort. We particularly appreciate the work of Craig Peeper, Loren McQuade, Dave Aronson, Anuj Gosalia, Chas Boyd, and Mike Toelle.

We acknowledge the pioneering research on hardware shading languages conducted at the University of North Carolina and Stanford University. Obviously, Pixar's Render-Man Shading Language provided a great deal of inspiration for NVIDIA's efforts to develop a real-time language for mass-market graphics hardware. Ken Perlin's work on the Pixel Stream Editor, not to mention his early Cg compiler testing, deserves recognition as well.

On the hardware front, we acknowledge the fundamental work of Erik Lindholm and Henry Moreton, who architected the user-programmable vertex processing engine inside NVIDIA's GeForce3 GPU. OpenGL's and Direct3D's support for general programmable vertex processing, and hence Cg's support for the same, are indebted to this work.

The hard work and dedication of NVIDIA's architecture, hardware, and software engineers to deliver ever faster and ever more programmable graphics processors was and still is the overriding justification for Cg. We acknowledge the efforts of all the engineers at NVIDIA who strive to make real-time programmable shading a reality for everyone.

We thank the Addison-Wesley production team for making this book a reality. We particularly thank Chris Keane for manhandling our manuscript into shape.

Finally, we thank the thousands of Cg developers for their feedback, bug reports, patience, and enthusiasm.

The Cg Tutorial

Chapter 1

Introduction

This chapter has the following four sections:

- **"What Is Cg?"** introduces the Cg programming language.
- **"Vertices, Fragments, and the Graphics Pipeline"** describes the data flow of modern graphics hardware and explains how Cg fits into this data flow.
- **"Cg's Historical Development"** provides some background on how Cg was developed.
- **"The Cg Environment"** explains how applications go about using Cg programs through the Cg runtime and existing 3D application programming interfaces (APIs).

1.1 What Is Cg?

This book teaches you how to use a programming language called Cg. The Cg language makes it possible for you to control the shape, appearance, and motion of objects drawn using programmable graphics hardware. It marries programmatic control of these attributes with the incredible speed and capabilities of today's graphics processors. Never before have computer graphics practitioners, whether artists or programmers, had so much control over the real-time images they generate.

Cg provides developers with a complete programming platform that is easy to use and enables the fast creation of special effects and real-time cinematic-quality experiences on multiple platforms. By providing a new level of abstraction, Cg removes the need for developers to program directly to the graphics hardware assembly language, and thereby more easily target OpenGL, DirectX, Windows, Linux, Macintosh OS X, and console platforms such as the Xbox. Cg was developed in close collaboration with Microsoft Corporation and is compatible with both the OpenGL API and Microsoft's High-Level Shading Language (HLSL) for DirectX 9.0.

Cg stands for "C for graphics." The C programming language is a popular, general-purpose language invented in the 1970s. Because of its popularity and clean design, C provided the basis for several subsequent programming languages. For example, C++ and Java base their syntax and structure largely on C. The Cg language bases itself on C as well. If you are familiar with C or one of the many languages derived from C, then Cg will be easy to learn.

On the other hand, if you are not familiar with C or even programming languages in general but you enjoy computer graphics and want to learn something new, read on anyway. Cg programs tend to be short and understandable.

Much of this chapter is background that provides valuable context for understanding Cg and using it effectively. On the other hand, you may find Cg is easier to learn by doing. Feel free to skip to Chapter 2 at any time if you feel more comfortable just diving into the tutorial.

1.1.1   A Language for Programming Graphics Hardware

Cg is different from C, C++, and Java because it is very specialized. No one will ever write a spreadsheet or word processor in Cg. Instead, Cg targets the ability to programmatically control the shape, appearance, and motion of objects rendered using graphics hardware. Broadly, this type of language is called a *shading language*. However, Cg can do more than just shading. For example, Cg programs can perform physical simulation, compositing, and other nonshading tasks.

Think of a Cg program as a detailed recipe for how to render an object by using programmable graphics hardware. For example, you can write a Cg program to make a surface appear bumpy or to animate a virtual character. Later, in Section 1.3, you will learn more about the history of shading languages and where Cg fits into this history.

1.1.2   Cg's Data-Flow Model

In addition to being specialized for graphics, Cg and other shading languages are different from conventional programming languages because they are based on a data-flow computational model. In such a model, computation occurs in response to data that flows through a sequence of processing steps.

Cg programs operate on vertices and fragments (think "pixels" for now if you do not know what a fragment is) that are processed when rendering an image. Think of a Cg program as a black box into which vertices or fragments flow on one side, are somehow transformed, and then flow out on the other side. However, the box is not really a black box because you get to determine, by means of the Cg programs you write, exactly what happens inside.

Every time a vertex is processed or the rasterizer generates a fragment while rendering a 3D scene, your corresponding vertex or fragment Cg program executes. Section 1.3 explains Cg's data-flow model further.

Most recent personal computers—and all recent game consoles—contain a graphics processing unit (GPU) that is dedicated to graphics tasks such as transforming and rasterizing 3D models. Your Cg programs actually execute within the GPU of your computer.

1.1.3 GPU Specialization and CPU Generalization

Whether or not a personal computer or game console has a GPU, there must be a CPU that runs the operating system and application programs. CPUs are, by design, general purpose. CPUs execute applications (for example, word processors and accounting packages) written in general-purpose languages, such as C++ or Java.

Because of the GPU's specialized design, it is much faster at graphics tasks, such as rendering 3D scenes, than a general-purpose CPU would be. New GPUs process tens of millions of vertices per second and rasterize hundreds of millions or even billions of fragments per second. Future GPUs will be even speedier. This is overwhelmingly faster than the rate at which a CPU could process a similar number of vertices and fragments. However, the GPU cannot execute the same arbitrary, general-purpose programs that a CPU can.

The specialized, high-performance nature of the GPU is why Cg exists. General-purpose programming languages are too open-ended for the specialized task of processing vertices and fragments. In contrast, the Cg language is fully dedicated to this task. Cg also provides an abstract execution model that matches the GPU's execution model. You will learn about the unique execution model of GPUs in Section 1.2.

1.1.4 The Performance Rationale for Cg

To sustain the illusion of interactivity, a 3D application needs to maintain an animation rate of 15 or more images per second. Generally, we consider 60 or more frames per second to be "real time," the rate at which interaction with applications appears to occur instantaneously. The computer's display may have a million or more pixels that require redrawing. For 3D scenes, the GPU typically processes every pixel on the screen many times to account for how objects occlude each other, or to improve the appearance of each pixel. This means that real-time 3D applications can require hundreds of millions of pixel updates per second. Along with the required pixel processing, 3D models are composed of vertices that must be transformed properly before they are assembled into polygons, lines, and points that will be rasterized into pixels. This can require transforming tens of millions of vertices per second.

Moreover, this graphical processing happens in addition to the considerable amount of effort required of the CPU to update the animation for each new image. The reality is that we need both the CPU and the GPU's specialized graphics-oriented capabilities. Both are required to render scenes at the interactive rates and quality standards that users of 3D applications and games demand. This means a developer can write a 3D application or game in C++ and then use Cg to make the most of the GPU's additional graphics horsepower.

1.1.5 Coexistence with Conventional Languages

In no way does Cg replace any existing general-purpose languages. Cg is an auxiliary language, designed specifically for GPUs. Programs written for the CPU in conventional languages such as C or C++ can use the Cg runtime (described in Section 1.4.2) to load Cg programs for GPUs to execute. The Cg runtime is a standard set of subroutines used to load, compile, manipulate, and configure Cg programs for execution by the GPU. Applications supply Cg programs to instruct GPUs on how to accomplish the programmable rendering effects that would not otherwise be possible on a CPU at the rendering rates a GPU is capable of achieving.

Cg enables a specialized style of parallel processing. While your CPU executes a conventional application, that application also orchestrates the parallel processing of vertices and fragments on the GPU, by programs written in Cg.

If a real-time shading language is such a good idea, why didn't someone invent Cg sooner? The answer has to do with the evolution of computer graphics hardware. Prior to 2001, most computer graphics hardware—certainly the kind of inexpensive graphics hardware in PCs and game consoles—was hard-wired to the specific tasks of vertex and fragment processing. By "hard-wired," we mean that the algorithms were fixed within the hardware, as opposed to being programmable in a way that is accessible to graphics applications. Even though these hard-wired graphics algorithms could be configured by graphics applications in a variety of ways, the applications could not reprogram the hardware to do tasks unanticipated by the designers of the hardware. Fortunately, this situation has changed.

Graphics hardware design has advanced, and vertex and fragment processing units in recent GPUs are truly programmable. Before the advent of programmable graphics hardware, there was no point in providing a programming language for it. Now that such hardware is available, there is a clear need to make it easier to program this hardware. Cg makes it much easier to program GPUs in the same manner that C made it much easier to program CPUs.

Before Cg existed, addressing the programmable capabilities of the GPU was possible only through low-level assembly language. The cryptic instruction syntax and manual hardware register manipulation required by assembly languages—such as DirectX 8 vertex and pixel shaders and some OpenGL extensions—made it a painful task for most developers. As GPU technology made longer and more complex assembly language programs possible, the need for a high-level language became clear. The extensive low-level programming that had been required to achieve optimal performance could now be delegated to a compiler, which optimizes the code output and handles tedious instruction scheduling. Figure 1-1 is a small portion of a complex assembly language fragment program used to represent skin. Clearly, it is hard to comprehend, particularly with the specific references to hardware registers.

In contrast, well-commented Cg code is more portable, more legible, easier to debug, and easier to reuse. Cg gives you the advantages of a high-level language such as C while delivering the performance of low-level assembly code.

1.1.6 Other Aspects of Cg

Cg is a language for programming "in the small." That makes it much simpler than a modern general-purpose language such as C++. Because Cg specializes in transforming vertices and fragments, it does not currently include many of the complex features required for massive software engineering tasks. Unlike C++ and Java, Cg does not support classes and other features used in object-oriented programming. Current Cg

5

5

```
. . .
DEFINE LUMINANCE = {0.299, 0.587, 0.114, 0.0};
TEX   H0, f[TEX0], TEX4, 2D;
TEX   H1, f[TEX2], TEX5, CUBE;
DP3X  H1.xyz, H1, LUMINANCE;
MULX  H0.w, H0.w, LUMINANCE.w;
MULX  H1.w, H1.x, H1.x;
MOVH  H2, f[TEX3].wxyz;
MULX  H1.w, H1.x, H1.w;
DP3X  H0.xyz, H2.xzyw, H0;
MULX  H0.xyz, H0, H1.w;
TEX   H1, f[TEX0], TEX1, 2D;
TEX   H3, f[TEX0], TEX3, 2D;
MULX  H0.xyz, H0, H3;
MADX  H1.w, H1.w, 0.5, 0.5;
MULX  H1.xyz, H1, {0.15, 0.15, 1.0, 0.0};
MOVX  H0.w, H1.w;
TEX   H1, H1, TEX7, CUBE;
TEX   H3, f[TEX3], TEX2, 1D;
MULX  H3.w, H0.w, H2.w;
MULX  H3.xyz, H3, H3.w;
. . .
```

Figure 1-1. A Snippet of Assembly Language Code

implementations do not provide pointers or even memory allocation (though future implementations may, and keywords are appropriately reserved). Cg has absolutely no support for file input/output operations. By and large, these restrictions are not permanent limitations in the language, but rather are indicative of the capabilities of today's highest performance GPUs. As technology advances to permit more general programmability on the GPU, you can expect Cg to grow appropriately. Because Cg is closely based on C, future updates to Cg are likely to adopt language features from C and C++.

Cg provides arrays and structures. It has all the flow-control constructs of a modern language: loops, conditionals, and function calls.

Cg natively supports vectors and matrices because these data types and related math operations are fundamental to graphics and most graphics hardware directly supports vector data types. Cg has a library of functions, called the Standard Library, that is well suited for the kind of operations required for graphics. For example, the Cg Standard Library includes a **reflect** function for computing reflection vectors.

Cg programs execute in relative isolation. This means that the processing of a particular vertex or fragment has no effect on other vertices or fragments processed at the same time. There are no side effects to the execution of a Cg program. This lack of interdependency among vertices and fragments makes Cg programs extremely well suited for hardware execution by highly pipelined and parallel hardware.

1.1.7 The Limited Execution Environment of Cg Programs

When you write a program in a language designed for modern CPUs using a modern operating system, you expect that a more-or-less arbitrary program, as long as it is correct, will compile and execute properly. This is because CPUs, by design, execute general-purpose programs for which the overall system has more than sufficient resources.

However, GPUs are specialized rather than general-purpose, and the feature set of GPUs is still evolving. Not everything you can write in Cg can be compiled to execute on a given GPU. Cg includes the concept of hardware "profiles," one of which you specify when you compile a Cg program. Each profile corresponds to a particular combination of GPU architecture and graphics API. Your program not only must be correct, but it also must limit itself to the restrictions imposed by the particular profile used to compile your Cg program. For example, a given fragment profile may limit you to no more than four texture accesses per fragment.

As GPUs evolve, additional profiles will be supported by Cg that correspond to more capable GPU architectures. In the future, profiles will be less important as GPUs become more full-featured. But for now Cg programmers will need to limit programs to ensure that they can compile and execute on existing GPUs. In general, future profiles will be supersets of current profiles, so that programs written for today's profiles will compile without change using future profiles.

This situation may sound limiting, but in practice the Cg programs shown in this book work on tens of millions of GPUs and produce compelling rendering effects. Another reason for limiting program size and scope is that the smaller and more efficient your Cg programs are, the faster they will run. Real-time graphics is often about balancing increased scene complexity, animation rates, and improved shading. So it's always good to maximize rendering efficiency through judicious Cg programming.

Keep in mind that the restrictions imposed by profiles are really limitations of current GPUs, not Cg. The Cg language is powerful enough to express shading techniques that are not yet possible with all GPUs. With time, GPU functionality will evolve far enough that Cg profiles will be able to run amazingly complex Cg programs. Cg is a language for both current and future GPUs.

1.2   Vertices, Fragments, and the Graphics Pipeline

To put Cg into its proper context, you need to understand how GPUs render images. This section explains how graphics hardware is evolving and then explores the modern graphics hardware-rendering pipeline.

1.2.1   The Evolution of Computer Graphics Hardware

Computer graphics hardware is advancing at incredible rates. Three forces are driving this rapid pace of innovation, as shown in Figure 1-2. First, the semiconductor industry has committed itself to doubling the number of transistors (the basic unit of computer hardware) that fit on a microchip every 18 months. This constant redoubling of

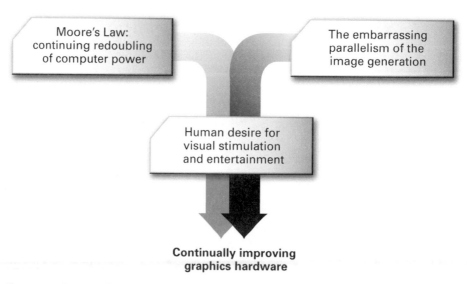

Figure 1-2. Forces Driving Graphics Hardware Innovation

computer power, historically known as Moore's Law, means cheaper and faster computer hardware, and is the norm for our age.

The second force is the vast amount of computation required to simulate the world around us. Our eyes consume and our brains comprehend images of our 3D world at an astounding rate and with startling acuity. We are unlikely ever to reach a point where computer graphics becomes a substitute for reality. Reality is just too real. Undaunted, computer graphics practitioners continue to rise to the challenge. Fortunately, generating images is an embarrassingly parallel problem. What we mean by "embarrassingly parallel" is that graphics hardware designers can repeatedly split up the problem of creating realistic images into more chunks of work that are smaller and easier to tackle. Then hardware engineers can arrange, in parallel, the ever-greater number of transistors available to execute all these various chunks of work.

Our third force is the sustained desire we all have to be stimulated and entertained visually. This is the force that "connects" the source of our continued redoubling of computer hardware resources to the task of approximating visual reality ever more realistically than before.

As Figure 1-2 illustrates, these insights let us confidently predict that computer graphics hardware is going to get much faster. These innovations whet our collective appetite for more interactive and compelling 3D experiences. Satisfying this demand is what motivated the development of the Cg language.

1.2.2 Four Generations of Computer Graphics Hardware

In the mid-1990s, the world's fastest graphics hardware consisted of multiple chips that worked together to render images and display them to a screen. The most complex computer graphics systems consisted of dozens of chips spread over several boards. As time progressed and semiconductor technology improved, hardware engineers incorporated the functionality of complicated multichip designs into a single graphics chip. This development resulted in tremendous economies of integration and scale.

You may be surprised to learn that the GPU now exceeds the CPU in the number of transistors present in each microchip. Transistor count is a rough measure of how much computer hardware is devoted to a microchip. For example, Intel packed its 2.4 GHz Pentium 4 with 55 million transistors; NVIDIA used over 125 million transistors in the original GeForce FX GPU.

NVIDIA introduced the term "GPU" in the late 1990s when the legacy term "VGA controller" was no longer an accurate description of the graphics hardware in a PC. IBM had introduced Video Graphics Array (VGA) hardware in 1987. At that time, the VGA controller was what we now call a "dumb" frame buffer. This meant that the CPU was responsible for updating all the pixels. Today the CPU rarely manipulates pixels directly. Instead, graphics hardware designers build the "smarts" of pixel updates into the GPU.

Industry observers have identified four generations of GPU evolution so far. Each generation delivers better performance and evolving programmability of the GPU feature set. Each generation also influences and incorporates the functionality of the two major 3D programming interfaces, OpenGL and DirectX. OpenGL is an open standard for 3D programming for Windows, Linux, UNIX, and Macintosh computers. DirectX is an evolving set of Microsoft multimedia programming interfaces, including Direct3D for 3D programming.

Pre-GPU Graphics Acceleration

Prior to the introduction of GPUs, companies such as Silicon Graphics (SGI) and Evans & Sutherland designed specialized and expensive graphics hardware. The graphics systems developed by these companies introduced many of the concepts, such as vertex transformation and texture mapping, that we take for granted today. These systems were very important to the historical development of computer graphics, but because they were so expensive, they did not achieve the mass-market success of single-chip GPUs designed for PCs and video game consoles. Today, GPUs are far more powerful and much cheaper than any prior systems.

First-Generation GPUs

The first generation of GPUs (up to 1998) includes NVIDIA's TNT2, ATI's Rage, and 3dfx's Voodoo3. These GPUs are capable of rasterizing pre-transformed triangles and applying one or two textures. They also implement the DirectX 6 feature set. When running most 3D and 2D applications, these GPUs completely relieve the CPU from updating individual pixels. However, GPUs in this generation suffer from two clear limitations. First, they lack the ability to transform vertices of 3D objects; instead, vertex transformations occur in the CPU. Second, they have a quite limited set of math operations for combining textures to compute the color of rasterized pixels.

Second-Generation GPUs

The second generation of GPUs (1999–2000) includes NVIDIA's GeForce 256 and GeForce2, ATI's Radeon 7500, and S3's Savage3D. These GPUs offload 3D vertex transformation and lighting (T&L) from the CPU. Fast vertex transformation was one of the key capabilities that differentiated high-end workstations from PCs prior to this generation. Both OpenGL and DirectX 7 support hardware vertex transformation. Although the set of math operations for combining textures and coloring pixels expanded in this generation to include cube map textures and signed math operations, the possibilities are still limited. Put another way, this generation is more configurable, but still not truly programmable.

Third-Generation GPUs

The third generation of GPUs (2001) includes NVIDIA's GeForce3 and GeForce4 Ti, Microsoft's Xbox, and ATI's Radeon 8500. This generation provides vertex programmability rather than merely offering more configurability. Instead of supporting the conventional transformation and lighting modes specified by OpenGL and DirectX 7, these GPUs let the application specify a sequence of instructions for processing vertices. Considerably more pixel-level configurability is available, but these modes are not powerful enough to be considered truly programmable. Because these GPUs support vertex programmability but lack true pixel programmability, this generation is transitional. DirectX 8 and the multivendor **ARB_vertex_program** OpenGL extension expose vertex-level programmability to applications. DirectX 8 pixel shaders and various vendor-specific OpenGL extensions expose this generation's fragment-level configurability.

Fourth-Generation GPUs

The fourth and current generation of GPUs (2002 and on) includes NVIDIA's GeForce FX family with the CineFX architecture and ATI's Radeon 9700. These GPUs provide both vertex-level and pixel-level programmability. This level of programmability opens up the possibility of offloading complex vertex transformation and pixel-shading operations from the CPU to the GPU. DirectX 9 and various OpenGL extensions expose the vertex-level and pixel-level programmability of these GPUs. This is the generation of GPUs where Cg gets really interesting. Table 1-1 lists selected NVIDIA GPUs representing these various GPU generations.

Table 1-1. Features and Performance Evolution of Selected NVIDIA GPUs, by Generation

Generation	Year	Product Name	Process	Transistors	Antialiasing Fill Rate	Polygon Rate	Note
First	Late 1998	RIVA TNT	0.25 μ	7 M	*50 M*	6 M	1
First	Early 1999	RIVA TNT2	0.22 μ	9 M	*75 M*	9 M	2
Second	Late 1999	GeForce 256	0.22 μ	23 M	*120 M*	15 M	3
Second	Early 2000	GeForce2	0.18 μ	25 M	*200 M*	25 M	4
Third	Early 2001	GeForce3	0.15 μ	57 M	800 M	30 M	5
Third	Early 2002	GeForce4 Ti	0.15 μ	63 M	1200 M	60 M	6
Fourth	Early 2003	GeForce FX	0.13 μ	125 M	2000 M	200 M	7

Notes
1. Dual texture DirectX 6
2. AGP 4×
3. Fixed-function vertex hardware, register combiners, cube maps, DirectX 7
4. Performance, double data-rate (DDR) memory
5. Vertex programs, quad-texturing, texture shaders, DirectX 8
6. Performance, antialiasing
7. Massive vertex and fragment programmability, floating-point pixels, DirectX 9, AGP 8×

The table uses the following terms:

- *Process*—the minimum feature size in microns (μ, millionths of a meter) for the semiconductor process used to fabricate each microchip

- *Transistors*—an approximate measure, in millions (M), of the chips' design and manufacturing complexity

- *Antialiasing fill rate*—a GPU's ability to fill pixels, measured in millions (M) of 32-bit RGBA pixels per second, assuming two-sample antialiasing; numbers in *italics* indicate fill rates that are de-rated because the hardware lacks true antialiased rendering

- *Polygon rate*—a GPU's ability to draw triangles, measured in millions (M) of triangles per second

The notes highlight the most significant improvements in each design. Performance rates may not be comparable with designs from other hardware vendors.

Future GPUs will further generalize the programmable aspects of current GPUs, and Cg will make this additional programmability easy to use.

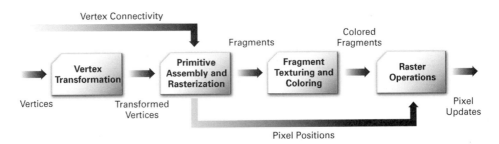

Figure 1-3. The Graphics Hardware Pipeline

1.2.3 The Graphics Hardware Pipeline

A *pipeline* is a sequence of stages operating in parallel and in a fixed order. Each stage receives its input from the prior stage and sends its output to the subsequent stage. Like an assembly line where dozens of automobiles are manufactured at the same time, with each automobile at a different stage of the line, a conventional graphics hardware pipeline processes a multitude of vertices, geometric primitives, and fragments in a pipelined fashion.

Figure 1-3 shows the graphics hardware pipeline used by today's GPUs. The 3D application sends the GPU a sequence of vertices batched into geometric primitives: typically polygons, lines, and points. As shown in Figure 1-4, there are many ways to specify geometric primitives.

Every vertex has a position but also usually has several other attributes such as a color, a secondary (or *specular*) color, one or multiple texture coordinate sets, and a normal vector. The normal vector indicates what direction the surface faces at the vertex, and is typically used in lighting calculations.

Vertex Transformation

Vertex transformation is the first processing stage in the graphics hardware pipeline. Vertex transformation performs a sequence of math operations on each vertex. These operations include transforming the vertex position into a screen position for use by the rasterizer, generating texture coordinates for texturing, and lighting the vertex to determine its color. We will explain many of these tasks in subsequent chapters.

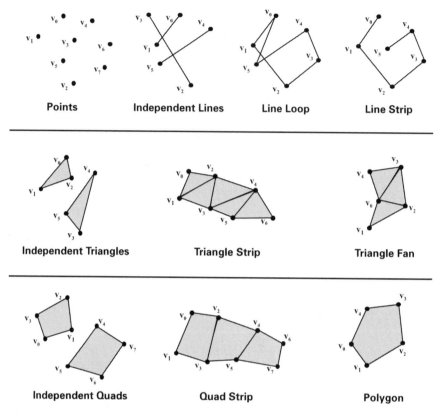

Figure 1-4. Types of Geometric Primitives

Primitive Assembly and Rasterization

The transformed vertices flow in sequence to the next stage, called *primitive assembly and rasterization*. First, the primitive assembly step assembles vertices into geometric primitives based on the geometric primitive batching information that accompanies the sequence of vertices. This results in a sequence of triangles, lines, or points. These primitives may require clipping to the *view frustum* (the view's visible region of 3D space), as well as any enabled application-specified clip planes. The rasterizer may also discard polygons based on whether they face forward or backward. This process is known as *culling*.

Polygons that survive these clipping and culling steps must be rasterized. Rasterization is the process of determining the set of pixels covered by a geometric primitive. Polygons, lines, and points are each rasterized according to the rules specified for each type of primitive. The results of rasterization are a set of pixel locations as well as a set of fragments. There is no relationship between the number of vertices a primitive has and the number of fragments that are generated when it is rasterized. For example, a triangle made up of just three vertices could take up the entire screen, and therefore generate millions of fragments!

Earlier, we told you to think of a fragment as a pixel if you did not know precisely what a fragment was. At this point, however, the distinction between a fragment and a pixel becomes important. The term *pixel* is short for "picture element." A pixel represents the contents of the frame buffer at a specific location, such as the color, depth, and any other values associated with that location. A *fragment* is the state required potentially to update a particular pixel.

The term "fragment" is used because rasterization breaks up each geometric primitive, such as a triangle, into pixel-sized fragments for each pixel that the primitive covers. A fragment has an associated pixel location, a depth value, and a set of interpolated parameters such as a color, a secondary (specular) color, and one or more texture coordinate sets. These various interpolated parameters are derived from the transformed vertices that make up the particular geometric primitive used to generate the fragments. You can think of a fragment as a "potential pixel." If a fragment passes the various rasterization tests (in the raster operations stage, which is described shortly), the fragment updates a pixel in the frame buffer.

Interpolation, Texturing, and Coloring

Once a primitive is rasterized into a collection of zero or more fragments, the *interpolation, texturing, and coloring* stage interpolates the fragment parameters as necessary, performs a sequence of texturing and math operations, and determines a final color for each fragment. In addition to determining the fragment's final color, this stage may also determine a new depth or may even discard the fragment to avoid updating the frame buffer's corresponding pixel. Allowing for the possibility that the stage may discard a fragment, this stage emits one or zero colored fragments for every input fragment it receives.

Raster Operations

The *raster operations* stage performs a final sequence of per-fragment operations immediately before updating the frame buffer. These operations are a standard part of OpenGL and Direct3D. During this stage, hidden surfaces are eliminated through a

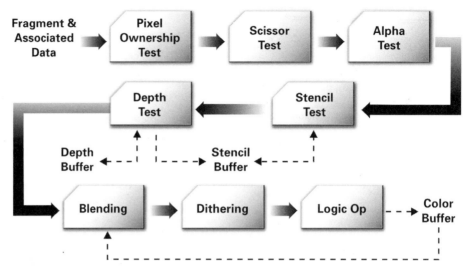

Figure 1-5. Standard OpenGL and Direct3D Raster Operations

process known as *depth testing*. Other effects, such as blending and stencil-based shadowing, also occur during this stage.

The raster operations stage checks each fragment based on a number of tests, including the scissor, alpha, stencil, and depth tests. These tests involve the fragment's final color or depth, the pixel location, and per-pixel values such as the depth value and stencil value of the pixel. If any test fails, this stage discards the fragment without updating the pixel's color value (though a stencil write operation may occur). Passing the depth test may replace the pixel's depth value with the fragment's depth. After the tests, a blending operation combines the final color of the fragment with the corresponding pixel's color value. Finally, a frame buffer write operation replaces the pixel's color with the blended color. Figure 1-5 shows this sequence of operations.

Figure 1-5 shows that the raster operations stage is actually itself a series of pipeline stages. In fact, all of the previously described stages can be broken down into substages as well.

Visualizing the Graphics Pipeline

Figure 1-6 depicts the stages of the graphics pipeline. In the figure, two triangles are rasterized. The process starts with the transformation and coloring of vertices. Next, the primitive assembly step creates triangles from the vertices, as the dotted lines indi-

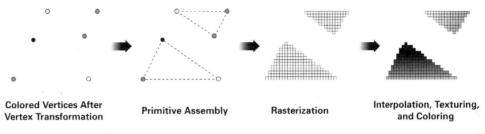

| Colored Vertices After Vertex Transformation | Primitive Assembly | Rasterization | Interpolation, Texturing, and Coloring |

Figure 1-6. Visualizing the Graphics Pipeline

cate. After this, the rasterizer "fills in" the triangles with fragments. Finally, the register values from the vertices are interpolated and used for texturing and coloring. Notice that many fragments are generated from just a few vertices.

1.2.4 The Programmable Graphics Pipeline

The dominant trend in graphics hardware design today is the effort to expose more programmability within the GPU. Figure 1-7 shows the vertex processing and fragment processing stages in the pipeline of a programmable GPU.

Figure 1-7 shows more detail than Figure 1-3, but more important, it shows the vertex and fragment processing broken out into programmable units. The *programmable*

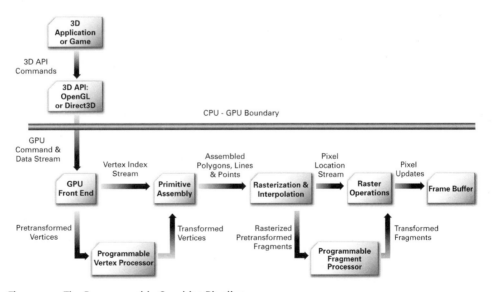

Figure 1-7. The Programmable Graphics Pipeline

vertex processor is the hardware unit that runs your Cg vertex programs, whereas the *programmable fragment processor* is the unit that runs your Cg fragment programs.

As explained in Section 1.2.2, GPU designs have evolved, and the vertex and fragment processors within the GPU have transitioned from being configurable to being programmable. The descriptions in the next two sections present the critical functional features of programmable vertex and fragment processors.

The Programmable Vertex Processor

Figure 1-8 shows a flow chart for a typical programmable vertex processor. The dataflow model for vertex processing begins by loading each vertex's attributes (such as

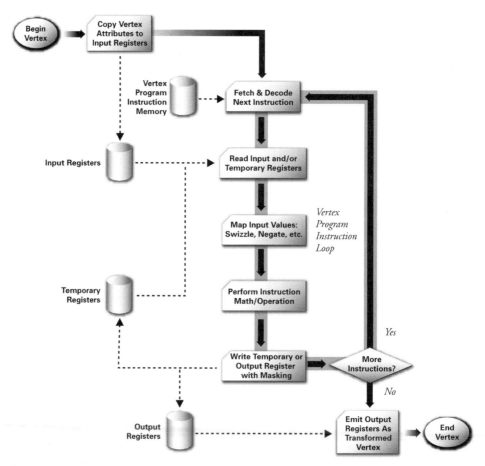

Figure 1-8. Programmable Vertex Processor Flow Chart

position, color, texture coordinates, and so on) into the vertex processor. The vertex processor then repeatedly fetches the next instruction and executes it until the vertex program terminates. Instructions access several distinct sets of registers banks that contain vector values, such as position, normal, or color. The vertex attribute registers are read-only and contain the application-specified set of attributes for the vertex. The temporary registers can be read and written and are used for computing intermediate results. The output result registers are write-only. The program is responsible for writing its results to these registers. When the vertex program terminates, the output result registers contain the newly transformed vertex. After triangle setup and rasterization, the interpolated values for each register are passed to the fragment processor.

Most vertex processing uses a limited palette of operations. Vector math operations on floating-point vectors of two, three, or four components are necessary. These operations include add, multiply, multiply-add, dot product, minimum, and maximum. Hardware support for vector negation and component-wise swizzling (the ability to reorder vector components arbitrarily) generalizes these vector math instructions to provide negation, subtraction, and cross products. Component-wise write masking controls the output of all instructions. Combining reciprocal and reciprocal square root operations with vector multiplication and dot products, respectively, enables vector-by-scalar division and vector normalization. Exponential, logarithmic, and trigonometric approximations facilitate lighting, fog, and geometric computations. Specialized instructions can make lighting and attenuation functions easier to compute.

Further functionality, such as relative addressing of constants and flow-control support for branching and looping, is also available in more recent programmable vertex processors.

The Programmable Fragment Processor

Programmable fragment processors require many of the same math operations as programmable vertex processors do, but they also support texturing operations. Texturing operations enable the processor to access a texture image using a set of texture coordinates and then to return a filtered sample of the texture image.

Newer GPUs offer full support for floating-point values; older GPUs have more limited fixed-point data types. Even when floating-point operations are available, fragment operations are often more efficient when using lower-precision data types. GPUs must process so many fragments at once that arbitrary branching is not available in current GPU generations, but this is likely to change over time as hardware evolves.

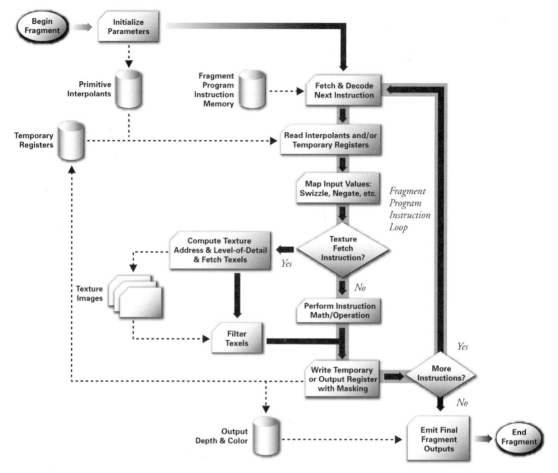

Figure 1-9. Programmable Fragment Processor Flow Chart

Cg still allows you to write fragment programs that branch and iterate by simulating such constructs with conditional assignment operations or loop unrolling.

Figure 1-9 shows the flow chart for a current programmable fragment processor. As with a programmable vertex processor, the data flow involves executing a sequence of instructions until the program terminates. Again, there is a set of input registers. However, rather than vertex attributes, the fragment processor's read-only input registers contain interpolated per-fragment parameters derived from the per-vertex parameters of the fragment's primitive. Read/write temporary registers store intermediate values. Write operations to write-only output registers become the color and optionally the new depth of the fragment. Fragment program instructions include texture fetches.

1.2.5 Cg Provides Vertex and Fragment Programmability

These two programmable processors in your GPU require you, the application programmer, to supply a program for each processor to execute. What Cg provides is a language and a compiler that can translate your shading algorithm into a form that your GPU's hardware can execute. With Cg, rather than program at the level shown in Figures 1-8 and 1-9, you can program in a high-level language very similar to C.

1.3   Cg's Historical Development

Cg's heritage comes from three sources, as shown in Figure 1-10. First, Cg bases its syntax and semantics on the general-purpose C programming language. Second, Cg incorporates many concepts from offline shading languages such as the RenderMan Shading Language, as well as prior hardware shading languages developed by academia. Third, Cg bases its graphics functionality on the OpenGL and Direct3D programming interfaces for real-time 3D.

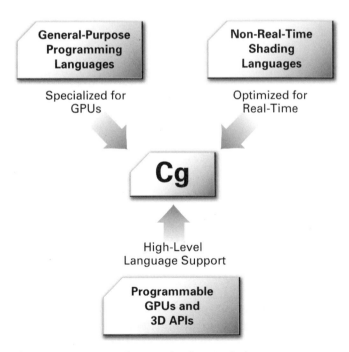

Figure 1-10. Sources of Cg's Technology Heritage

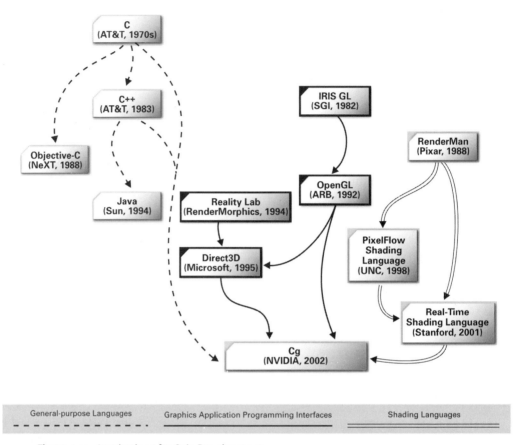

Figure 1-11. Inspirations for Cg's Development

Figure 1-11 shows the general-purpose programming languages, 3D application programming interfaces, and shading languages that inspired Cg's development.

Earlier, we mentioned how Cg leverages C's syntax and semantics. Over the course of this book, you will find that Cg mostly does what C programmers expect. Cg differs from C in situations where either Cg's specialization for GPUs or performance justifies a change.

1.3.1 Microsoft and NVIDIA's Collaboration to Develop Cg and HLSL

NVIDIA and Microsoft collaborated to develop the Cg language. Microsoft calls its implementation High-Level Shading Language, or HLSL for short. HLSL and Cg are the same language but reflect the different names each company uses to identify the language and its underlying technology. HLSL is a part of Microsoft's DirectX Graphics, a component of the DirectX 9 multimedia framework. Direct3D is the 3D component of Microsoft's DirectX Graphics. Cg is independent of the 3D programming interface and fully integrates with either Direct3D or OpenGL. A properly written Cg application can be written once and then work with either OpenGL or Direct3D.

This flexibility means that NVIDIA's Cg implementation provides a way to author programs that work with both dominant 3D programming interfaces and whatever operating system you choose. Cg works whether you choose Windows, Linux, Mac OS X, a game console, or embedded 3D hardware as your 3D computing platform. Cg programs work with hardware from multiple hardware vendors because Cg layers cleanly upon either Direct3D or OpenGL. Cg programs work on programmable GPUs from all the major graphics hardware vendors, such as 3Dlabs, ATI, Matrox, and NVIDIA.

The multivendor, cross-API, and multiplatform nature of the Cg language makes it the best choice when writing programs for programmable GPUs.

1.3.2 Noninteractive Shading Languages

The RenderMan Interface Standard describes the best-known shading language for noninteractive shading. Pixar developed the language in the late 1980s to generate high-quality computer animation with sophisticated shading for films and commercials. Pixar has created a complete rendering system with its implementation of the RenderMan Interface Standard, the offline renderer PRMan (PhotoRealistic RenderMan). The RenderMan Shading Language is just one component of this system.

Shade Trees

The inspiration for the RenderMan Shading Language came from an earlier idea called *shade trees*. Rob Cook, then at Lucasfilm Ltd., which later spun off Pixar, published a SIGGRAPH paper about shade trees in 1984. A shade tree organizes various shading operations as nodes within a tree structure. Figure 1-12 shows a shade tree for rendering a copper surface. The leaf nodes are data inputs to the shade tree. The non-leaf nodes represent simple shading operations. During the process of rendering, the renderer evaluates the shade tree associated with a given surface to determine the color of the surface in the rendered image. To evaluate a shade tree, a renderer performs the

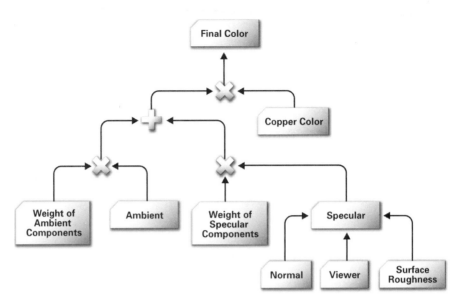

Figure 1-12. A Shade Tree Example, Based on Rob Cook's Original SIGGRAPH Paper

shading operation associated with the topmost node in the shade tree. However, to evaluate a given node, the renderer must first evaluate the node's child nodes. This rule is applied recursively to evaluate the shade tree fully. The result of a shade tree evaluation at a given point on a surface is the color of that point.

Shade trees grew out of the realization that a single predefined shading model would never be sufficient for all the objects and scenes one might want to render.

Shade tree diagrams are great for visualizing a data flow of shading operations. However, if the shade trees are complex, their diagrams become unwieldy. Researchers at Pixar and elsewhere recognized that each shade tree is a limited kind of program. This realization provided the impetus for a new kind of programming language known as a shading language.

The RenderMan Shading Language

The RenderMan Shading Language grew out of shade trees and the realization that open-ended control of the appearance of rendered surfaces in the pursuit of photorealism requires programmability.

Today most offline renderers used in actual production have some type of support for a shading language. The RenderMan Shading Language is the most established and best known for offline rendering, and it was significantly overhauled and extended in the late 1990s.

Hardware-Amenable Shading Languages

A hardware implementation of an algorithm is most efficient when the task decomposes into a long sequence of stages in which each stage's communication is limited to its prior stage and its subsequent stage (that is, when it can be pipelined).

The vertex-based and fragment-based pipeline described in Section 1.2 is extremely amenable to hardware implementation. However, the Reyes algorithm used by Photo-Realistic RenderMan is not very suitable for efficient hardware implementation, primarily due to its higher-level geometry handling. Contemporary GPUs rely completely on a graphics pipeline based on vertices and fragments.

Researchers at the University of North Carolina (UNC) began investigating programmable graphics hardware in the mid-1990s, when UNC was developing a new programmable graphics hardware architecture called PixelFlow. This project fostered a new line of computer graphics research into hardware-amenable shading languages by Marc Olano and others at UNC. Unfortunately, PixelFlow was too expensive and failed commercially.

Subsequently, researchers at Silicon Graphics worked on a system to translate shaders into multiple passes of OpenGL rendering. Although the targeted OpenGL hardware was not programmable in the way GPUs are today, the OpenGL Shader system orchestrates numerous rendering passes to achieve a shader's intended effect.

Researchers at Stanford University, including Kekoa Proudfoot, Bill Mark, Svetoslav Tzvetkov, and Pat Hanrahan, began building a shading language designed specifically for second-generation and third-generation GPUs. This language, known as the Stanford Real-Time Shading Language (RTSL), could compile shaders written in RTSL into one or more OpenGL rendering passes.

The research at Stanford inspired NVIDIA's own effort to develop a commercial-quality hardware-amenable shading language. Bill Mark joined NVIDIA in 2001 to lead the effort to define and implement the shading language we now call Cg. During this time, NVIDIA collaborated with Microsoft to agree on a common language syntax and feature set.

1.3.3 Programming Interfaces for 3D Graphics

The third influence on Cg was the pair of standard 3D programming interfaces, OpenGL and Direct3D. The influence of these programming interfaces on Cg is ongoing, as is explained in the next section.

1.4 The Cg Environment

Cg is just one component of the overall software and hardware infrastructure for rendering complex 3D scenes with programmable GPUs at real-time rates. This section explains how Cg interacts with actual 3D applications and games.

1.4.1 Standard 3D Programming Interfaces: OpenGL and Direct3D

In the old days of 3D graphics on a PC (before there were GPUs), the CPU handled all the vertex transformation and pixel-pushing tasks required to render a 3D scene. The graphics hardware provided only the buffer of pixels that the hardware displayed to the screen. Programmers had to implement their own 3D graphics rendering algorithms in software. In a sense, everything about vertex and fragment processing back then was completely programmable. Unfortunately, the CPU was too slow to produce compelling 3D effects.

These days, 3D applications no longer implement their own 3D rendering algorithms using the CPU; rather, they rely on either OpenGL or Direct3D, the two standard 3D programming interfaces, to communicate rendering commands to the GPU.

OpenGL

In the early 1990s, Silicon Graphics developed OpenGL in coordination with an organization called the OpenGL Architecture Review Board (ARB), which comprised all the major computer graphics system vendors. Originally, OpenGL ran only on powerful UNIX graphics workstations. Microsoft, a founding member of the ARB, then implemented OpenGL as a way to support 3D graphics for its Windows NT operating system. Microsoft later added OpenGL support to Windows 95 and all of Microsoft's desktop operating systems.

OpenGL is not limited to a single operating or windowing system. In addition to supporting UNIX workstations and Windows PCs, OpenGL is supported by Apple for its Macintosh personal computers. Linux users can use either the Mesa open-source implementation of OpenGL or a hardware-accelerated implementation such as NVIDIA's OpenGL driver for Linux. This flexibility makes OpenGL the industry's best cross-platform programming interface for 3D graphics.

Over the last decade, OpenGL has evolved along with graphics hardware. OpenGL is extensible, meaning that OpenGL implementers can add new functionality to OpenGL in an incremental way. Today, scores of OpenGL extensions provide access to all the latest GPU features. This includes ARB-standardized extensions for vertex and fragment programmability. As extensions are established, they are often rolled into the core OpenGL standard so that the standard as a whole advances. At the time of this writing, the current version of OpenGL is 1.4. Ongoing work to evolve OpenGL is underway in various OpenGL ARB working groups. This work includes both assembly-level and high-level programmable interfaces. Because Cg operates as a layer above such interfaces, it will continue to function with future revisions of OpenGL in a compatible manner.

Direct3D

Microsoft began developing the Direct3D programming interface about 1995 as part of its DirectX multimedia initiative. Direct3D is one of the programming interfaces that make up DirectX. Microsoft introduced DirectX and Direct3D to jump-start the consumer market for 3D graphics, particularly gaming, on Windows PCs. Microsoft's Xbox game console also supports Direct3D. Direct3D is the most popular graphics API for games on Windows, due to its history of closely matching the capabilities of available graphics hardware.

Every year or so, Microsoft has updated DirectX, including Direct3D, to keep up with the rapid pace of PC hardware innovation. The current version of DirectX at the time of this writing is DirectX 9, which includes HLSL, Microsoft's implementation of the same language syntax and constructs found in Cg.

3D Programming Interface Détente

A few years ago, OpenGL and Direct3D competed to see which programming interface would dominate, particularly in the domain of Windows PCs. The competition continues to be good for both programming interfaces, and each has improved in performance, quality, and functionality. In the area of GPU programmability that Cg addresses, both programming interfaces have comparable capabilities. This is because both OpenGL and Direct3D run on the same GPU hardware and the graphics hardware determines the available functionality and performance. OpenGL has a slight advantage in functionality because hardware vendors are better able to expose their entire feature set through OpenGL, though vendor-specific extensions do add some complexity for developers.

Most software developers now choose a 3D programming interface based on programmer preference, history, and their target market and hardware platform, rather than on technical grounds.

Cg supports either programming interface. You can write Cg programs so that they work with either the OpenGL or Direct3D programming interface. This is a huge boon for 3D content developers. They can pair their 3D content with programs written in Cg and then render the content no matter what programming interface the final application uses for 3D rendering.

1.4.2   The Cg Compiler and Runtime

No GPU can execute Cg programs directly from their textual form. A process known as compilation must translate Cg programs into a form that the GPU can execute. The Cg compiler first translates your Cg program into a form accepted by the application's choice of 3D programming interface, either OpenGL or Direct3D. Then your application transfers the OpenGL or Direct3D translation of your Cg program to the GPU using the appropriate OpenGL or Direct3D commands. The OpenGL or Direct3D driver performs the final translation into the hardware-executable form your GPU requires.

The details of this translation depend on the combined capabilities of the GPU and 3D programming interface. How a Cg program compiles its intermediate OpenGL or Direct3D form depends on the type and generation of GPU in your computer. It may be that your GPU is not capable of supporting a particular valid Cg program because of limitations of the GPU itself. For example, your Cg fragment program will not compile if your program accesses more texture units than your target GPU supports.

Support for Dynamic Compilation

When you compile a program with a conventional programming language such as C or C++, compilation is an offline process. Your compiler compiles the program into an executable that runs directly on the CPU. Once compiled, your program does not need to be recompiled, unless you change the program code. We call this *static compilation*.

Cg is different because it encourages *dynamic compilation,* although static compilation is also supported. The Cg compiler is not a separate program but part of a library known as the Cg runtime. 3D applications and games using Cg programs must link with the Cg runtime. Applications using Cg then call Cg runtime routines, all prefixed with the letters **cg**, to compile and manipulate Cg programs. Dynamic compilation allows Cg programs to be optimized for the particular model of GPU installed in the user's machine.

CgGL and CgD3D, the 3D-API-Specific Cg Libraries

In addition to the core Cg runtime, Cg provides two closely related libraries. If your application uses OpenGL, you will use the CgGL library to invoke the appropriate OpenGL routines to pass your translated Cg program to the OpenGL driver. Likewise, if your application uses Direct3D, you will use the CgD3D library to invoke the appropriate Direct3D routines to pass your translated Cg program to the Direct3D driver. Normally, you would use either the CgGL or the CgD3D library, but not both, because most applications use either OpenGL or Direct3D, not both.

Compared with the core Cg runtime library that contains the Cg compiler, the CgGL and CgD3D libraries are relatively small. Their job is to make the appropriate OpenGL or Direct3D calls for you to configure Cg programs for execution. These calls transfer a translated Cg program to the appropriate driver that will further translate the program into a form your GPU can execute. For the most part, the CgGL and CgD3D libraries have similar routines. The routines in the CgGL library begin with **cgGL**; the routines in the CgD3D library begin with **cgD3D**.

How the Cg Runtime Fits into Your Application

Figure 1-13 shows how a typical 3D application uses the Cg libraries. If you are a programmer, you will want to learn more about the Cg runtime and the specific library for the 3D API your application uses to render 3D graphics. Most of this book focuses on the Cg language itself and on how to write Cg programs, but Appendix B has more information about the Cg runtime library.

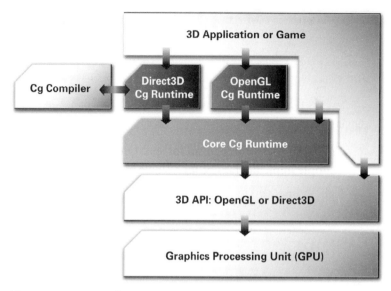

Figure 1-13. How Cg Fits into a Standard Cg Application

1.4.3   The CgFX Toolkit and File Format

Cg programs need 3D models, textures, and other data to operate on. A Cg program without any associated data is useless. Cg programs and data also require the correct 3D programming interface configuration and state. It is often helpful to have a way to bundle all the information required to render a 3D model, including its associated Cg program.

What CgFX Provides

CgFX is a standardized file format for representing complete effects and appearances. As they did with Cg, Microsoft and NVIDIA collaborated to develop the CgFX format. CgFX files are text-based, with a syntax that is a superset of Cg's, and may contain any number of Cg programs. The **.fx** suffix identifies CgFX files. A CgFX file describes the complete render state for a particular effect: multiple passes, texture states, and any number of individual vertex and fragment programs may be defined to create a complete appearance or effect. An accompanying development toolkit is provided for using and parsing CgFX files. The toolkit exposes user-interface hooks to host applications, so that CgFX-aware applications can automatically supply meaningful controls and semantics to users and developers alike.

Cg programs describe the vertex or fragment processing that takes place in a single rendering pass, but some complex shading algorithms require multiple rendering passes. CgFX offers a format to encode complex multipass effects, including designating which Cg program is used for each rendering pass.

More specifically, CgFX supports three additional capabilities beyond what the core Cg language supports:

1. CgFX provides a mechanism for specifying multiple rendering passes and optional multiple implementations for a single effect.

2. CgFX allows you to specify nonprogrammable rendering states, such as alpha-test modes and texture-filtering. The settings for these render states may take the form of simple expressions, which are evaluated on the CPU when the effect is initialized.

3. CgFX allows annotations to be added to shaders and shader parameters. These annotations provide additional information to applications, including content creation applications. For example, an annotation can specify the allowed range of values for a shader parameter.

Multiple Shader Instancing

The CgFX file format encapsulates multiple implementations of Cg programs for a given shader. This means you can have one Cg shader program written for a third-generation or fourth-generation GPU, while also including a simpler program that supports a less capable, second-generation GPU. An application loading the CgFX file can determine at runtime the most appropriate shader implementation to use based on the computer's available GPU.

Multiple instancing of Cg programs with CgFX is one way to address the functional variations in GPUs of different generations or different hardware vendors. Multiple instancing also lets you develop a Cg program specialized for a particular 3D API—for example, if OpenGL exposes extra functionality through an extension. Cg programs specialized for Direct3D, standard OpenGL, or OpenGL with extensions can all be contained in a single CgFX file.

CgFX and Digital Content Creation

The CgFX Toolkit consists of the CgFX compiler, which supports the full CgFX syntax; the CgFX runtime API, for loading and manipulating CgFX files; and plug-in modules for major digital content creation (DCC) applications such as

Alias|Wavefront's Maya and Discreet's 3ds max. Figure 1-14 shows these applications making use of CgFX. Softimage|XSI 3.0 provides direct support for Cg compilation in its Render Tree.

Prior to CgFX, there was no standard way for a DCC application to export 3D content with all the associated shading knowledge necessary to render the content in real time. Now the major DCC applications use CgFX in their content creation process and support the CgFX file format. This means that CgFX can significantly improve the artistic workflow from DCC applications to real-time games and other 3D applications. Using CgFX, artists can view and tweak Cg shaders and associated 3D content to see, from within the DCC tool of their choice, how their work will appear in a 3D game or application.

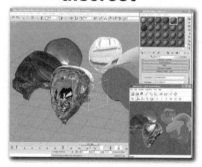

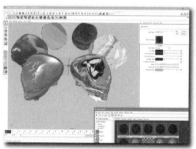

Figure 1-14. Digital Content Creation Applications That Use Cg and CgFX

How CgFX Fits into Your Application

Figure 1-15 shows how a CgFX file containing multiple instanced shaders is used by an application in conjunction with the Cg runtime and your choice of rendering API. Most of this book focuses on the Cg language itself and on how to write Cg programs, rather than CgFX, but see Appendix C for more information about the CgFX file format and its associated runtime API.

Onward to the Tutorial

Having finished this introduction to the Cg programming language, you are now ready to take on the tutorial chapters, which will teach you how to write Cg programs.

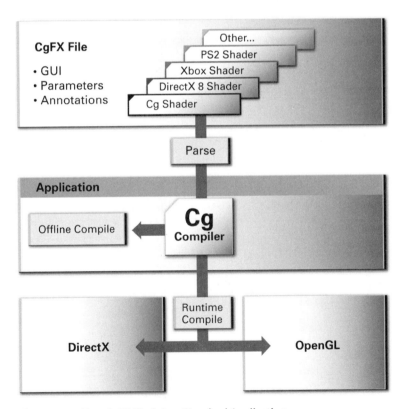

Figure 1-15. How CgFX Fits into a Standard Application

1.5   Exercises

The exercises at the end of each chapter help you review your knowledge and develop practical programming skills.

1. **Answer this:** Name two standard 3D programming interfaces for which you can compile Cg programs. What operating systems does each programming interface support?

2. **Answer this:** What are the major stages of the graphics pipeline? In what order are the stages arranged?

3. **Answer this:** Where do vertex and fragment programs fit into the pipeline?

4. **Answer this:** What is a vertex? What is a fragment? Distinguish a fragment from a pixel.

5. **Try this yourself:** We haven't begun writing Cg programs yet (we'll get there soon enough in the next chapter), so take a break and watch a good feature-length computer graphics animation such as *Monsters, Inc.*

1.6   Further Reading

Cg builds on a host of concepts in computer language design, computer hardware design, and computer graphics. Doing justice to all these contributions in the context of this tutorial is not always practical. What we attempt in the "Further Reading" section at the end of each chapter is to offer you pointers to learn more about the contributions that underlie the topics in each chapter.

There are plenty of books on C. *The C Programming Language, Third Edition* (Prentice Hall, 2000), by Brian Kernighan and Dennis Ritchie, is a classic; the authors invented the C language. Cg includes concepts from both C and C++. There now may actually be more books about C++ than about C. The classic C++ book is *The C++ Programming Language, Third Edition* (Addison-Wesley, 2000), by Bjarne Stroustrup, who invented the language.

To learn more about the RenderMan Shading Language, read *The RenderMan Companion: A Programmer's Guide to Realistic Computer Graphics* (Addison-Wesley, 1989), by Steve Upstill. Pat Hanrahan and Jim Lawson published a SIGGRAPH paper about

RenderMan called "A Language for Shading and Lighting Calculations" (ACM Press) in 1990.

Robert Cook's 1984 SIGGRAPH paper titled "Shade Trees" (ACM Press) motivated the development of RenderMan.

The development of programmable graphics hardware and its associated languages has been an active and fruitful research area for almost a decade. Anselmo Lastra, Steven Molnar, Marc Olano, and Yulan Wang at UNC published an early research paper in 1995 titled "Real-Time Programmable Shading" (ACM Press). Researchers at UNC also published several papers about their programmable PixelFlow graphics architecture. Marc Olano and Anselmo Lastra published a SIGGRAPH paper titled "A Shading Language on Graphics Hardware: The PixelFlow Shading System" (ACM Press) in 1998.

Kekoa Proudfoot, Bill Mark, Svetoslav Tzvetkov, and Pat Hanrahan published a SIGGRAPH paper in 2001 titled "A Real-Time Procedural Shading System for Programmable Graphics Hardware" (ACM Press) that describes a GPU-oriented shading language developed at Stanford.

Real-Time Rendering, Second Edition (A. K. Peters, 2002), written by Eric Haines and Tomas Akenine-Möller, is an excellent resource for further information about graphics hardware and interactive techniques.

The OpenGL Graphics System: A Specification documents the OpenGL 3D programming interface. The best tutorial for learning OpenGL programming is the *OpenGL Programming Guide: The Official Guide to Learning OpenGL, Third Edition* (Addison-Wesley, 1999), by Mason Woo, Jackie Neider, Tom Davis, and Dave Shreiner. The **www.opengl.org** Web site serves up much more information about OpenGL.

Documentation for the Direct3D programming interface is available from Microsoft's **msdn.microsoft.com** Web site.

NVIDIA provides further information about the Cg runtime, CgFX, and Cg itself on its Developer Web site at **developer.nvidia.com/Cg**.

Chapter 2

The Simplest Programs

This chapter introduces Cg programming through a series of simple vertex and fragment programs. The chapter has the following four sections:

- **"A Simple Vertex Program"** presents a straightforward vertex program and explains the basic elements and syntax of the Cg language.

- **"Compiling Your Example"** explains how to compile programs for different GPUs, using the concept of profiles.

- **"A Simple Fragment Program"** defines a basic fragment program and introduces fragment profiles.

- **"Rendering with Your Vertex and Fragment Program Examples"** shows how to render simple geometry with OpenGL or Direct3D. This section also mentions the concept of clipping.

2.1 A Simple Vertex Program

Green is the color associated with inexperience and growth, so a Cg program for rendering a green 2D triangle is a fitting way to start learning Cg.

Example 2-1 shows the complete source code for your first vertex program in Cg. Source code examples in this book use **boldface** to indicate Cg keywords, built-in functions, and built-in data types. This notation will help you identify words in programs that have special meaning to the Cg compiler. In addition, comments in code samples are set in gray type, to distinguish them from the rest of the code. Comments in Cg work just as in C++: you can use the **/*** and ***/** delimiters, or you can precede comments with the **//** characters.

The Naming Convention for Examples

The vertex program in Example 2-1 is quite simple. The "**C2E1v**" prefix used in various parts of the program stands for "Chapter 2, Example 1 vertex program." We use this notation to make it easier to find examples across chapters and in the accompanying software framework. This convention makes it easier to keep track of the various examples in this book, but it is not a requirement of the Cg language itself and indeed is not a convention intended for your own programs.

```
struct C2E1v_Output {
  float4 position : POSITION;
  float4 color    : COLOR;
};


C2E1v_Output C2E1v_green(float2 position : POSITION)
{
  C2E1v_Output OUT;

  OUT.position = float4(position, 0, 1);
  OUT.color    = float4(0, 1, 0, 1);   // RGBA green

  return OUT;
}
```

Example 2-1. The **C2E1v_green** Vertex Program

If you are familiar with C or C++, you can probably deduce what the program does. The program assigns the vertex's incoming 2D position to the vertex's output 2D position. In addition, it assigns the RGBA (red, green, blue, alpha) constant representing green to the output color of the vertex.

2.1.1   Output Structures

The **C2E1v_green** program begins with this declaration:

```
struct C2E1v_Output {
  float4 position : POSITION;
  float4 color    : COLOR;
};
```

This declaration is for a special structure known as an *output structure*. This structure contains the bundle of values that represent the output (or result) of a given Cg program.

A program written in a general-purpose CPU language such as C can perform a wide variety of tasks, such as reading and writing files, soliciting input from users, printing text, displaying graphics, and communicating over a network. Cg programs, on the other hand, are limited to outputting a bundle of values. A Cg program's output structure encapsulates the potential range of output values for a given Cg program.

Cg declares structures with the same syntax used in C and C++. A structure declaration begins with the **struct** keyword, followed by the name of the structure. Enclosed in curly brackets, a structure definition contains a list of structure members, each with a name and a type.

An output structure differs from a conventional C or C++ structure because it includes *semantics* for each member. We will return to the concept of semantics soon in Section 2.1.6.

2.1.2 Identifiers

When you declare a structure, you provide an *identifier,* or name, after the **struct** keyword; you do this for each structure you declare. An identifier in Cg has the same form as in C and C++. Identifiers consist of a sequence of one or more uppercase or lowercase alphabetic characters, the digits 0 to 9, and the underscore character (_). For example, **Matrix_B** and **pi2** are valid identifiers. An identifier cannot begin with a digit and cannot be a keyword.

Identifiers not only name structures, but also name type declarations, members of structures, variables, functions, and semantics (you will learn more about each of these shortly). Other identifiers in Example 2-1 are these:

- **C2E1v_green**—the entry function name
- **position**—a function parameter
- **OUT**—a local variable

- **float4**—a vector data type that is part of Cg's Standard Library
- **color** and **position**—structure members
- **POSITION** and **COLOR**—semantics

Cg maintains different namespaces, based on the context of an identifier, in the same manner as C and C++. For example, the identifier **position** identifies a function parameter and a member of the **C2E1v_Output** structure.

Keywords in Cg

Many Cg keywords are also C and C++ keywords, but Cg uses additional keywords not found in C or C++. Over the course of the book, we will explain most of these keywords. Appendix D contains the complete list of Cg keywords. As in C and C++, Cg's keywords are not available for use as identifiers.

2.1.3　Structure Members

Within the curly brackets of a structure declaration, you will find one or more structure members. Each member is a data type with an associated member name.

In the **C2E1v_Output** structure, there are two members: **position** and **color**. Both members are four-component floating-point vectors, as indicated by their type, **float4**.

2.1.4　Vectors

The fundamental data types in C or C++ are scalar quantities, such as **int** or **float**. In C or C++, there is no native "vector" type, so vectors are typically just arrays of scalar values. Because vectors are essential to vertex and fragment processing and because GPUs have built-in support for vector data types, Cg has vector data types.

The members (**position** and **color**) are declared using the **float4** data type. This name is not a reserved word in Cg; it is a standard type definition in the Cg Standard Library. Unlike in C and C++, there is no need to specify a preprocessor statement (such as **#include**) to include declarations for Cg's Standard Library. Instead, Cg automatically includes the declarations needed by most Cg programs.

You should rely on the predefined vector data types provided by the Cg Standard Library, such as **float2**, **float3**, **float4**, and other such types to ensure that your programs make the most efficient use of the vector processing capabilities of your programmable GPU.

Vector types in Cg, such as **float3** and **float4**, are not 100 percent equivalent to arrays of however many **float**s. For example, **float x[4]** is not the same declaration as **float4 x**. These vector types are, in fact, *packed arrays*. Packed arrays, often just called vectors, tell the compiler to allocate the elements of packed arrays so that vector operations on these variables are most efficient. If two input vectors are stored in packed form, programmable graphics hardware typically performs three-component or four-component math operations—such as multiplications, additions, and dot products—in a single instruction.

Packed arrays are not available in conventional programming languages like C and C++. Recent CPU instruction sets—such as Intel's SSE2, SSE, and MMX; AMD's 3DNow!; and Motorola's AltiVec—have additional vector instructions, but packed arrays are not natively supported by most general-purpose programming languages. Cg, however, provides specific support for packed arrays because vector quantities are integral to vertex and fragment processing. Packed arrays help the Cg compiler take advantage of the fast vector operations provided by programmable GPUs.

As with many aspects of Cg, how you use packed arrays depends on the Cg profile you select. For example, packed arrays are usually limited to four or fewer components. They are often extremely efficient for vector operations such as assignment, negation, absolute value, multiplication, addition, linear interpolation, maximum, and minimum. Dot-product and cross-product operations with packed operands are also very efficient.

On the other hand, accessing packed arrays with a nonconstant array index is either inefficient or unsupported, depending on the profile. For example:

```
float4 data = { 0.5, -2, 3, 3.14159 }; // Initializer,
                                        // as in C

int index = 3;
float scalar;
scalar = data[3];      // Efficient
scalar = data[index];  // Inefficient or unsupported
```

The rule of thumb is to declare all vectors that consist of two, three, or four components (such as colors, positions, texture coordinate sets, and directions) as packed arrays by using Cg's built-in vector types.

2.1 A Simple Vertex Program

2.1.5 Matrices

In addition to vector types, Cg natively supports matrix types. Here are some examples of matrix declarations in Cg:

```
float4x4 matrix1;  // Four-by-four matrix with 16 elements
half3x2 matrix2;   // Three-by-two matrix with 6 elements
fixed2x4 matrix3;  // Two-by-four matrix with 8 elements
```

You can declare and initialize a matrix with the same notation that would be used to initialize an array in C or C++:

```
float2x3 matrix4 = { 1.0, 2.0,
                     3.0, 4.0,
                     5.0, 6.0 };
```

Like vectors, matrices are packed data types in Cg, so operations using standard matrix types execute very efficiently on the GPU.

2.1.6 Semantics

A colon and a special word, known as a *semantic*, follow the **position** and color members of the **C2E1v_Output** structure. Semantics are, in a sense, the glue that binds a Cg program to the rest of the graphics pipeline. The semantics **POSITION** and **COLOR** indicate the hardware resource that the respective member feeds when the Cg program returns its output structure. They indicate how the variables preceding them connect to the rest of the graphics pipeline.

The **POSITION** semantic (in this case, in an output structure used by a Cg vertex program) is the clip-space position for the transformed vertex. Later graphics pipeline stages will use the output vector associated with this semantic as the post-transform, clip-space position of the vertex for primitive assembly, clipping, and rasterization. You will be introduced to clip space later in this chapter, and more formally in Chapter 4. For now, you can think of a 2D vertex's clip-space position simply as its position within a window.

The **COLOR** semantic in this context is what Direct3D calls the "diffuse vertex color" and OpenGL calls the "primary vertex color." Color interpolation for a triangle or other geometric primitive during rasterization depends on the primitive's per-vertex colors.

Do not confuse a member name with its semantic. In Example 2-1, the `position` member is associated with the `POSITION` semantic. However, it is the use of the `POSITION` semantic after the member name—not the name of the member itself—that makes the rasterizer treat the `position` member as a position. In the following output structure, the member names `density` and `position` are poorly chosen, but Cg abides by the specified semantics despite the misleading names:

```
struct misleadingButLegal {
  float4 density  : POSITION;   // Works, but confusing
  float4 position : COLOR;      // Also confusing
};
```

Subsequent examples will introduce other output semantic names. Not all semantics are available in all profiles, but in our examples, we will use the semantics that are broadly supported by existing profiles.

You can also create your own semantic names, but in this book, we limit our examples to the standard set of semantics. For more information about using your own semantic names, see the *Cg Toolkit User's Manual: A Developer's Guide to Programmable Graphics.*

2.1.7 Functions

Declaring functions in Cg works in much the same way as it does in C and C++. You specify a return type for the function (or **void** if nothing is returned), its name, and a comma-separated parameter list in parentheses. After the declaration, the body of the function describes the computation performed by the function.

Functions can be either entry functions or internal functions.

Entry Functions

An *entry function* defines a vertex program or fragment program; it is analogous to the **main** function in C or C++. A program's execution starts in its entry function. In Example 2-1, the entry function called **C2E1v_green** is defined as follows:

```
C2E1v_Output C2E1v_green(float2 position : POSITION)
```

This function returns the output structure **C2E1v_Output** described earlier. This means that the function outputs both a position and a color. These outputs have semantics defined by the structure.

The function also accepts an input parameter named **position**. This parameter has the type **float2**, so it is a floating-point vector with two components. When a colon and semantic name follow an input parameter name, this indicates the semantic associated with that input parameter. When **POSITION** is used as an input semantic, this tells the vertex processor to initialize this parameter with the application-specified position of every vertex processed by the function.

Internal Functions

Internal functions are helper functions called by entry functions or other internal functions. You can use the internal functions provided by the Cg Standard Library, and you can define your own internal functions as well.

Internal functions ignore any semantics applied to their input or output parameters or return values; only entry functions use semantics.

2.1.8 Input and Output Semantics Are Different

Figure 2-1 shows the flow of input and output semantics for the **C2E1v_green** vertex program.

Input and output semantics are not the same, even though some have the same names. For example, for an input parameter to a vertex program, **POSITION** refers to the application-specified position assigned by the application when it sends a vertex to the GPU. However, an output structure element with the **POSITION** semantic represents the clip-space position that is fed to the hardware rasterizer.

Both semantics are named **POSITION** and, indeed, each is a position. However, each position semantic refers to a position at different points along the graphics pipeline. Your Cg vertex program transforms the application-supplied vertex position into a vertex suited for primitive assembly, clipping, and rasterization. In the **C2E1v_green** program, this transformation is trivial (the vertex position is passed along unchanged), but later in this book, particularly in Chapters 4 and 5, you will learn more useful and interesting ways to transform vertices.

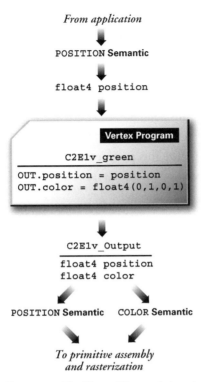

From application

↓

POSITION Semantic

↓

float4 position

↓

Vertex Program

C2E1v_green
_____

OUT.position = position
OUT.color = float4(0,1,0,1)

↓

C2E1v_Output
_____

float4 position
float4 color

↙   ↘

POSITION Semantic   COLOR Semantic

↘   ↙

*To primitive assembly
and rasterization*

Figure 2-1. The Flow of Semantic Inputs and Outputs for **C2E1v_green**

2.1.9   The Function Body

The substance of the **C2E1v_green** function is contained in its body:

```
{
  C2E1v_Output OUT;

  OUT.position = float4(position, 0, 1);
  OUT.color    = float4(0, 1, 0, 1);  // RGBA green

  return OUT;
}
```

Because the function's return type is **C2E1v_Output**, you must declare a variable of this type to hold the value that the function returns. We often call a structure returned by an entry function an *output structure*. The function body sets both elements of this structure variable and returns the structure. (Note that the entry function's return type is not required to have the same prefix as the entry function, although we've chosen to make them the same in our examples.)

The dot between **OUT** and **position**, as well as **OUT** and **color**, is the *member operator* and gives access to a member within a structure. This is the same way that C and C++ access structure members. Think of a structure as a container for multiple values. The member operator lets you retrieve the values contained in a structure:

```
OUT.position = float4(position, 0, 1);
OUT.color    = float4(0, 1, 0, 1);  // RGBA green
```

First, the program assigns the **position** input parameter to **OUT.position**. However, the output structure member **OUT.position** is of type **float4** (Chapter 4 explains why). The expression **float4(position, 0, 1)** converts a two-component position vector to a four-component vector by setting the third and fourth components to 0 and 1, respectively.

Second, the program assigns the RGBA color value for green to **OUT.color**. To provide the numeric value for green, construct the appropriate four-component color vector. The type of the **color** member is **float4** because the color is an RGBA color. The "A" in RGBA stands for "alpha," which normally encodes a measure of how opaque or transparent a color value is. The value 1 for alpha means the color is fully opaque.

When you use the **float4** or similar vector type name like a function (for example, **float4(0, 1, 0, 1)**), this is a called a *constructor*. This constructor creates a value of the type specified out of the values listed in the parentheses. C++ has the concept of constructors, but C does not. Constructors in Cg are provided for vectors and matrices.

The syntax **float4(0, 1, 0, 1)** creates a vector $\langle 0, 1, 0, 1 \rangle$ that is assigned to the **color** member of type **float4** in **OUT**. The vector $\langle 0, 1, 0, 1 \rangle$ is green because the color components are in the red, green, blue, alpha (RGBA) order with a green (and alpha) contribution specified, but no red or blue contribution.

```
return OUT;
```

Finally, the **return** statement returns the output structure you initialized. The collection of values within **OUT** is passed along to the next stage of the graphics pipeline, as indicated by the semantics assigned to each member.

2.2 Compiling Your Example

You use the Cg runtime to load and compile Cg programs. When you compile a program, you must specify two things in addition to the text of the program:

- The name of the entry function to compile
- The profile name for the entry function to compile

The name of the entry function in Example 2-1 is **C2E1v_green**.

C2E1v_green is a vertex program, so you need to compile for a vertex profile. The vertex profile you choose depends on the programming interface your application uses for 3D rendering (OpenGL or Direct3D), as well as the hardware capabilities of your GPU.

2.2.1 Vertex Program Profiles

There are several appropriate vertex profiles for compiling our example, as listed in Table 2-1. Future GPUs will no doubt support profiles that are more capable.

Your first example is very simple, so there is no problem compiling it with any of the profiles in Table 2-1, or any future vertex profile for that matter. As you progress through the book, you'll encounter some complex Cg programs that will require advanced vertex or fragment profiles. When an advanced profile is required, we are careful

Table 2-1. Cg Vertex Profiles

Profile Name	Programming Interface	Description
arbvp1	OpenGL	Basic multivendor vertex programmability (corresponding to **ARB_vertex_program** functionality)
vs_1_1	DirectX 8	Basic multivendor vertex programmability
vp20	OpenGL	Basic NVIDIA vertex programmability (corresponding to **NV_vertex_program** functionality)
vs_2_0 **vs_2_x**	DirectX 9	Advanced multivendor vertex programmability
vp30	OpenGL	Advanced NVIDIA vertex programmability (corresponding to **NV_vertex_program2** functionality)

to point that out. Most examples in this book are written to compile for a broad range of Cg profiles.

Because you'll want your **C2E1v_green** example to compile on the broadest range of GPUs, the best profiles for your example are **arbvp1** for OpenGL and **vs_1_1** for DirectX 8. Is there any reason to choose another profile? Yes, if you want to use advanced vertex programmability functionality, such as complex flow control or fast hardware instructions, which are not available in the basic profiles. For example, if you choose the **vp30** profile, you can write a Cg vertex program that loops a varying (nonconstant) number of times.

 If there is a basic profile that is sufficient for compiling your Cg example, use it to gain the broadest hardware support. However, if you choose a more advanced profile, your Cg program may execute more efficiently and you can program using more general programming practices.

So what is the disadvantage of a more advanced profile? It may limit your program to newer GPUs. To get the best of both worlds—broad hardware support as well as the latest available hardware—you might provide both a fallback Cg program for basic profiles and a more advanced Cg program for more advanced profiles. The CgFX format simplifies this approach by providing a unified way to encapsulate multiple Cg implementations of a given rendering effect in a single source file. Appendix C explains more about CgFX.

Refer to Appendix B to learn how an application can use the Cg runtime library to load and compile Cg programs. In general, you call a set of Cg runtime routines that require your program text, your entry function name, and your chosen profile. If there are errors in your program, the compilation will fail. You can request a list of compile errors to assist you in correcting your code. Once your program compiles successfully, other Cg runtime routines assist you in configuring your 3D programming interface of choice (OpenGL or Direct3D) to render with your program.

2.2.2   Classes of Cg Compilation Errors

There are two classes of compilation errors for Cg programs: conventional and profile-dependent.

Conventional errors are caused either by incorrect syntax, usually due to typos, or by incorrect semantics, such as calling a function with the wrong number of parameters.

These types of errors are not fundamentally different from the everyday compile errors that C and C++ programmers deal with.

Profile-dependent errors result from using Cg in a way that is syntactically and semantically correct but not supported by your specified profile. You may have written valid Cg code, but it might not compile because of the profile you specified. General-purpose programming languages do not have this type of error.

2.2.3 Profile-Dependent Errors

Profile-dependent errors are usually caused by limitations of the 3D programming interface and the underlying GPU hardware for which you are attempting to compile your program. There are three categories of profile-dependent errors: capability, context, and capacity.

Capability

All current profiles for fragment programs permit texture accesses, but no current vertex profiles do. The reason for this is simple. The programmable vertex processors in most current GPUs do not support texture accesses. Future vertex profiles are likely to permit texture accesses.

Cg does not allow you to compile a program that is impossible to execute, given the specified profile for compilation. If a vertex profile does not support texture accesses, a profile-dependent error of capability occurs. The hardware, or the 3D programming interface, lacks the ability to do what Cg allows you to express.

Context

An error of profile-dependent context is more fundamental, though rare. For example, it is an error to write a vertex program that does not return exactly one parameter that is bound to the **POSITION** semantic. This is because the remainder of the graphics pipeline assumes that all vertices have a position.

Likewise, a fragment profile cannot return a **POSITION** the way a vertex profile must. Such errors are caused by using Cg in a manner inconsistent with the data flow of the graphics pipeline.

Capacity

Capacity errors stem from a limit on a GPU's capability. Some GPUs can perform only four texture accesses in a single rendering pass. Other GPUs can perform any number of texture accesses in a single rendering pass, restricted only by the number of fragment program instructions the hardware supports. If you access more than four textures in a profile that does not permit access to more than four textures, you receive a capacity error.

Capacity errors are probably the most frustrating, because it may not be apparent from looking at your program what the exceeded capacity is. For example, you may have exceeded the maximum number of vertex program instructions allowed by the GPU in a single program, but that fact may not be obvious.

Preventing Errors

There are two ways to avoid these frustrating errors. One is to use a more advanced profile. The more advanced a profile is, the less chance you have of bumping into the capability and capacity limits of the profile. As the functionality of programmable graphics hardware improves, you will worry less and less about capability and capacity limits.

Another solution is to educate yourself about the limitations of capability, context, and capacity for the profiles you use in your 3D application. Consult the documentation that accompanies the Cg Toolkit to learn about these limits.

You can often get a good sense of the profile-dependent restrictions by knowing the limitations of the raw 3D programming interface you are using. Consult your OpenGL and Direct3D documentation; it will help you identify Cg constructs that might be subject to profile-dependent limitations.

2.2.4   The Norm: Multiple Entry Functions

C and C++ programs begin executing when the operating system invokes a program instance and calls the program's **main** routine (or **WinMain** routine for Windows programs). Example 2-1 is complete, but it has no routine named **main**. Why? Because, instead, we named the entry function **C2E1v_green**. In this book, we adhere to our naming convention to distinguish our examples from each other and to make them easy to locate. In your own 3D application, however, you can name the entry function whatever you choose, as long as the name is a valid identifier.

Your 3D application will typically use a collection of Cg programs, not just one. At a minimum, you will probably have one vertex program and one fragment program, though you can use the fixed-function pipeline for vertex processing, fragment processing, or even both if you wish. A complex application may have hundreds of Cg programs. Because Cg programs can be compiled at runtime, you can even generate new Cg programs while your application is running, by formatting Cg program text procedurally.

Of course, you can still use the name **main**, which is the default entry function name for Cg programs if no explicit entry function name is specified when you compile Cg source code.

 To avoid confusion, find descriptive names for your entry functions. If all your entry functions are named **main**, it will be difficult to have several entry functions in a single Cg source file—even if that is the default entry function name assumed by the runtime.

2.2.5   Downloading and Configuring Vertex and Fragment Programs

In a general-purpose language, the operating system invokes the **main** (or **WinMain**) routine and the program executes the code contained in that **main** routine. If the **main** routine returns, the program terminates.

However, in Cg, you do not invoke a program that runs until it terminates, as you would in C or C++. Instead, the Cg compiler translates your program into a form that your 3D programming interface can download to hardware. It is up to your application to call the necessary Cg runtime and 3D programming interface routines to download and configure your program for use by the GPU.

Figure 2-2 shows how an application compiles a Cg program and converts it into a binary microcode that the GPU's vertex processor directly executes when transforming vertices.

Once loaded with a vertex program, the programmable vertex processor in your GPU runs that program every time the application feeds a vertex to the GPU. When it renders a complex model with thousands of vertices, your current vertex program processes every vertex in the model. The vertex program runs once for each vertex.

2.2 Compiling Your Example

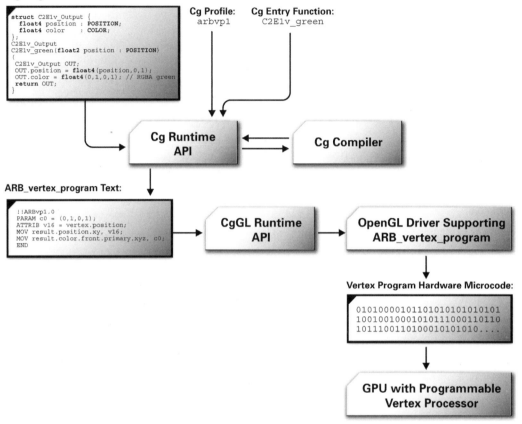

Cg Program Text:

```
struct C2E1v_Output {
    float4 position : POSITION;
    float4 color    : COLOR;
};
C2E1v_Output
C2E1v_green(float2 position : POSITION)
{
    C2E1v_Output OUT;
    OUT.position = float4(position,0,1);
    OUT.color = float4(0,1,0,1); // RGBA green
    return OUT;
}
```

Cg Profile:
arbvp1

Cg Entry Function:
C2E1v_green

Cg Runtime API

Cg Compiler

ARB_vertex_program Text:

```
!!ARBvp1.0
PARAM c0 = (0,1,0,1);
ATTRIB v16 = vertex.position;
MOV result.position.xy, v16;
MOV result.color.front.primary.xyz, c0;
END
```

CgGL Runtime API

OpenGL Driver Supporting ARB_vertex_program

Vertex Program Hardware Microcode:

```
010100001011010101010101
100100100010101111000110110
101110011010001010101010....
```

GPU with Programmable Vertex Processor

Figure 2-2. Compiling and Loading a Cg Program into the GPU

A single current vertex program is loaded in the programmable vertex processor for execution at any one time. However, your application may change the current vertex program, as needed.

This same concept of a single current program applies to the programmable fragment processor in your GPU too. You compile your Cg fragment program and use the Cg runtime, along with your 3D programming interface, to download your program and bind it as the current fragment program for processing fragments generated by the rasterizer. After your fragment program is bound, 3D primitives are rasterized into fragments and your current fragment program processes each generated fragment. The fragment program runs once for each fragment.

Typically, 3D applications co-program the programmable vertex and fragment processors in the GPU to achieve a particular rendering effect. This approach is very efficient because of the parallel and highly pipelined nature of the programmable vertex and fragment processors in GPUs.

2.3 A Simple Fragment Program

So far, our example involves only a vertex program, **C2E1v_green**. This section presents a simple fragment program that you can use with our vertex program.

Example 2-2 shows the complete Cg source code for our first fragment program.

```
struct C2E2f_Output {
  float4 color : COLOR;
};


C2E2f_Output C2E2f_passthrough(float4 color : COLOR)
{
  C2E2f_Output OUT;
  OUT.color = color;
  return OUT;
}
```

Example 2-2. The **C2E2f_passthrough** Fragment Program

This program is even simpler than the example for the **C2E1v_green** vertex program. In fact, it does almost nothing. The program outputs the unchanged interpolated color assigned for every fragment generated by the rasterizer. The GPU's raster operation hardware uses this color to update the frame buffer if the fragment survives the various raster operations, such as scissoring and depth testing.

Here is the output structure returned by **C2E2f_passthrough**:

```
struct C2E2f_Output {
  float4 color : COLOR;
};
```

Fragment programs have a simpler output structure than vertex programs. A vertex program must output a position and may return one or more colors, texture coordinate sets, and other per-vertex outputs. A fragment program, however, must reduce everything to a single color that will update the frame buffer. (In some advanced profiles, fragment programs can write additional data such as a depth value as well.) The **COLOR** semantic assigned to the **color** member in a fragment program indicates that the member is the color to be used to update the frame buffer.

The entry function declaration for **C2E2f_passthrough** is this:

```
C2E2_Output C2E2f_passthrough(float4 color : COLOR)
```

The function returns the **C2E2f_Output** output structure with one color. The function receives a single four-component vector, named "color," bound to the **COLOR** input semantic. The **COLOR** input semantic for a fragment program is the color of the fragment interpolated by the rasterizer, based on the primitive's assigned vertex colors.

The body of **C2E2f_passthrough** is this:

```
{
  C2E2f_Output OUT;
  OUT.color = color;
  return OUT;
}
```

After declaring an **OUT** variable with the **C2E2f_Output** output structure type, the program assigns the fragment's interpolated color (the single input parameter) to the final fragment color in the output structure. Finally, the program returns the **OUT** structure.

2.3.1   Fragment Program Profiles

Just as you needed a profile to compile the **C2E1v_green** example, you also need a profile to compile the **C2E2f_passthrough** example. However, the profiles for compiling the **C2E1v_green** example were for vertex programs. To compile **C2E2f_passthrough**, you must choose an appropriate fragment profile.

Table 2-2 lists various profiles for compiling fragment programs.

Like the earlier vertex program example, this first fragment program example is so simple that you can compile the **C2E2f_passthrough** example with any of the profiles in Table 2-2.

Table 2-2. Cg Fragment Profiles

Profile Name	Programming Interface	Description
ps_1_1 **ps_1_2** **ps_1_3**	DirectX 8	Basic multivendor fragment programmability
fp20	OpenGL	Basic NVIDIA fragment programmability (corresponding to **NV_texture_shader** and **NV_register_combiners** functionality)
arbfp1	OpenGL	Advanced multivendor fragment programmability (corresponding to **ARB_fragment_program** functionality)
ps_2_0 **ps_2_x**	DirectX 9	Advanced multivendor fragment programmability
fp30	OpenGL	Advanced NVIDIA fragment programmability (corresponding to **NV_fragment_program** functionality)

Cg has a command-line compiler known as **cgc**, which is short for "Cg compiler." Dynamic compilation at runtime can be very powerful and is highly recommended. However, when you are writing Cg programs, you often want to verify that they compile correctly without having to run your 3D application. To detect Cg compiler errors while writing programs, try running **cgc**. It will "test compile" the Cg program files used by your application as part of your regular application build process. Using **cgc** in an integrated development environment (IDE) such as Microsoft's Visual C++ can make it quick and easy to find compilation errors. A good IDE will even help you quickly locate the appropriate line of code, based on line numbers in the error message, just as you would with C or C++ programs. Figure 2-3 shows an example of debugging compiler errors in Microsoft Visual Studio.

Cg developers often write a single Cg program that works for both OpenGL and Direct3D, even if they predominantly use one programming interface or the other. However, profile-dependent differences can exist between what is valid in the corresponding profiles for these 3D programming interfaces. So make it your practice to compile your Cg programs twice with **cgc**: once for the appropriate OpenGL profile, and again for the appropriate Direct3D profile.

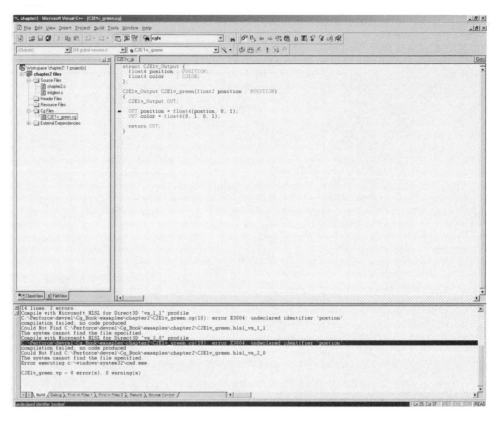

Figure 2-3. Locating Error Lines in an Integrated Development Environment

2.4 Rendering with Your Vertex and Fragment Program Examples

Now it's time to see your two simple Cg programs in action. Don't expect too much, because these are both very simple programs. However, you can still learn a lot by examining how the programs work together—and with the rest of the graphics pipeline—to draw a green triangle.

Look at the 2D triangle in Figure 2-4. This is the geometry that your vertex and fragment program will operate on in this example.

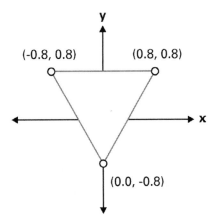

Figure 2-4. A 2D Triangle for Rendering

2.4.1 Rendering a Triangle with OpenGL

In OpenGL, you can render this 2D triangle with the following commands:

```
glBegin(GL_TRIANGLES);
  glVertex2f(-0.8, 0.8);
  glVertex2f(0.8, 0.8);
  glVertex2f(0.0, -0.8);
glEnd();
```

2.4.2 Rendering a Triangle with Direct3D

In Direct3D, you can render the same triangle with the following code:

```
D3DXVECTOR4 vertices[3] =
{
    D3DXVECTOR4(-0.8f,  0.8f, 0.f, 1.f),
    D3DXVECTOR4( 0.8f,  0.8f, 0.f, 1.f),
    D3DXVECTOR4( 0.0f, -0.8f, 0.f, 1.f),
};

m_pD3DDevice->DrawPrimitiveUP(D3DPT_TRIANGLELIST, 1,
  vertices, sizeof(D3DXVECTOR4));
```

There are other, more efficient ways to transfer vertices to the GPU in OpenGL or Direct3D. When you use Cg programs to process vertices, it doesn't matter how the application sends the vertices to the GPU.

2.4.3 Getting the Same Results

Figure 2-5 shows the result of rendering this triangle with the **C2E1v_green** vertex program and **C2E2f_passthrough** fragment program configured. The result is the same, whether rendered with OpenGL or Direct3D. Admittedly, it's not very exciting, but the triangle is solid green.

Figure 2-5. Rendering a Triangle with **C2E1v_green** and **C2E2f_passthrough**

The vertex program passes the specified 2D position of each vertex to the rasterizer. The rasterizer expects positions to be specified as coordinates in clip space. Clip space defines what is visible from the current viewpoint. If the vertex program supplies 2D coordinates, as is the case in Figure 2-5, the portion of the primitive that is rasterized is the portion of the primitive where x and y are between -1 and +1. The entire triangle is within the clipping region, so the complete triangle is rasterized.

Figure 2-6 shows the region of rasterization for 2D clip space.

Primitives are rendered into the frame buffer if they fall within the gray region (the region of clip space where x and y are between -1 and +1). You'll learn more about clip space in Chapter 4.

Figure 2-7 shows what happens when you use the **C2E1v_green** vertex program and **C2E2f_passthrough** fragment program with 2D geometry that is not entirely within the visible region of 2D clip space. When the stars include vertices that have x

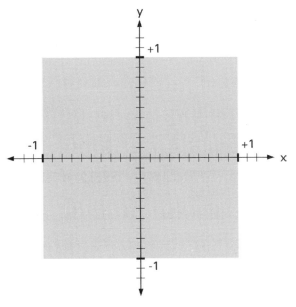

Figure 2-6. A 2D View of Clip Space

or *y* coordinates outside the -1 to +1 region, the rasterizer clips some of the green stars by the edge of the visible region. If no part of a primitive is within the viewable region of clip space, the rasterizer eliminates the primitive.

The GPU then transforms clip space automatically (by a simple scale and bias) into window space coordinates for the rasterizer. Effectively, the GPU stretches clip-space coordinates as necessary, prior to rasterization, to fit the rendering viewport and window position.

Figure 2-7. Primitives Rendered with `C2E1v_green` and `C2E2f_passthrough` Require 2D Clipping

Chapter 4 generalizes this 2D notion of clip space to 3D, and includes perspective views. But in this chapter and Chapter 3, the examples use 2D rendering to keep things simple.

2.5   Exercises

1. **Answer this:** What GPU profiles does your Cg compiler support? Consult your compiler's documentation or try running **cgc -help** at the command line. Which profiles are vertex profiles and which are fragment profiles?

2. **Try this yourself:** Modify the **C2E1v_green** vertex program to color the vertices red instead of green.

3. **Try this yourself:** Change the one triangle vertex position by extending the vertex coordinates outside the [-1, +1] range. Run the example. Is the triangle clipped as you would expect?

2.6   Further Reading

Check out the documentation, such as the *Cg Toolkit User's Manual: A Developer's Guide to Programmable Graphics*, that accompanies the Cg Toolkit software distribution.

Also, visit the Web site **www.cgshaders.org** for current Cg information. This site has articles, forums where you can ask questions, and freely available sample shader code.

Chapter 3

Parameters, Textures, and Expressions

This chapter continues to present Cg concepts through a series of simple vertex and fragment programs. The chapter has the following three sections:

- "Parameters" explains how Cg programs handle parameters.
- "Texture Samplers" explains how fragment programs access textures.
- "Math Expressions" shows how math expressions compute new vertex and fragment values.

3.1 Parameters

The **C2E1v_green** and **C2E2f_passthrough** examples from Chapter 2 are very basic. We will now broaden these examples to introduce additional parameters.

3.1.1 Uniform Parameters

C2E1v_green (see page 38 in Chapter 2) always assigns green for the vertex color. If you rename the **C2E1v_green** program and change the line that assigns the value of **OUT.color**, you can potentially make a different vertex program for any color you like.

For example, changing the appropriate line results in a hot pink shader:

```
OUT.color = float4(1.0, 0.41, 0.70, 1.0); // RGBA hot pink
```

The world is a colorful place, so you wouldn't want to have to write a different Cg program for every color under the sun. Instead, you can generalize the program by passing it a parameter that indicates the currently requested color.

The **C3E1v_anyColor** vertex program in Example 3-1 provides a **constantColor** parameter that your application can assign to any color, rather than just a particular constant color.

```
struct C3E1v_Output {
  float4 position : POSITION;
  float4 color    : COLOR;
};

C3E1v_Output C3E1v_anyColor(float2 position : POSITION,
                            uniform float4 constantColor)
{
  C3E1v_Output OUT;

  OUT.position = float4(position, 0, 1);
  OUT.color = constantColor;  // Some RGBA color

  return OUT;
}
```

Example 3-1. The **C3E1v_anyColor** Vertex Program

The difference between **C3E1v_anyColor** and **C2E1v_green** is the function interface definition and what each program assigns to **OUT.color**.

The updated function definition is this:

```
C3E1v_Output C3E1v_anyColor(float2 position : POSITION,
                            uniform float4 constantColor)
```

In addition to the position parameter, the new function definition has a parameter named **constantColor** that the program defines as type **uniform float4**. As we discussed earlier, the **float4** type is a vector of four floating-point values—in this case, assumed to be an RGBA color. What we have not discussed is the **uniform** type qualifier.

The **uniform** Type Qualifier

The **uniform** qualifier indicates the source of a variable's initial value. When a Cg program declares a variable as **uniform**, it conveys that the variable's initial value comes from an environment that is external to the specified Cg program. This external environment contains your 3D programming interface state and other name/value pairs established through the Cg runtime.

In the case of the **constantColor** variable in the **C3E1v_anyColor** example, the Cg compiler generates a vertex program that retrieves the variable's initial value from a vertex processor constant register within the GPU.

Using the Cg runtime, your 3D application can query a parameter handle for a uniform parameter name within a Cg program—in this case, **constantColor**—and use the handle to load the proper value for the particular uniform variable into the GPU. The details of how uniform parameter values are specified and loaded vary by profile, but the Cg runtime makes this process easy. Appendix B explains how to do this.

Our **C3E1v_anyColor** vertex program assigns the vertex output color to the value of its **constantColor** uniform variable, as shown:

```
OUT.color = constantColor;   // Some RGBA color
```

Whatever color the application specifies for the **constantColor** uniform variable is the color that the Cg program assigns to the output vertex color when **C3E1v_anyColor** transforms a vertex.

The addition of a uniform parameter lets us generalize our initial example to render any color, when originally it could render only green.

When There Is No **uniform** Qualifier

When a Cg program does *not* include the **uniform** qualifier to specify a variable, you can assign the initial value for the variable in one of the following ways:

- Using an explicit initial assignment:
```
float4 green = float4(0, 1, 0, 1);
```

- Using a semantic:
```
float4 position : POSITION;
```

- Leaving it undefined or equal to zero, depending on the profile:

```
float whatever;    // May be initially undefined or zero
```

What uniform Means in RenderMan vs. Cg

 The **uniform** reserved word will be familiar to programmers who have written shaders in Render-Man. However, the meaning of **uniform** in Cg is different from its meaning in RenderMan.

In RenderMan, the **uniform** storage modifier indicates variables whose values are constant over a shaded surface, whereas **varying** variables are those whose values can vary over the surface.

Cg does not have this same distinction. In Cg, a **uniform**-qualified variable obtains its initial value from an external environment and, except for this initialization difference, is the same as any other variable. Cg permits all variables to vary, unless the variable has the **const** type qualifier specified. Unlike RenderMan, Cg has no **varying** reserved word.

Despite the semantic difference between RenderMan's concept of **uniform** and Cg's concept of it, variables declared **uniform** in RenderMan correspond to variables declared **uniform** in Cg, and vice versa.

3.1.2   The const Type Qualifier

Cg also provides the **const** qualifier. The **const** qualifier affects variables the same way that the **const** qualifier does in C and C++: it restricts how a variable in your program may be used. You cannot assign a value to, or otherwise change, a variable that is specified as constant. Use the **const** qualifier to indicate that a certain value should never change. The Cg compiler will generate an error if it detects usage that would modify a variable declared as **const**.

Here are some examples of usage *not* allowed when a program qualifies a variable with **const**:

```
const float pi = 3.14159;
pi = 0.4;        // An error because pi is specified const
float a = pi++;  // Implicit modification is also an error
```

The **const** and **uniform** type qualifiers are independent, so a variable can be specified using **const** or **uniform**, both **const** and **uniform**, or neither.

3.1.3 Varying Parameters

You have already seen examples of a per-vertex varying parameter in both **C2E1v_green** and **C3E1v_anyColor**. The **POSITION** input semantic that follows the **position** parameter in **C2E1v_green** and **C3E1v_anyColor** indicates that the GPU is to initialize each respective **position** parameter with the input position of each vertex processed by each respective program.

Semantics provide a way to initialize Cg program parameters with values that vary either from vertex to vertex (in vertex programs) or fragment to fragment (in fragment programs).

A slight modification to **C3E1v_anyColor**, called **C3E2v_varying**, in Example 3-2, lets the program output not merely a single constant color, but rather a color and texture coordinate set (used for accessing textures) that can vary per vertex.

```
struct C3E2v_Output {
  float4 position : POSITION;
  float4 color    : COLOR;
  float2 texCoord : TEXCOORD0;
};

C3E2v_Output C3E2v_varying(float2 position : POSITION,
                           float4 color    : COLOR,
                           float2 texCoord : TEXCOORD0)
{
  C3E2v_Output OUT;

  OUT.position = float4(position, 0, 1);
  OUT.color    = color;
  OUT.texCoord = texCoord;

  return OUT;
}
```

Example 3-2. The **C3E2v_varying** Vertex Program

The **C3E2v_varying** example prototypes its vertex program as:

```
C3E2v_Output C3E2v_varying(float2 position : POSITION,
                           float4 color    : COLOR,
                           float2 texCoord : TEXCOORD0)
```

The **C3E2v_varying** example replaces the **constantColor** parameter declared as a uniform parameter in the **C3E1v_anyColor** example with two new nonuniform parameters, **color** and **texCoord**. The program assigns the **COLOR** and **TEXCOORD0** semantics, respectively, to the two parameters. These two semantics correspond to the application-specified vertex color and texture coordinate set zero, respectively.

Instead of outputting the per-vertex position and a constant color, this new program transforms each vertex by outputting each vertex's position, color, and a single texture coordinate set with the following code:

```
OUT.position = float4(position, 0, 1);
OUT.color    = color;
OUT.texCoord = texCoord;
```

Figure 3-1 shows the result of rendering our original triangle using the **C3E2v_varying** vertex program and the **C2E2f_passthrough** fragment program. Here, we assume that you have used OpenGL or Direct3D to assign the vertices of the triangle the per-vertex colors bright blue for the top two vertices and off-blue for the bottom vertex. Color interpolation performed by the rasterization hardware smoothly shades the interior fragments of the triangle. Although per-vertex texture coordinates are input and output by the **C3E2v_varying** vertex program, the subsequent **C2E2f_passthrough** fragment program ignores the texture coordinates.

Figure 3-1. Rendering a Gradiated 2D Triangle with **C3E2v_varying** and **C2E2f_passthrough**

Chapter 3: Parameters, Textures, and Expressions

3.2   Texture Samplers

The **C3E2v_varying** example passed per-vertex texture coordinates through the vertex program. Although the **C2E2f_passthrough** fragment program ignores texture coordinates, this next fragment program, called **C3E3f_texture** and shown in Example 3-3, uses the texture coordinates to sample a texture image.

```
struct C3E3f_Output {
  float4 color : COLOR;
};

C3E3f_Output C3E3f_texture(float2 texCoord : TEXCOORD0,
                           uniform sampler2D decal)
{
  C3E3f_Output OUT;
  OUT.color = tex2D(decal, texCoord);
  return OUT;
}
```

Example 3-3. The **C3E3f_texture** Fragment Program

The **C3E3f_Output** structure is essentially the same as the **C2E2f_Output** structure used by **C2E2f_passthrough**, our prior fragment program example. What is new about the **C3E3f_texture** example is in its declaration:

```
C3E3f_Output C3E3f_texture(float2 texCoord : TEXCOORD0,
                           uniform sampler2D decal)
```

The **C3E3f_texture** fragment program receives an interpolated texture coordinate set but ignores the interpolated color. The program also receives a uniform parameter called **decal** of type **sampler2D**.

3.2.1   Sampler Objects

A *sampler* in Cg refers to an external object that Cg can sample, such as a texture. The **2D** suffix for the **sampler2D** type indicates that the texture is a conventional two-dimensional texture. Table 3-1 lists other sampler types supported by Cg that correspond to different kinds of textures. You will encounter some of these in later chapters.

Table 3-1. Cg Sampler Types

Sampler Type	Texture Type	Applications
`sampler1D`	One-dimensional texture	1D functions
`sampler2D`	Two-dimensional texture	Decals, normal maps, gloss maps, shadow maps, and others
`sampler3D`	Three-dimensional texture	Volumetric data, 3D attenuation functions
`samplerCUBE`	Cube map texture	Environment maps, normalization cube maps
`samplerRECT`	Non-power-of-two, non-mipmapped 2D texture	Video images, photographs, temporary buffers

Texture coordinates specify where to look when accessing a texture. Figure 3-2 shows a 2D texture, along with a query based on the texture coordinates (0.6, 0.4). Typically, texture coordinates range from 0 to 1, but you can also use values outside the range. We will not go into detail about this here, because the resulting behavior depends on how you set up your texture in OpenGL or Direct3D.

The semantic for the texture coordinate set named **texCoord** in Example 3-3 is **TEXCOORD0**, corresponding to the texture coordinate set for texture unit 0. As the name of the sampler parameter **decal** implies, the intent of this fragment program is to use the fragment's interpolated texture coordinate set to access a texture.

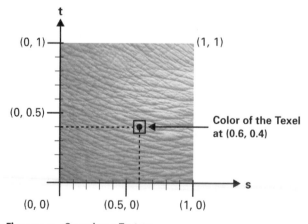

Figure 3-2. Querying a Texture

Chapter 3: Parameters, Textures, and Expressions

3.2.2 Sampling Textures

The next interesting line of **C3E3f_texture** accesses the decal texture with the interpolated texture coordinates:

```
OUT.color = tex2D(decal, texCoord);
```

The routine **tex2D** belongs to the Cg Standard Library. It is a member of a family of routines that access different types of samplers with a specified texture coordinate set and then return a vector result. The result is the sampled data at the location indicated by the texture coordinate set in the sampler object.

In practice, this amounts to a texture lookup. How the texture is sampled and filtered depends on the texture type and texture parameters of the texture object associated with the Cg sampler variable. You can determine the texture properties for a given texture by using OpenGL or Direct3D texture specification commands, depending on your choice of 3D programming interface. Your application is likely to establish this association by using the Cg runtime.

The **2D** suffix indicates that **tex2D** must sample a sampler object of type **sampler2D**. Likewise, the **texCUBE** routine returns a vector, accepts a sampler of type **samplerCUBE** for its first argument, and requires a three-component texture coordinate set for its second argument.

Basic fragment profiles (such as **ps_1_1** and **fp20**) limit texture-sampling routines, such as **tex2D** and **texCUBE**, to the texture coordinate set that corresponds to the sampler's texture unit. To be as simple as possible and support all fragment profiles, the **C3E3f_texture** example follows this restriction. (See Section 2.3.1 for a brief introduction to profiles.)

Advanced fragment profiles (such as **ps_2_x**, **arbfp1**, and **fp30**) allow a sampler to be sampled using texture coordinate sets from other texture units, or even texture coordinates computed in your Cg program.

3.2.3 Sending Texture Coordinates While Sampling a Texture

The **C3E2v_varying** vertex program passes a per-vertex position, color, and texture coordinate set to the rasterizer. The **C3E3f_texture** fragment program ignores the interpolated color, but samples a texture image with the interpolated texture coordinate set. Figure 3-3 shows what happens when you first bind both Cg programs with a

Figure 3-3. Rendering a Textured 2D Triangle with `C3E2v_varying` and `C3E3f_texture`

texture that contains the image of a gruesome face, and then render our simple triangle with additional per-vertex texture coordinates assigned.

3.3 Math Expressions

So far, all the Cg examples we've presented have done little more than pass along parameters, or use a parameter to sample a texture. Conventional nonprogrammable 3D programming interfaces can accomplish just as much. The point of these examples was to introduce you to Cg and show the structure of simple Cg programs.

More interesting Cg programs perform computations on input parameters by using operators and built-in functions provided by the Cg Standard Library.

3.3.1 Operators

Cg supports the same arithmetic, relational, and other operators provided by C and C++. This means that addition is expressed with a + sign, multiplication with a * symbol, and greater-than-or-equal-to with the **>=** operator. You have already seen in prior examples that assignment is accomplished with the **=** sign.

Here are some examples of Cg expressions:

```
float total = 0.333 * (red + green + blue);
total += 0.333 * alpha;
float smaller = (a < b) ? a : b;
float eitherOption = optionA || optionB;
float allTrue = v[0] && v[1] && v[2];
```

Cg is different from C and C++ because it provides built-in support for arithmetic operations on vector quantities. You can accomplish this in C++ by writing your own classes that use operator loading, but vector math operations are a standard part of the language in Cg.

The following operators work on vectors in a component-wise fashion:

*	Multiplication
/	Division
–	Negation
+	Addition
–	Subtraction

When a scalar and a vector are used as operands of one of these component-wise operators, the scalar value is replicated (sometimes called "smeared") into a vector of the matching size.

Here are some examples of vector Cg expressions:

```
float3 modulatedColor = color * float3(0.2, 0.4, 0.5);
modulatedColor *= 0.5;
float3 specular = float3(0.1, 0.0, 0.2);
modulatedColor += specular;
negatedColor = -modulatedColor;
float3 direction = positionA - positionB;
```

Table 3-2. Precedence, Associativity, and Usage of Operators

Operators	Associativity	Usage
( ) [ ] `->` .	Left to right	Function call, array reference, structure reference, component selection
! `~` ++ — + – `*` `&` (`type`) `sizeof`	Right to left	Unary operators: negation, increment, decrement, positive, negative, indirection, address, cast
* / `%`	Left to right	Multiplication, division, remainder
+ –	Left to right	Addition, subtraction
`<<` `>>`	Left to right	Shift operators
< <= > >=	Left to right	Relational operators
== !=	Left to right	Equality, inequality
`&`	Left to right	Bitwise AND
`^`	Left to right	Bitwise exclusive OR
`|`	Left to right	Bitwise OR
&&	Left to right	Logical AND
||	Left to right	Logical OR
? :	Right to left	Conditional expression

= += -= *= /=
 `%=` `&=` `^=` `|=`
 `<<=` `>>=`
	Right to left	Assignment, assignment expressions

,	Left to right	Comma operator

Notes
- Operators are listed top to bottom, from highest to lowest precedence.
- Operators in the same row have the same precedence.
- Operators marked with a reverse highlight are currently reserved for future use.

Chapter 3: Parameters, Textures, and Expressions

Table 3-2 presents the complete list of operators, along with their precedence, associativity, and usage. Operators marked with a reverse highlight are currently reserved. However, no existing Cg profiles support these reserved operators because current graphics hardware does not support bitwise integer operations.

3.3.2 Profile-Dependent Numeric Data Types

When you program in C or C++ and declare variables, you pick from a few different-sized integer data types (**int**, **long**, **short**, **char**) and a couple of different-sized floating-point data types (**float**, **double**).

Your CPU provides the hardware support for all these basic data types. However, GPUs do not generally support so many data types—though, as GPUs evolve, they promise to provide more data types. For example, existing GPUs do not support pointer types in vertex or fragment programs.

Representing Continuous Data Types

Cg provides the **float**, **half**, and **double** floating-point types. Cg's approach to defining these types is similar to C's—the language does not mandate particular precisions. It is understood that **half** has a range and precision less than or equal to the range and precision of **float**, and **float** has a range and precision less than or equal to the range and precision of **double**.

The **half** data type does not exist in C or C++. This new data type introduced by Cg holds a half-precision floating-point value (typically 16-bit) that is more efficient in storage and performance than standard-precision floating-point (typically 32-bit) types.

The NVIDIA CineFX GPU architecture supports half-precision values for fragment programs. The **half** data type is often appropriate for intermediate values in fragment programs, such as colors and normalized vectors. By using **half** values when possible rather than **float**, you speed up the performance of your fragment programs.

GPUs, by design, provide data types that represent continuous quantities, such as colors and vectors. GPUs do not (currently) support data types that represent inherently discrete quantities, such as alphanumeric characters and bit masks, because GPUs do not typically operate on this kind of data.

Continuous quantities are not limited to integer values. When programming a CPU, programmers typically use floating-point data types to represent continuous values because floating-point types can represent fractional values. Continuous values processed by GPUs, particularly at the fragment level, have been limited to narrow ranges such as [0, 1] or [-1, +1], rather than supporting the expansive range provided by floating-point. For example, colors are often limited to the [0, 1] range, and normalized vectors are, by definition, confined to the [-1, +1] range. These range-limited data types are known as "fixed-point," rather than floating-point.

Although fixed-point data types use limited precision, they can represent continuous quantities. However, they lack the range of floating-point data types, whose encoding is similar to scientific notation. A floating-point value encodes a variable exponent in addition to a mantissa (similar to how numbers are written in scientific notation, such as 2.99×10^8), whereas a fixed-point value assumes a fixed exponent. For example, an unnormalized vector or a sufficiently large texture coordinate may require floating-point for the value to avoid overflowing a given fixed-point range.

Current GPUs handle floating-point equally well when executing vertex and fragment programs. However, earlier programmable GPUs provide floating-point data types only for vertex processing; they offer only fixed-point data types for fragment processing.

Cg must be able to manipulate fixed-point data types to support programmability for GPUs that lack floating-point fragment programmability. This means that certain fragment profiles use fixed-point values. Table 3-3 lists various Cg profiles and describes how they represent various data types. The implication for Cg programmers is that **float** may not actually mean floating-point in all profiles in all contexts.

 The **fp20** and **ps_1_1** profiles treat variables in fragment coloring as fixed-point values in the range [-1, +1]. By *fragment coloring,* we mean math operations performed after the texture mapping results. If you want true floating-point data types, use the **arbfp1, fp30,** or **vp_2_0** profiles, but be aware these are advanced profiles not supported by older GPUs.

 The CineFX architecture also supports a special high-performance continuous data type called **fixed** for fragment programs. The **fixed** data type has a [-2, +2) range (meaning, ranging from negative 2 to not quite positive 2) for the **fp30** profile. In other profiles, the **fixed** data type is synonymous with the smallest continuous data type available. Although the Cg compiler (**cgc**) and runtime support the **fixed** data type (and vector versions such as **fixed3** and **fixed4**), Microsoft's HLSL compiler (**fxc**) does not.

Chapter 3: Parameters, Textures, and Expressions

Table 3-3. Data Types for Various Profiles

Profile Names	Types	Numerics
arbfp1 arbvp1 vs_1_1 vs_2_0 vp20 vp30	float double half fixed	Floating-point
	int	Floating-point clamped to integers
fp20	float double half int fixed	Floating-point for texture mapping; fixed point with [-1, +1] range for fragment coloring
ps_1_1 ps_1_2 ps_1_3	float double half int fixed	Floating-point for texture mapping; fixed-point with GPU-dependent range for fragment coloring; range depends on underlying Direct3D capability
ps_2_0 ps_2_x	float double	24-bit floating-point (minimum)
	int	Floating-point clamped to integers
	half	16-bit floating-point (minimum)
	fixed	Depends on compiler settings
fp30	float double	Floating-point
	int	Floating-point clamped to integers
	half	16-bit floating-point
	fixed	Fixed-point with [-2, 2) range

3.3.3 Standard Library Built-In Functions

The Cg Standard Library contains many built-in functions that simplify GPU programming. In many cases, the functions map to a single native GPU instruction, so they can be very efficient.

Table 3-4. Selected Cg Standard Library Functions

Function Prototype	Profile Usage	Description
abs(x)	All	Absolute value
cos(x)	Vertex, advanced fragment	Cosine of angle in radians
cross(v1, v2)	Vertex, advanced fragment	Cross product of two vectors
ddx(a) ddy(a)	Advanced fragment	Approximate partial derivatives of a with respect to window-space x or y coordinate, respectively
determinant(M)	Vertex, advanced fragment	Determinant of a matrix
dot(a, b)	All, but restricted basic fragment	Dot product of two vectors
floor(x)	Vertex, advanced fragment	Largest integer not greater than x
isnan(x)	Advanced vertex and fragment	True if x is not a number (NaN)
lerp(a, b, f)	All	Linear interpolation between a and b based on f
log2(x)	Vertex, advanced fragment	Base 2 logarithm of x
max(a, b)	All	Maximum of a and b
mul(M, N) mul(M, v) mul(v, M)	Vertex, advanced fragment	Matrix-by-matrix multiplication Matrix-by-vector multiplication Vector-by-matrix multiplication
pow(x, y)	Vertex, advanced fragment	Raise x to the power y
radians(x)	Vertex, advanced fragment	Degrees-to-radians conversion
reflect(v, n)	Vertex, advanced fragment	Reflection vector of entering ray v and normal vector n

Table 3-4 (*continued*). Selected Cg Standard Library Functions

Function Prototype	Profile Usage	Description
`round(x)`	Vertex, advanced fragment	Round *x* to nearest integer
`rsqrt(x)`	Vertex, advanced fragment	Reciprocal square root
`tex2D(sampler, x)`	Fragment, restricted for basic	2D texture lookup
`tex3Dproj(sampler, x)`	Fragment, restricted for basic	Projective 3D texture lookup
`texCUBE(sampler, x)`	Fragment, restricted for basic	Cube-map texture lookup

These built-in functions are similar to C's Standard Library functions. The Cg Standard Library provides a practical set of trigonometric, exponential, vector, matrix, and texture functions. But there are no Cg Standard Library routines for input/output, string manipulation, or memory allocation, because Cg does not support these operations (though your C or C++ application certainly could).

We already used one Cg Standard Library function, **tex2D**, in Example 3-3. Refer to Table 3-4 for a select list of other functions that the Cg Standard Library provides. You can find a complete list of Cg Standard Library functions in Appendix E.

Function Overloading

The Cg Standard Library "overloads" most of its routines so that the same routine works for multiple data types. As in C++, function overloading provides multiple implementations for a routine by using a single name and differently typed parameters.

Overloading is very convenient. It means you can use a function, for example **abs**, with a scalar parameter, a two-component parameter, a three-component parameter, or a four-component parameter. In each case, Cg "calls" the appropriate version of the absolute value function:

```
float4 a4 = float4(0.4, -1.2, 0.3, 0.2);
float2 b2 = float2(-0.3, 0.9);
float4 a4abs = abs(a4);
float2 b2abs = abs(b2);
```

The code fragment calls the **abs** routine twice. In the first instance, **abs** accepts a four-component vector. In the second instance, **abs** accepts a two-component vector. The compiler automatically calls the appropriate version of **abs**, based on the parameters passed to the routine. The extensive use of function overloading in the Cg Standard Library means you do not need to think about what routine to call for a given-size vector or other parameter. Cg automatically picks the appropriate implementation of the routine you name.

Function overloading is not limited to the Cg Standard Library. Additionally, you can write your own internal functions with function overloading.

Function overloading in Cg can even apply to different implementations of the same routine name for different profiles. For example, an advanced vertex profile for a new GPU may have special instructions to compute the trigonometric sine and cosine functions. A basic vertex profile for older GPUs may lack that special instruction. However, you may be able to approximate sine or cosine with a sequence of supported vertex instructions, although with less accuracy. You could write two functions and specify that each require a particular profile.

Cg's support for profile-dependent overloading helps you isolate profile-dependent limitations in your Cg programs to helper functions. The *Cg Toolkit User's Manual: A Developer's Guide to Programmable Graphics* has more information about profile-dependent overloading.

The Cg Standard Library's Efficiency and Precision

Whenever possible, use the Cg Standard Library to do math or other operations it supports. The Cg Standard Library functions are as efficient and precise as—or more efficient and precise than—similar functions you might write yourself.

For example, the **dot** function computes the dot product of two vectors. You might write a dot product function yourself, such as this one:

```
float myDot(float3 a, float3 b)
{
  return a[0]*b[0] + a[1]*b[1] + a[2]*b[2];
}
```

This is the same math that the **dot** function implements. However, the **dot** function maps to a special GPU instruction, so the dot product provided by the Cg Standard Library is very likely to be faster and more accurate than the **myDot** routine.

By using Cg Standard Library functions wherever possible, you guide the Cg compiler to generate the most efficient and precise program for your particular GPU.

3.3.4   2D Twisting

In the next example you will put expressions, operators, and the Cg Standard Library to work. This example demonstrates how to twist 2D geometry. The farther a vertex is from the center of the window, the more the vertex program rotates the vertex around the center of the window.

The **C3E4v_twist** program shown in Example 3-4 demonstrates scalar-by-vector multiplication, scalar addition and multiplication, scalar negation, the **length** Standard Library routine, and the **sincos** Standard Library routine.

```
struct C3E4_Output {
  float4 position : POSITION;
  float4 color    : COLOR;
};

C3E4_Output C3E4v_twist(float2 position : POSITION,
                        float4 color    : COLOR,

                        uniform float twisting)
{
  C3E4_Output OUT;
  float angle = twisting * length(position);
  float cosLength, sinLength;
  sincos(angle, sinLength, cosLength);
  OUT.position[0] = cosLength * position[0] +
                    -sinLength * position[1];
  OUT.position[1] = sinLength * position[0] +
                    cosLength * position[1];
  OUT.position[2] = 0;
  OUT.position[3] = 1;
  OUT.color = color;
  return OUT;
}
```

Example 3-4. The **C3E4v_twist** Vertex Program

3.3 Math Expressions

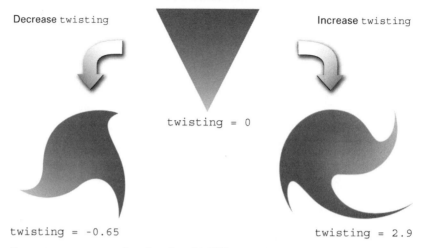

Decrease `twisting`

Increase `twisting`

twisting = 0

twisting = -0.65

twisting = 2.9

Figure 3-4. `C3E4v_twist` Results with Different `twisting` Parameter Settings

The **C3E4v_twist** program inputs the vertex **position** and **color** as varying parameters and a uniform scalar **twisting** scale factor. Figure 3-4 shows the example with various amounts of twisting.

The `length` and `sincos` Standard Library Routines

The **length** routine has an overloaded prototype, where *SCALAR* is any scalar data type and *VECTOR* is a vector of the same scalar data type as *SCALAR* with one, two, three, or four components:

```
SCALAR length(VECTOR x);
```

The Cg Standard Library routine **length** returns the scalar length of its single input parameter:

```
float angle = twisting * length(position);
```

The program computes an angle in radians that is the **twisting** parameter times the length of the input position. Then the **sincos** Standard Library routine computes the sine and cosine of this angle.

The **sincos** routine has the following overloaded prototype, where *SCALAR* is any scalar data type:

```
void sincos(SCALAR angle, out SCALAR s, out SCALAR c);
```

When **sincos** returns, Cg updates the calling parameters **s** and **c** with the sine and cosine, respectively, of the **angle** parameter (assumed to be in radians).

Call-by-Result Parameter Passing

An **out** qualifier indicates that when the routine returns, Cg must assign the final value of a formal parameter qualified by **out** to its corresponding caller parameter. Initially, the value of an **out** parameter is undefined. This convention is known as *call-by-result* (or *copy-out*) parameter passing.

C has no similar parameter-passing convention. C++ allows a reference parameter to function (indicated by **&** prefixed to formal parameters), but this is a *call-by-reference* parameter-passing convention, not Cg's call-by-result convention.

Cg also provides the **in** and **inout** keywords. The **in** type qualifier indicates that Cg passes the parameter by value, effectively *call-by-value*. The calling routine's parameter value initializes the corresponding formal parameter of the routine called. When a routine with **in**-qualified parameters returns, Cg discards the values of these parameters unless the parameter is also **out**-qualified.

C uses the copy-by-value parameter-passing convention for all parameters. C++ uses copy-by-value for all parameters, except those passed by reference.

The **inout** type qualifier (or the **in** and **out** type qualifiers that are specified for a single parameter) combine call-by-value with call-by-result (otherwise known as *call-by-value-result* or *copy-in-copy-out*).

The **in** qualifier is optional because if you do not specify an **in**, **out**, or **inout** qualifier, the **in** qualifier is assumed.

You can use **out** and **inout** parameters and still return a conventional return value.

Rotating Vertices

Once the program has computed the sine and cosine of the angle of rotation for the vertex, it applies a rotation transformation. Equation 3-1 expresses 2D rotation.

$$\begin{bmatrix} x' \\ y' \end{bmatrix} = \begin{bmatrix} \cos\theta & -\sin\theta \\ \sin\theta & \cos\theta \end{bmatrix} \begin{bmatrix} x \\ y \end{bmatrix}$$

Equation 3-1. 2D Rotation

The following code fragment implements this equation. In Chapter 4, you will learn how to express this type of matrix math more succinctly and efficiently, but for now we'll implement the math the straightforward way:

```
OUT.position[0] = cosLength * position[0] +
                  -sinLength * position[1];
OUT.position[1] = sinLength * position[0] +
                  cosLength * position[1];
```

The Importance of Tessellation for Vertex Programs

The **C3E4v_twist** program works by rotating vertices around the center of the image. As the magnitude of the twist rotation increases, an object may require more vertices—thus higher tessellation—to reproduce the twisting effect reasonably.

Generally, when a vertex program involves nonlinear computations, such as the trigonometric functions in this example, sufficient tessellation is required for acceptable results. This is because the values of the vertices are interpolated linearly by the rasterizer as it creates fragments. If there is insufficient tessellation, the vertex program may reveal the tessellated nature of the underlying geometry. Figure 3-5 shows how increasing the amount of tessellation improves the twisted appearance of the **C3E4v_twist** example.

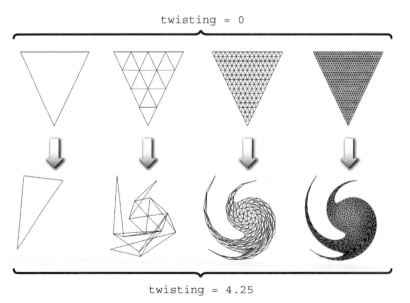

Figure 3-5. Improving the Fidelity of **C3E4v_twist** by Increasing Tessellation

3.3.5 Double Vision

Now we demonstrate how to combine a vertex program and a fragment program to achieve a textured "double vision" effect. The idea is to sample the same texture twice, based on slightly shifted texture coordinates, and then blend the samples equally.

The **C3E5v_twoTextures** vertex program shown in Example 3-5 shifts a single texture coordinate position twice, using two distinct offsets to generate two slightly separated texture coordinate sets. The fragment program then accesses a texture image at the two offset locations and equally blends the two texture results. Figure 3-6 shows the rendering results and the required inputs.

```
void C3E5v_twoTextures(float2 position : POSITION,
                       float2 texCoord : TEXCOORD0,

              out float4 oPosition : POSITION,
              out float2 leftTexCoord : TEXCOORD0,
              out float2 rightTexCoord : TEXCOORD1,

           uniform float2 leftSeparation,
           uniform float2 rightSeparation)
{
  C3E5v_Output OUT;

  oPosition     = float4(position, 0, 1);
  leftTexCoord  = texCoord + leftSeparation;
  rightTexCoord = texCoord + rightSeparation;

  return OUT;
}
```

Example 3-5. The **C3E5v_twoTextures** Vertex Program

The Double Vision Vertex Program

The **C3E5v_twoTextures** program in Example 3-5 passes through the vertex position. The program outputs the single input texture coordinate twice, once shifted by the **leftSeparation** uniform parameter and then shifted by the **rightSeparation** uniform parameter.

```
  oPosition     = float4(position, 0, 1);
  leftTexCoord  = texCoord + leftSeparation;
  rightTexCoord = texCoord + rightSeparation;
```

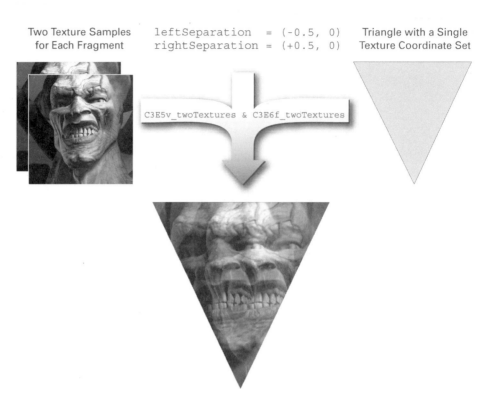

Two Texture Samples for Each Fragment

leftSeparation = (-0.5, 0)
rightSeparation = (+0.5, 0)

Triangle with a Single Texture Coordinate Set

`C3E5v_twoTextures & C3E6f_twoTextures`

Figure 3-6. Creating a Double Vision Effect with `C3E5v_twoTextures` and `C3E6f_twoTextures`

Out Parameters vs. Output Structures

The `C3E5v_twoTextures` example also shows a different approach to outputting parameters. Rather than return an output structure, as all our previous examples have done, the `C3E5v_twoTextures` example returns nothing; the function's return type is **void**. Instead, **out** parameters with associated semantics, which are part of the entry function's prototype, indicate which parameters are output parameters. The choice of using **out** parameters or an output return structure to output parameters from an entry function is up to you. There is no functional difference between the two approaches. You can even mix them.

The remainder of this book uses the **out** parameter approach, because it avoids having to specify output structures. We add an "**o**" prefix for **out** parameters to distinguish input and output parameters that would otherwise have the same name—for example, the **position** and **oPosition** parameters.

Chapter 3: Parameters, Textures, and Expressions

```
void C3E6f_twoTextures(float2 leftTexCoord  : TEXCOORD0,
                       float2 rightTexCoord : TEXCOORD1,

                   out float4 color : COLOR,

               uniform sampler2D decal)
{
  float4 leftColor  = tex2D(decal, leftTexCoord);
  float4 rightColor = tex2D(decal, rightTexCoord);
  color = lerp(leftColor, rightColor, 0.5);
}
```

Example 3-6. The `C3E6f_twoTextures` Fragment Program

In Example 3-5 and subsequent examples, we also line up and group the parameters to the entry function as input, output, and uniform parameters. This style takes extra work to format code, but we use it in this book to make the examples easier to read, particularly when the examples have many parameters.

The Double Vision Fragment Program for Advanced Fragment Profiles

The **C3E6f_twoTextures** fragment program in Example 3-6 takes the two shifted and interpolated texture coordinate sets computed by **C3E5v_twoTextures** and uses them to sample the same texture image twice, as shown in Figure 3-6.

```
  float4 leftColor  = tex2D(decal, leftTexCoord);
  float4 rightColor = tex2D(decal, rightTexCoord);
```

Then the program computes the average of the two color samples:

```
  color = lerp(leftColor, rightColor, 0.5);
```

The **lerp** routine computes a weighted linear interpolation of two same-sized vectors. The mnemonic *lerp* stands for "linear interpolation." The routine has an overloaded prototype in which *VECTOR* is a vector with one, two, three, or four components and *TYPE* is a scalar or vector with the same number of components and element types as *VECTOR*:

```
VECTOR lerp(VECTOR a, VECTOR b, TYPE weight);
```

3.3 Math Expressions

The **lerp** routine computes:

$$result = (1 - weight) \times a + weight \times b$$

A *weight* of 0.5 gives a uniform average. There is no requirement that the weight be within the 0 to 1 range.

Unfortunately, the **C3E6f_twoTextures** fragment program will not compile with basic fragment profiles such as **fp20** and **ps_1_1** (you will learn why shortly). It compiles fine, however, with advanced fragment profiles, such as **fp30** and **ps_2_0**.

The Double Vision Fragment Program for Basic Fragment Profiles

The **C3E6f_twoTextures** example uses two texture coordinate sets, 0 and 1, to access texture unit 0. Because of this, the program does not compile with basic fragment program profiles. Such profiles can use only a given texture coordinate set with the set's corresponding texture unit due to limitations in third-generation and earlier GPUs.

You can alter the **C3E6f_twoTextures** program slightly so that it works with basic and advanced fragment profiles. The **C3E7f_twoTextures** version in Example 3-7 contains the necessary alterations.

```
void C3E7f_twoTextures(float2 leftTexCoord  : TEXCOORD0,
                       float2 rightTexCoord : TEXCOORD1,

                  out float4 color : COLOR;

              uniform sampler2D decal0,
              uniform sampler2D decal1)
{
  float4 leftColor  = tex2D(decal0, leftTexCoord);
  float4 rightColor = tex2D(decal1, rightTexCoord);
  color = lerp(leftColor, rightColor, 0.5);
}
```

Example 3-7. The **C3E7f_twoTextures** Fragment Program

The modified program requires two texture units:

```
              uniform sampler2D decal0,
              uniform sampler2D decal1
```

So that the two texture units sample the *same* texture image, the **C3E7f_twoTextures** fragment program requires the application to bind the same texture for two separate texture units. The original **C3E6f_twoTextures** program did not require the application to bind the texture twice.

When the program samples the two textures, it samples each texture unit with its corresponding texture coordinate set, as required by basic fragment program profiles:

```
float4 leftColor  = tex2D(decal0, leftTexCoord);
float4 rightColor = tex2D(decal1, rightTexCoord);
```

The performance of these two approaches is comparable. This example demonstrates that *simpler* Cg programs—those that are not too complicated—can often be written with a little extra care to run on older GPUs, which support basic vertex and fragment profiles, as well as on recent GPUs, which support advanced profiles.

3.4 Exercises

1. **Answer this:** Beyond mere convenience, why do you suppose the **sincos** Standard Library routine returns both the sine and the cosine of an angle? *Hint:* Think trigonometric identities.

2. **Answer this:** Explain in your own words why the increased tessellation shown in Figure 3-5 is required for the twisted triangle to look good.

3. **Try this yourself:** Modify the **C3E4v_twist** example so that the twisting centers on some arbitrary 2D point specified as a **uniform float2** parameter, rather than on the origin (0, 0).

4. **Try this yourself:** Modify the **C3E5v_twoTextures** and **C3E7f_twoTextures** programs to provide "quadruple vision." Make sure your new program works on both basic and advanced profiles. Assume that your GPU supports four texture units.

5. **Try this yourself:** Modify the **C3E5v_twoTextures** example to return an output structure rather than use **out** parameters. Also, modify an earlier example, such as **C3E4v_twist**, to use **out** parameters rather than return an output structure. Which approach do you prefer?

3.5 Further Reading

You can learn more about 2×2 matrices, such as the rotation matrix in the twist example, in *The Geometry Toolbox for Graphics and Modeling* (A. K. Peters, 1998), by Gerald Farin and Dianne Hansford.

Chapter 4

Transformations

When you write vertex or fragment programs, it is important to understand the coordinate systems that you are working with. This chapter explains the transformations that take place in the graphics pipeline, without going into detail about the underlying mathematics. The chapter has the following two sections:

- **"Coordinate Systems"** explains the various coordinate systems used to represent vertex positions as they are transformed prior to rasterization.

- **"Applying the Theory"** describes how to apply the theory of coordinate systems and matrices in Cg.

4.1   Coordinate Systems

The purpose of the graphics pipeline is to create images and display them on your screen. The graphics pipeline takes geometric data representing an object or scene (typically in three dimensions) and creates a two-dimensional image from it. Your application supplies the geometric data as a collection of vertices that form polygons, lines, and points. The resulting image typically represents what an observer or camera would see from a particular vantage point.

As the geometric data flows through the pipeline, the GPU's vertex processor transforms the constituent vertices into one or more different coordinate systems, each of which serves a particular purpose. Cg vertex programs provide a way for you to program these transformations yourself.

Vertex programs may perform other tasks, such as lighting (discussed in Chapter 5) and animation (discussed in Chapter 6), but transforming vertex positions is a task *required* by all vertex programs. You cannot write a vertex program that does not output a transformed position, because the rasterizer needs transformed positions in order to assemble primitives and generate fragments.

So far, the vertex program examples you've encountered limited their position processing to simple 2D transformations. This chapter explains how to implement conventional 3D transformations to render 3D objects.

Figure 4-1 illustrates the conventional arrangement of transforms used to process vertex positions. The diagram annotates the transitions between each transform with the coordinate space used for vertex positions as the positions pass from one transform to the next.

The following sections describe each coordinate system and transform in this sequence. We assume that you have some basic knowledge of matrices and transformations, and so we explain each stage of the pipeline with a high-level overview.

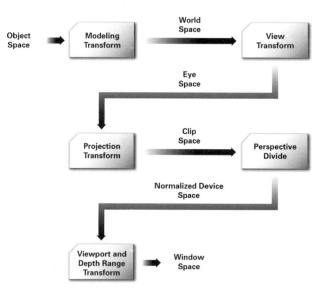

Figure 4-1. Coordinate Systems and Transforms for Vertex Processing

4.1.1 Object Space

Applications specify vertex positions in a coordinate system known as *object space* (also called *model space*). When an artist creates a 3D model of an object, the artist selects a convenient orientation, scale, and position with which to place the model's constituent vertices. The object space for one object may have no relationship to the object space of another object. For example, a cylinder may have an object-space coordinate system in which the origin lies at the center of the base and the *z* direction points along the axis of symmetry.

You represent each vertex position, whether in object space or in one of the subsequent spaces, as a vector. Typically, your application maintains each object-space 3D vertex position as an $\langle x, y, z \rangle$ vector. Each vertex may also have an accompanying object-space surface normal, also stored as an $\langle x, y, z \rangle$ vector.

4.1.2 Homogeneous Coordinates

More generally, we consider the $\langle x, y, z \rangle$ position vector to be merely a special case of the four-component $\langle x, y, z, w \rangle$ form. This type of four-component position vector is called a *homogeneous position*. When we express a vector position as an $\langle x, y, z \rangle$ quantity, we assume that there is an implicit 1 for its *w* component.

Mathematically, the *w* value is the value by which you would divide the *x*, *y*, and *z* components to obtain the conventional 3D (nonhomogeneous) position, as shown in Equation 4-1.

$$\left\langle \frac{x}{w}, \frac{y}{w}, \frac{z}{w}, 1 \right\rangle = \langle x, y, z, w \rangle$$

Equation 4-1. Converting Between Nonhomogeneous and Homogeneous Positions

Expressing positions in this homogeneous form has many advantages. For one, multiple transformations, including projective transformations required for perspective 3D views, can be combined efficiently into a single 4×4 matrix. This technique is explained in Section 4.2. Also, using homogeneous positions makes it unnecessary to perform expensive intermediate divisions and to create special cases involving perspective views. Homogeneous positions are also handy for representing directions and curved surfaces described by rational polynomials.

We will return to the *w* component when discussing the projection transform.

4.1.3 World Space

Object space for a particular object gives it no spatial relationship with respect to other objects. The purpose of *world space* is to provide some absolute reference for all the objects in your scene. How a world-space coordinate system is established is arbitrary. For example, you may decide that the origin of world space is the center of your room. Objects in the room are then positioned relative to the center of the room and some notion of scale (Is a unit of distance a foot or a meter?) and some notion of orientation (Does the positive *y*-axis point "up"? Is north in the direction of the positive *x*-axis?).

4.1.4 The Modeling Transform

The way an object, specified in object space, is positioned within world space is by means of a modeling transform. For example, you may need to rotate, translate, and scale the 3D model of a chair so that the chair is placed properly within your room's world-space coordinate system. Two chairs in the same room may use the same 3D chair model but have different modeling transforms, so that each chair exists at a distinct location in the room.

You can mathematically represent all the transforms in this chapter as a 4×4 matrix. Using the properties of matrices, you can combine several translations, rotations, scales, and projections into a single 4×4 matrix by multiplying them together. When you concatenate matrices in this way, the combined matrix also represents the combination of the respective transforms. This turns out to be very powerful, as you will see.

If you multiply the 4×4 matrix representing the modeling transform by the object-space position in homogeneous form (assuming a 1 for the *w* component if there is no explicit *w* component), the result is the same position transformed into world space. This same matrix math principle applies to all subsequent transforms discussed in this chapter.

Figure 4-2 illustrates the effect of several different modeling transformations. The left side of the figure shows a robot modeled in a basic pose with no modeling transformations applied. The right side shows what happens to the robot after you apply a series of modeling transformations to its various body parts. For example, you must rotate

Chapter 4: Transformations

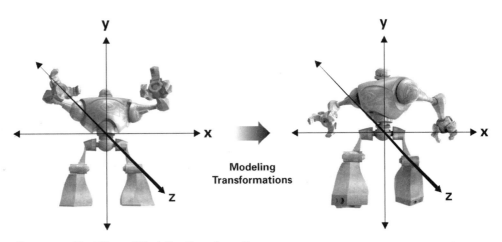

Figure 4-2. The Effect of Modeling Transformations

and translate the right arm to position it as shown. Further transformations may be required to translate and rotate the newly posed robot into the proper position and orientation in world space.

4.1.5 Eye Space

Ultimately, you want to look at your scene from a particular viewpoint (the "eye"). In the coordinate system known as *eye space* (or *view space*), the eye is located at the origin of the coordinate system. Following the standard convention, you orient the scene so the eye is looking down one direction of the z-axis. The "up" direction is typically the positive y direction.

Eye space, which is particularly useful for lighting, will be discussed in Chapter 5.

4.1.6 The View Transform

The transform that converts world-space positions to eye-space positions is the *view transform*. Once again, you express the view transform with a 4×4 matrix.

The typical view transform combines a translation that moves the eye position in world space to the origin of eye space and then rotates the eye appropriately. By doing this, the view transform defines the position and orientation of the viewpoint.

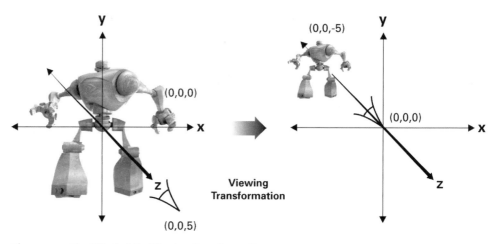

Figure 4-3. The Effect of the Viewing Transformation

Figure 4-3 illustrates the view transform. The left side of the figure shows the robot from Figure 4-2 along with the eye, which is positioned at $\langle 0, 0, 5 \rangle$ in the world-space coordinate system. The right side shows them in eye space. Observe that eye space positions the origin at the eye. In this example, the view transform translates the robot in order to move it to the correct position in eye space. After the translation, the robot ends up at $\langle 0, 0, -5 \rangle$ in eye space, while the eye is at the origin. In this example, eye space and world space share the positive y-axis as their "up" direction and the translation is purely in the z direction. Otherwise, a rotation might be required as well as a translation.

The Modelview Matrix

Most lighting and other shading computations involve quantities such as positions and surface normals. In general, these computations tend to be more efficient when performed in either eye space or object space. World space is useful in your application for establishing the overall spatial relationships between objects in a scene, but it is not particularly efficient for lighting and other shading computations.

For this reason, we typically combine the two matrices that represent the modeling and view transforms into a single matrix known as the *modelview matrix*. You can combine the two matrices by simply multiplying the view matrix by the modeling matrix.

4.1.7   Clip Space

Once positions are in eye space, the next step is to determine what positions are actually viewable in the image you eventually intend to render. The coordinate system subsequent to eye space is known as *clip space*, and coordinates in this space are called *clip coordinates*.

The vertex position that a Cg vertex program outputs is in clip space. Every vertex program optionally outputs parameters such as texture coordinates and colors, but a vertex program *always* outputs a clip-space position. As you have seen in earlier examples, the **POSITION** semantic is used to indicate that a particular vertex program output is the clip-space position.

4.1.8   The Projection Transform

The transform that converts eye-space coordinates into clip-space coordinates is known as the *projection transform*.

The projection transform defines a *view frustum* that represents the region of eye space where objects are viewable. Only polygons, lines, and points that are within the view frustum are potentially viewable when rasterized into an image. OpenGL and Direct3D have slightly different rules for clip space. In OpenGL, everything that is viewable must be within an axis-aligned cube such that the x, y, and z components of its clip-space position are less than or equal to its corresponding w component. This implies that $-w \leq x \leq w$, $-w \leq y \leq w$, and $-w \leq z \leq w$. Direct3D has the same clipping requirement for x and y, but the z requirement is $0 \leq z \leq w$. These clipping rules assume that the clip-space position is in homogeneous form, because they rely on w.

The projection transform provides the mapping to this clip-space axis-aligned cube containing the viewable region of clip space from the viewable region of eye space—otherwise known as the view frustum. You can express this mapping as a 4×4 matrix.

The Projection Matrix

The 4×4 matrix that corresponds to the projection transform is known as the *projection matrix*.

Figure 4-4 illustrates how the projection matrix transforms the robot in eye space from Figure 4-3 into clip space. The entire robot fits into clip space, so the resulting image should picture the robot without any portion of the robot being clipped.

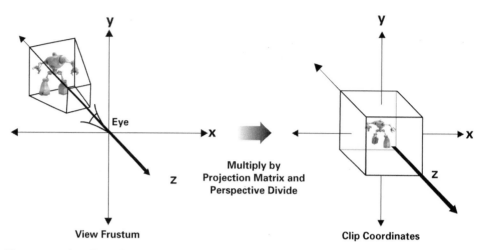

Multiply by
Projection Matrix and
Perspective Divide

View Frustum

Clip Coordinates

Figure 4-4. The Effect of the Projection Matrix

The clip-space rules are different for OpenGL and Direct3D and are built into the projection matrix for each respective API. As a result, if Cg programmers rely on the appropriate projection matrix for their choice of 3D programming interface, the distinction between the two clip-space definitions is not apparent. Typically, the application is responsible for providing the appropriate projection matrix to Cg programs.

4.1.9   Normalized Device Coordinates

Clip coordinates are in the homogenous form of $\langle x, y, z, w \rangle$, but we need to compute a 2D position (an x and y pair) along with a depth value. (The depth value is for *depth buffering*, a hardware-accelerated way to render visible surfaces.)

Perspective Division

Dividing x, y, and z by w accomplishes this. The resulting coordinates are called *normalized device coordinates*. Now all the visible geometric data lies in a cube with positions between $\langle -1, -1, -1 \rangle$ and $\langle 1, 1, 1 \rangle$ in OpenGL, and between $\langle -1, -1, 0 \rangle$ and $\langle 1, 1, 1 \rangle$ in Direct3D.

The 2D vertex programs in Chapters 2 and 3 output what you now know as normalized device coordinates. The 2D output position in these examples assumed an implicit z value of 0 and a w value of 1.

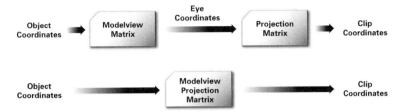

Figure 4-5. Optimizations for Transforming to Clip Space

4.1.10 Window Coordinates

The final step is to take each vertex's normalized device coordinates and convert them into a final coordinate system that is measured in pixels for x and y. This step, called the *viewport transform,* feeds the GPU's rasterizer. The rasterizer then forms points, lines, or polygons from the vertices, and generates fragments that determine the final image. Another transform, called the *depth range transform,* scales the z value of the vertices into the range of the depth buffer for use in depth buffering.

4.2 Applying the Theory

Despite all the discussion about coordinate spaces, the Cg code you need for transforming vertices correctly is quite trivial. Normally, the vertex program receives vertex positions in object space. The program then multiplies each vertex by the modelview and projection matrices to get that vertex into clip space. In practice, you would concatenate these two matrices so that just one multiplication is needed instead of two. Figure 4-5 illustrates this principle by showing two ways to get from object coordinates to clip coordinates.

Example 4-1 shows how a typical Cg program would efficiently handle 3D vertex transformations from object space directly to clip space.

```
void C4E1v_transform(float4 position  : POSITION,
                 out float4 oPosition : POSITION,
               uniform float4x4 modelViewProj)
{
  // Transform position from object space to clip space
  oPosition = mul(modelViewProj, position);
}
```

Example 4-1. The **C4E1v_transform** Vertex Program

The program takes the object-space position (**position**) and concatenated modelview and projection matrices (**modelViewProj**) as input parameters. Your OpenGL or Direct3D application would be responsible for providing this data. There are Cg runtime routines that help you load the appropriate matrix based on the current OpenGL or Direct3D transformation state. The **position** parameter is then transformed with a matrix multiplication, and the result is written out to **oPosition**:

```
// Transform position from object space to clip space
oPosition = mul(modelViewProj, position);
```

In this book, we explicitly assign all output parameters, even if they are simply being passed through. We use the "**o**" prefix to differentiate input and output parameters that have the same names.

4.3   Exercises

1. **Answer this:** List the various coordinate spaces and the sequence of transformations used to move from one to the next.

2. **Answer this:** If you are interested in the theory of transformations, list some situations where you can use just a 3×3 matrix for the modelview and projection matrices instead of a complete 4×4 matrix.

3. **Try this yourself:** Use **cgc** to output the vertex program assembly for the **C4E1v_transform** example. The **DP4** instruction computes a four-component dot product. How many such instructions are generated by the program's **mul** routine?

4.4   Further Reading

Computer graphics textbooks explain vertex transformation and develop more of the matrix math underlying the topic than presented here. We recommend Edward Angel's *Interactive Computer Graphics: A Top-Down Approach with OpenGL, Third Edition* (Addison-Wesley, 2002).

If you want to develop your intuition for the projective transformations that underlie vertex transformation and be entertained at the same time, read *Jim Blinn's Corner: A Trip Down the Graphics Pipeline* (Morgan Kaufmann, 1996).

Graphics Gems (Academic Press, 1994), edited by Andrew Glassner, has many useful short articles about modeling, transformation, and matrix techniques.

Chapter 5

Lighting

This chapter shows you how to illuminate the objects in your scenes with light sources. We start by building a simplified version of a commonly used lighting model. Then, we gradually add functionality to the basic model to make it more useful in common situations. This chapter has the following five sections:

- **"Lighting and Lighting Models"** explains the importance of lighting and introduces the concept of a lighting model.

- **"Implementing the Basic Per-Vertex Lighting Model"** presents a simplified version of the lighting model used in OpenGL and Direct3D. This section also goes through a step-by-step implementation of this lighting model in a vertex program.

- **"Per-Fragment Lighting"** describes the differences between per-vertex and per-fragment lighting and shows you how to implement per-fragment lighting.

- **"Creating a Lighting Function"** explains how to create your own functions.

- **"Extending the Basic Model"** describes several improvements to the basic lighting model, including texturing, attenuation, and spotlight effects. While explaining these improvements, we introduce several key Cg concepts, such as creating functions, arrays, and structures.

5.1   Lighting and Lighting Models

So far, all our examples have been straightforward, focusing on the fundamental concepts that you need to start writing programs. The next few chapters will show you how to add some more interesting effects. This chapter explains lighting.

Adding a light to a scene causes many variations in shading and creates more interesting images. This is why movie directors pay such close attention to lighting: it plays a big part in telling a compelling story. Dark areas of a scene can evoke a sense of mystery and heightened tension. (Unfortunately, in computer graphics, shadows do not come "for free" when you add lights to a scene. Chapter 9 visits the separate topic of shadow generation.)

Together, lighting and an object's material properties determine its appearance. A lighting model describes the way light interacts with an object, based on the light's characteristics and the object material's characteristics. Over the years, numerous lighting models have been developed and used, ranging from simple approximations to extremely accurate simulations.

Figure 5-1 shows a set of objects that were rendered using various lighting models. Notice how the different formulations resemble an assortment of real-world materials.

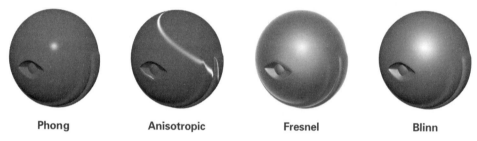

| Phong | Anisotropic | Fresnel | Blinn |

Figure 5-1. Different Lighting Models

In the past, fixed-function graphics pipelines were limited to one lighting model, which we call the *fixed-function lighting model*. The fixed-function model is based on what is known as the Phong lighting model, but with some tweaks and additions. The fixed-function lighting model has several advantages: it looks adequate, it's cheap to compute, and it has a number of intuitive parameters that can be tweaked to control appearance. The problem with it, however, is that it works well for only a limited set of materials. A plastic or rubbery appearance is the most common symptom of using the fixed-function lighting model, and this explains why many computer graphics images do not look realistic.

To get around the limitations of the fixed-function lighting model, graphics programmers found innovative ways to use other features of the pipeline. For example, clever programs used texture-based methods to mimic the surface characteristics of a wider range of materials.

With the advent of Cg and programmable hardware, you can now express complicated lighting models concisely using a high-level language. You no longer have to configure a limited set of graphics pipeline states or program tedious assembly language routines. And, you don't have to limit your lighting model to fit the fixed-function pipeline's capabilities. Instead, you can express your own custom lighting model as a Cg program that executes within your programmable GPU.

5.2 Implementing the Basic Per-Vertex Lighting Model

This section explains how to implement a simplified version of the fixed-function lighting model using a vertex program. The familiarity and simplicity of this lighting model make it an excellent starting point. First we give some background about the fixed-function lighting model. If you are already familiar with this lighting model, feel free to skip ahead to the implementation in Section 5.2.2.

5.2.1 The Basic Lighting Model

OpenGL and Direct3D provide almost identical fixed-function lighting models. In our example, we will use a simplified version that we will refer to as the "Basic" model. The Basic model, like the OpenGL and Direct3D models, modifies and extends the classic Phong model. In the Basic model, an object's surface color is the sum of emissive, ambient, diffuse, and specular lighting contributions. Each contribution depends on the combination of the surface's material properties (such as shininess and material color) and the light source's properties (such as light color and position). We represent each contribution as a **float3** vector that contains the red, green, and blue color components.

This high-level equation describes the Basic model mathematically:

$$surfaceColor = emissive + ambient + diffuse + specular$$

The Emissive Term

The emissive term represents light emitted or given off by a surface. This contribution is independent of all light sources. The emissive term is an RGB value that indicates

Emissive

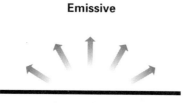

Object Surface

Figure 5-2. The Emissive Term

Figure 5-3. Rendering the Emissive Term

the color of the emitted light. If you were to view an emissive material in a completely dark room, it would appear to be this color. The emissive term can simulate glowing. Figure 5-2 illustrates the emissive term conceptually, and Figure 5-3 shows a rendering of a purely emissive object. The rendering is understandably boring, because the emissive color is the same all over the object. Unlike in the real world, an object's emissive glow does not actually illuminate other nearby objects in the scene. An emissive object is not itself a light source—it does not illuminate other objects or cast shadows. Another way to think of the emissive term is that it is a color added after computing all the other lighting terms. More advanced global illumination models would simulate how the emitted light affects the rest of the scene, but these models are beyond the scope of this book.

Here is the mathematical formulation we use for the emissive term:

$$emissive = K_e$$

where:

- K_e is the material's emissive color.

The Ambient Term

The ambient term accounts for light that has bounced around so much in the scene that it seems to come from everywhere. Ambient light does not appear to come from any particular direction; rather, it appears to come from all directions. Because of this, the ambient lighting term does not depend on the light source position. Figure 5-4 illustrates this concept, and Figure 5-5 shows a rendering of an object that receives only ambient light. The ambient term depends on a material's ambient reflectance, as

Incoming Ambient Light   **Reflected Ambient Light**

Object Surface   **Object Surface**

Figure 5-4. The Ambient Term

Figure 5-5. Rendering the Ambient Term

well as the color of the ambient light that is incident on the material. Like the emissive term, the ambient term on its own is just a constant color. Unlike the emissive color, however, the ambient term is affected by the global ambient lighting.

Here is the mathematical formulation we use for the ambient term:

$$ambient = K_a \times globalAmbient$$

where:

- K_a is the material's ambient reflectance and
- *globalAmbient* is the color of the incoming ambient light.

The Diffuse Term

The diffuse term accounts for directed light reflected off a surface equally in all directions. In general, diffuse surfaces are rough on a microscopic scale, with small nooks and crannies that reflect light in many directions. When incoming rays of light hit these nooks and crannies, the light bounces off in all directions, as shown in Figure 5-6.

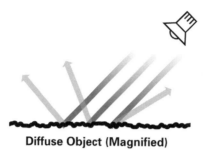

Diffuse Object (Magnified)

Figure 5-6. Diffuse Light Scattering

The amount of light reflected is proportional to the angle of incidence of the light striking the surface. Surfaces with a dull finish, such as a dusty chalkboard, are said to be diffuse. The diffuse contribution at any particular point on a surface is the same, regardless of where the viewpoint is. Figure 5-7 illustrates the diffuse term, and Figure 5-8 shows a rendering of a diffuse object.

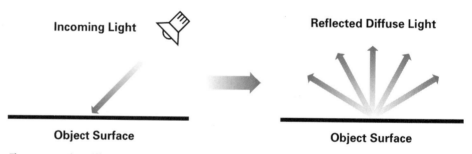

Figure 5-7. The Diffuse Term

Figure 5-8. Rendering the Diffuse Term

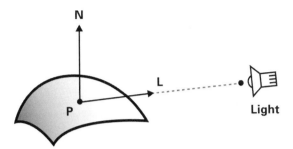

Figure 5-9. Calculating Diffuse Lighting

Here is the mathematical formulation we use for the diffuse term (illustrated in Figure 5-9):

$$diffuse = K_d \times lightColor \times \max(N \cdot L, 0)$$

where:

- K_d is the material's diffuse color,
- *lightColor* is the color of the incoming diffuse light,
- N is the normalized surface normal,
- L is the normalized vector toward the light source, and
- P is the point being shaded.

The vector dot product (or inner product) of the normalized vectors N and L is a measure of the angle between the two vectors. The smaller the angle between the vectors, the greater the dot-product value will be, and the more incident light the surface will receive. Surfaces that face away from the light will produce negative dot-product values, so the *max(N · L, 0)* in the equation ensures that these surfaces show no diffuse lighting.

The Specular Term

The specular term represents light scattered from a surface predominantly around the mirror direction. The specular term is most prominent on very smooth and shiny surfaces, such as polished metals. Figure 5-10 illustrates the concept of specular reflection, and Figure 5-11 shows a rendering of a completely specular object.

Unlike the emissive, ambient, and diffuse lighting terms, the specular contribution depends on the location of the viewer. If the viewer is not at a location that receives

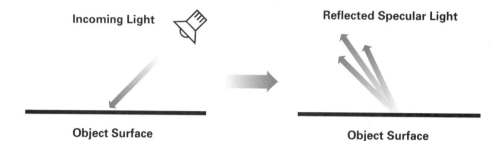

Incoming Light

Reflected Specular Light

Object Surface

Object Surface

Figure 5-10. The Specular Term

Figure 5-11. Rendering the Specular Term

the reflected rays, the viewer will not see a specular highlight on the surface. The specular term is affected not only by the specular color properties of the light source and material, but also by how shiny the surface is. Shinier materials have smaller, tighter highlights, whereas less shiny materials have highlights that are more spread out. Figure 5-12 shows some examples of shininess, with the shininess exponent increasing from left to right.

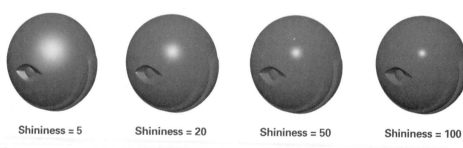

Shininess = 5   Shininess = 20   Shininess = 50   Shininess = 100

Figure 5-12. Examples of Different Shininess Exponents

Chapter 5: Lighting

Here is the mathematical formulation we use for the specular term (illustrated in Figure 5-13):

$$specular = K_s \times lightColor \times facing \times (\max(N \cdot H, 0))^{shininess}$$

where:

- K_s is the material's specular color,
- *lightColor* is the color of the incoming specular light,
- N is the normalized surface normal,
- V is the normalized vector toward the viewpoint,
- L is the normalized vector toward the light source,
- H is the normalized vector that is halfway between V and L,
- P is the point being shaded, and
- *facing* is 1 if $N \cdot L$ is greater than 0, and 0 otherwise.

When the angle between the view vector V and the half-angle vector H is small, the specular appearance of the material becomes apparent. The exponentiation of the dot product of N and H ensures that the specular appearance falls off quickly as H and V move farther apart.

Additionally, the specular term is forced to zero if the diffuse term is zero because $N \cdot L$ (from diffuse lighting) is negative. This ensures that specular highlights do not appear on geometry that faces away from the light.

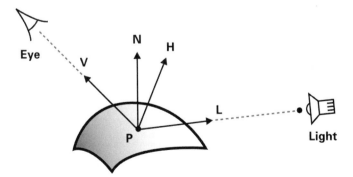

Figure 5-13. Calculating the Specular Term

Ambient   **Diffuse**   **Specular**   **Combined**

Figure 5-14. Putting the Terms Together

Adding the Terms Together

Combining the ambient, diffuse, and specular terms gives the final lighting, as shown in Figure 5-14. In the figure, we deliberately exclude the emissive term, because it is normally used to achieve special effects rather than for lighting ordinary objects.

Simplifications

If you are experienced with OpenGL or Direct3D, you might have noticed a number of simplifications for the Basic lighting model. We are using a global ambient color instead of a per-light ambient color. We are also using the same value for the light's diffuse and specular colors instead of allowing different values for each of these. In addition, we do not account for attenuation or spotlight effects.

5.2.2   A Vertex Program for Basic Per-Vertex Lighting

This section explains a Cg vertex program that implements the Basic lighting model described in Section 5.2.1

The **C5E1v_basicLight** vertex program in Example 5-1 does the following:

- Transforms the position from object space to clip space.
- Computes the illuminated color of the vertex, including the emissive, ambient, diffuse, and specular lighting contributions from a single light source.

In this example, we perform the lighting calculations in object space. You could also use other spaces, provided that you transform all necessary vectors into the appropriate coordinate system. For example, OpenGL and Direct3D perform their lighting computations in eye space rather than object space. Eye space is more efficient than object space when there are multiple lights, but object space is easier to implement.

```
void C5E1v_basicLight(float4 position  : POSITION,
                      float3 normal    : NORMAL,

                  out float4 oPosition : POSITION,
                  out float4 color     : COLOR,

                  uniform float4x4 modelViewProj,
                  uniform float3 globalAmbient,
                  uniform float3 lightColor,
                  uniform float3 lightPosition,
                  uniform float3 eyePosition,
                  uniform float3 Ke,
                  uniform float3 Ka,
                  uniform float3 Kd,
                  uniform float3 Ks,
                  uniform float  shininess)
{
  oPosition = mul(modelViewProj, position);

  float3 P = position.xyz;
  float3 N = normal;

  // Compute the emissive term
  float3 emissive = Ke;

  // Compute the ambient term
  float3 ambient = Ka * globalAmbient;

  // Compute the diffuse term
  float3 L = normalize(lightPosition - P);
  float diffuseLight = max(dot(N, L), 0);
  float3 diffuse = Kd * lightColor * diffuseLight;

  // Compute the specular term
  float3 V = normalize(eyePosition - P);
  float3 H = normalize(L + V);
  float specularLight = pow(max(dot(N, H), 0),
                            shininess);
  if (diffuseLight <= 0) specularLight = 0;
  float3 specular = Ks * lightColor * specularLight;

  color.xyz = emissive + ambient + diffuse + specular;
  color.w = 1;
}
```

Example 5-1. The **C5E1v_basicLight** Vertex Program

The exercises at the end of this chapter explore the trade-offs between eye-space and object-space lighting.

Application-Specified Data

Table 5-1 lists the various pieces of data that the application needs to send to the graphics pipeline. We classify each item as *varying* if the item changes with every vertex, or *uniform* if the item changes less frequently (such as on a per-object basis).

A Debugging Tip

As you can see, the code for lighting is significantly more complex than any Cg code you have seen so far. When you are working on a program that is not trivial, it is a

Table 5-1. Application-Specified Data for the Graphics Pipeline

Parameter	Variable Name	Type	Category
GEOMETRIC PARAMETERS			
Object-space vertex position	`position`	`float4`	Varying
Object-space vertex normal	`normal`	`float3`	Varying
Concatenated modelview and projection matrices	`modelViewProj`	`float4x4`	Uniform
Object-space light position	`lightPosition`	`float3`	Uniform
Object-space eye position	`eyePosition`	`float3`	Uniform
LIGHT PARAMETERS			
Light color	`lightColor`	`float3`	Uniform
Global ambient color	`globalAmbient`	`float3`	Uniform
MATERIAL PARAMETERS			
Emissive reflectance	`Ke`	`float3`	Uniform
Ambient reflectance	`Ka`	`float3`	Uniform
Diffuse reflectance	`Kd`	`float3`	Uniform
Specular reflectance	`Ks`	`float3`	Uniform
Shininess	`shininess`	`float`	Uniform

good idea to build it up slowly, piece by piece. Run the program as you make each incremental addition, and check to make sure that the results are what you expect. This is much smarter than writing all the code for the program and then hoping that it generates the right result. If you make a minor error, tracking down a problem will be a lot easier if you know the recent changes that probably caused it.

This tip applies particularly to lighting code, because lighting can be broken down into various contributions (emissive, ambient, diffuse, and specular). Therefore, a good approach is to calculate **emissive**, and then set **color** to just **emissive**. After that, calculate **ambient**, and set **color** to **emissive** plus **ambient**. By building up your Cg programs gradually in this manner, you will save yourself a lot of frustration.

The Vertex Program Body

Calculating the Clip-Space Position

We start by computing the usual clip-space position calculation for the rasterizer, as explained in Chapter 4:

```
oPosition = mul(modelViewProj, position);
```

Next, we instance a variable to store the object-space vertex position, because we will need this information later on. We are going to use a **float3** temporary variable because the other vectors used in lighting (such as the surface normal, light position, and eye position) are also **float3** types.

```
float3 P = position.xyz;
```

Here we see an interesting new piece of syntax: **position.xyz**. This is our first look at a feature of Cg called *swizzling*.

By ignoring the object-space *w* component, we are effectively assuming that *w* is 1.

Swizzling

Swizzling allows you to rearrange the components of a vector to create a new vector— in any way that you choose. Swizzling uses the same period operator that is used to access structure members, plus a suffix that indicates how you would like to rearrange the components of a vector that you're working on. The suffix is some combination of the letters **x**, **y**, **z**, and **w**. The letters **r**, **g**, **b**, and **a**—appropriate for RGBA colors— can also be used. However, the two sets of suffix letters cannot be mixed. These letters indicate which components of the original vector to use when constructing the new one. The letters **x** and **r** correspond to the first component of a vector, **y** and **g** to the second component, and so on. In the previous example, **position** is a **float4** variable. The **.xyz** suffix extracts the *x*, *y*, and *z* components of **position** and creates a new three-component vector from these three values. This new vector is then assigned to the **float3** variable called **P**.

Neither C nor C++ supports swizzling because neither language has built-in support for vector data types. However, swizzling is quite useful in Cg to manipulate vectors efficiently.

Here are some more examples of swizzling:

```
float4 vec1 = float4(4.0, -2.0, 5.0, 3.0);
float2 vec2 = vec1.yx;        // vec2 = (-2.0, 4.0)
float scalar = vec1.w;        // scalar = 3.0
float3 vec3 = scalar.xxx;     // vec3 = (3.0, 3.0, 3.0)
```

Take a closer look at these four lines of code. The first line declares a **float4** called **vec1**. The second line takes the **y** and **x** components of **vec1** and creates a swapped **float2** out of them. This vector is then assigned to **vec2**. In the third line, the **w** component of **vec1** is assigned to a single **float**, called **scalar**. Finally, in the last line, a **float3** vector is created by replicating **scalar** three times. This is known as *smearing*, and it illustrates that Cg treats scalar values just like one component vector (meaning that the **.x** suffix is used to access the scalar's value).

You can also swizzle matrices to create vectors based on a sequence of matrix elements. To do this, use the **._m**<*row*><*col*> notation. You can chain together a series of matrix swizzles, and the result will be an appropriately sized vector. For example:

```
float4x4 myMatrix;
float    myFloatScalar;
float4   myFloatVec4;'

// Set myFloatScalar to myMatrix[3][2]
myFloatScalar = myMatrix._m32;

// Assign the main diagonal of myMatrix to myFloatVec4
myFloatVec4 = myMatrix._m00_m11_m22_m33;
```

In addition, you can access an individual row of a matrix using the `[]` array operator. Using the variables declared in the preceding code sample:

```
// Set myFloatVector to the first row of myMatrix
myFloatVec4 = myMatrix[0];
```

Write Masking

Cg supports another operation, related to swizzling, called *write masking,* that allows only specified components of a vector to be updated by an assignment. For example, you could write to just the *x* and *w* components of a **float4** vector by using a **float2** vector:

```
// Assume that initially vec1 = (4.0, -2.0, 5.0, 3.0)
//                and vec2 = (-2.0, 4.0);
vec1.xw = vec2;    // Now vec1 = (-2.0, -2.0, 5.0, 4.0)
```

The write-masking suffix can list the **x**, **y**, **z**, and **w** (or **r**, **g**, **b**, and **a**) components in any order. Each letter can appear at most once in a given write-mask suffix, and you cannot mix the **xyzw** and **rgba** letters in a single write-mask suffix.

 On most modern GPUs, swizzling and write masking are operations that have no performance penalty. So use both features whenever they help improve the clarity or efficiency of your code.

The Emissive Light Contribution

There is nothing much to do for the emissive term. For the sake of coding clarity, we instance a variable, named **emissive**, for the emissive light contribution:

```
// Compute emissive term
float3 emissive = Ke;
```

 When the Cg compiler translates your program to executable code, it also optimizes the translated code so that there is no performance penalty for creating intermediate variables such as the **emissive** variable in the above code fragment. Because instancing such variables makes your code more readable, you are encouraged to instance named variables for intermediate results to improve the clarity of your code.

The Ambient Light Contribution

For the ambient term, recall that we have to take the material's ambient color, **Ka**, and multiply it by the global ambient light color. This is a per-component multiplication, meaning that we want to take each color component of **Ka** and multiply it with the corresponding color component of the global ambient light color. The following code, which uses both swizzling and write masking, would get the job done:

```
// An inefficient way to compute the ambient term
float3 ambient;
ambient.x = Ka.x * globalAmbient.x;
ambient.y = Ka.y * globalAmbient.y;
ambient.z = Ka.z * globalAmbient.z;
```

This code works, but it certainly looks like a lot of effort, and it isn't very elegant. Because Cg has native support for vectors, it allows you to express this type of operation concisely. Here is a much more compact way to scale a vector by another vector:

```
// Compute ambient term
float3 ambient = Ka * globalAmbient;
```

Pretty simple, isn't it? It is convenient to work in a language that has built-in support for vectors and matrices, as well as the common operations that you perform on them.

The Diffuse Light Contribution

Now we get to the more interesting parts of the lighting model. For the diffuse calculation, we need the vector from the vertex to the light source. To define a vector, you take the end point and subtract the starting point. In this case, the vector ends at **lightPosition** and starts at **P**:

```
// Compute the light vector
float3 L = normalize(lightPosition - P);
```

We are interested in direction only, not magnitude, so we need to normalize the vector. Fortunately, there is a **normalize** function, which is declared in the Cg Standard Library, that returns the normalized version of a vector. If the vector is not normalized correctly, the lighting will be either too bright or too dark.

---

normalize(v)   Returns a normalized version of vector **v**

Next, we need to do the actual lighting computation. This is a slightly complicated expression, so look at it in pieces. First, there is the dot product. Recall that the dot product is a basic math function that computes a single value, which represents the cosine of the angle between two unit-length vectors. In Cg, you can use the **dot** function to calculate the dot product between two vectors:

`dot(a, b)`	Returns the dot product of vectors **a** and **b**

Therefore, the code fragment that finds the dot product between **N** and **L** is this:

```
dot(N, L);
```

There is a problem with this, though. Surfaces that face away from the light are lit with "negative" light, because the dot product is negative when the normal faces away from the light source. Negative lighting values make no physical sense and will cause errors when added to other terms in the lighting equation. To deal with this problem, you must clamp the result to zero. This means that if the dot product value is less than zero, it is set to zero. The clamping operation is easy to perform using Cg's **max** function:

`max(a, b)`	Returns the maximum of **a** and **b**

Adding clamping to the previous expression gives:

```
max(dot(N, L), 0);
```

So the final piece of code looks like this:

```
float diffuseLight = max(dot(N, L), 0);
```

Finally, you have to factor in the diffuse material color (**Kd**) and the light color (**lightColor**). The **diffuseLight** value that you just calculated is a scalar quantity. Remember that in Cg, you can multiply a vector by a scalar; doing so will scale each component of the vector by the scalar. So you can combine all the colors easily with two multiplications:

```
float3 diffuse = Kd * lightColor * diffuseLight;
```

The Specular Light Contribution

The specular calculation requires a little more work. Take a look back at Figure 5-13, which shows the various vectors that you'll need. You already have the **L** vector from the diffuse lighting calculation, but the **V** and **H** vectors still need to be calculated. This is not too hard, given that you already have the eye position (**eyePosition**) and vertex position (**P**).

Start by finding the vector from the vertex to the eye. This is typically called the *view vector*, or simply **V** in the example code. Because we are trying to define a direction, we should normalize the vector. The following code is the result:

```
float3 V = normalize(eyePosition - P);
```

Next, you need **H**, the vector that is halfway between the light vector **L** and the view vector **V**. For this reason, **H** is known as the *half-angle vector*. Like **V**, **H** needs to be normalized, because it represents a direction. To find **H**, you could use the following expression:

```
// An inefficient way to calculate H
float3 H = normalize(0.5 * L + 0.5 * V);
```

However, since you are doing a normalize operation, scaling **L** and **V** by 0.5 has no effect, because the scaling factor cancels out during the normalization process. So the actual code looks like this:

```
float3 H = normalize(L + V);
```

At this point you're ready to calculate the specular term. As with the diffuse term, build up the expression for the specular term piece by piece. Start with the dot product of **H** and **N**:

```
dot(N, H)
```

This needs to be clamped to zero, just like the diffuse lighting:

```
max(dot(N, H), 0)
```

The result has to be raised to the power indicated by **shininess**. This has the effect of narrowing the specular highlight as the **shininess** value increases. To raise a quantity to a power, use Cg's **pow** function:

---

pow(x, y)   Returns x^y

Adding the **pow** function to the specular lighting expression gives:

```
pow(max(dot(N, H), 0), shininess)
```

Putting it all together, you've got the specular lighting:

```
float specularLight = pow(max(dot(N, H), 0),
                          shininess);
```

Finally, you must ensure that specular highlights do not show up when the diffuse lighting is zero (because the surface faces away from the light source). In other words, if the diffuse lighting is zero, then set the specular lighting to zero. Otherwise, use the calculated specular lighting value. This is a good opportunity to use Cg's conditional expression functionality.

Conditional Expressions

As in C, Cg allows you to use the keywords **if** and **else** to evaluate conditional expressions. For example:

```
if (value == 1) {
  color = float4(1.0, 0.0, 0.0, 1.0);     // Color is red
} else {
  color = float4(0.0, 1.0, 0.0, 1.0);     // Color is green
}
```

Also like C, you can use the **?:** notation to implement conditional expressions very concisely. The **?:** notation works as follows:

```
(test expression) ? (statements if true)
                  : (statements if false)
```

The previous example can therefore be expressed as:

```
color = (value == 1) ? float4(1.0, 0.0, 0.0, 1.0)
                     : float4(0.0, 1.0, 0.0, 1.0);
```

Getting back to the example, here is the specular lighting code, with the conditional test included:

```
  float specularLight = pow(max(dot(N, H), 0),
                            shininess);
  if (diffuseLight <= 0) specularLight = 0;
```

As with the diffuse lighting calculation, you have to factor in the material's specular color (**Ks**) as well as the light's color (**lightColor**). At first, it might seem odd to have two separate colors that control the specular highlight. However, this is useful because some materials (such as metals) have specular highlights that are similar to the material color, whereas other materials (such as plastics) have specular highlights that are white. Both kinds of highlights are then modulated by the light's color. The **Ks** and **lightColor** variables are convenient ways to tweak the lighting model to achieve a particular appearance.

The specular component is calculated as follows:

```
float3 specular = Ks * lightColor * specularLight;
```

Putting It All Together

The final step is to combine the emissive, ambient, diffuse, and specular contributions to get the final vertex color. You also need to assign this color to the output parameter called **color**.

```
color.xyz = emissive + ambient + diffuse + specular;
```

5.2.3   The Fragment Program for Per-Vertex Lighting

Because the vertex program has already performed the lighting calculations, your fragment program needs only to take the interpolated color and pass it to the frame buffer. We reuse the **C2E2f_passthrough** fragment program for this task, and we're done.

5.2.4   Per-Vertex Lighting Results

Figure 5-15 shows a sample rendering from the per-vertex lighting program.

Figure 5-15. Per-Vertex Lighting Results

5.3 Per-Fragment Lighting

You may have noticed that the per-vertex lighting results look somewhat coarse. The shading tends to be a bit "triangular" looking, meaning that you can make out the underlying mesh structure, if the model is simple enough. If the model has very few vertices, per-vertex lighting will often be inadequate. However, as your models acquire more and more vertices, you will find that the results start to improve considerably, as in Figure 5-16. The figure shows three tessellated cylinders with different levels of tessellation. Below each lit cylinder is the wireframe version of the model showing each cylinder's tessellation. As the amount of tessellation increases from left to right, notice that the lighting improves significantly.

Less tessellated models look bad with per-vertex lighting because of the way data is interpolated and used. With per-vertex lighting, lighting is calculated only at each vertex of each triangle. The lighting is then interpolated for each fragment that is generated for the triangle. This approach, called smooth color interpolation or *Gouraud shading*, can miss details because the lighting equation is not actually evaluated for

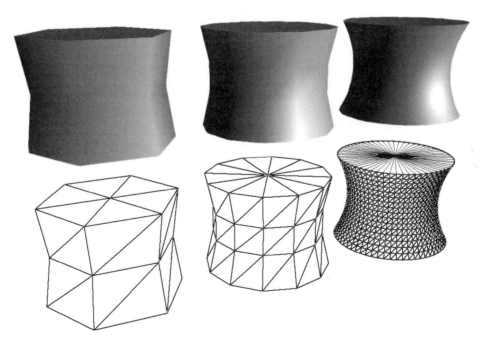

Figure 5-16. The Effects of Tessellation on Lighting

each fragment. For example, a specular highlight that is not captured at any of the triangle's vertices will not show up on the triangle, even if it should appear inside the triangle.

This is exactly what could happen with the preceding per-vertex lighting example: your vertex program calculated the lighting, and then the rasterizer interpolated the colors for each fragment.

To get a more accurate result, you need to evaluate the whole lighting model for each fragment, instead of just for each vertex. So instead of interpolating the final lit color, the surface normals are interpolated. Then, the fragment program uses the interpolated surface normals to calculate the lighting at each pixel. This technique is called *Phong shading* (not to be confused with the Phong lighting model, which refers to the specular approximation used in the Basic model) or, more commonly, *per-pixel lighting* or *per-fragment lighting*. As you might expect, per-fragment lighting gives much better results because the whole lighting equation is evaluated for each fragment of each triangle, as shown in Figure 5-17. The left side of the figure shows a tessellated cylinder rendered with per-vertex lighting, and the right side shows the same cylinder rendered

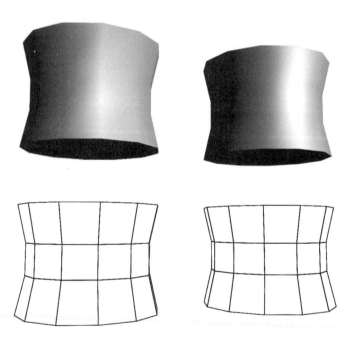

Figure 5-17. Comparing Per-Vertex and Per-Fragment Lighting

with per-fragment lighting. Each cylinder has the same coarse tessellation. Notice that the highlights are coarse on the left cylinder and much sharper on the right cylinder.

5.3.1   Implementing Per-Fragment Lighting

 The fragment program in this example requires a fourth-generation GPU, such as NVIDIA's GeForce FX or ATI's Radeon 9700.

In this example, the computational burden on vertex and fragment programs will be swapped; this time, the fragment program will do the interesting work. The vertex program will only help set the stage by passing some parameters over to the fragment program. Many advanced techniques follow this pattern as well, which is probably not very surprising, because fragment programs give you more detailed control over your final image than vertex programs do. Using a vertex or fragment program also has other implications, such as performance. Chapter 10 discusses this topic further.

You will find that the fragment program for per-fragment lighting looks remarkably similar to the vertex program for per-vertex lighting. Again, that is because Cg allows you to use a common language for both vertex and fragment programming. This capability turns out to be very useful for per-fragment lighting, because the required code will already be familiar to you. Like the per-vertex lighting, the per-fragment lighting is done in object space, for ease of implementation.

5.3.2   The Vertex Program for Per-Fragment Lighting

The vertex program for this example is just a conduit: it performs minimal computations and essentially forwards data down the pipeline, so that the fragment program can do the interesting work. After writing out the homogeneous position, the vertex program also passes along the object-space position and object-space normal, outputting them as texture coordinate sets 0 and 1.

Example 5-2 shows the complete source code for the vertex program. There are no new concepts here, so take this opportunity to make sure that you completely understand each line in the program.

```
void C5E2v_fragmentLighting(float4 position : POSITION,
                            float3 normal   : NORMAL,

                        out float4 oPosition : POSITION,
                        out float3 objectPos : TEXCOORD0,
                        out float3 oNormal   : TEXCOORD1,

                    uniform float4x4 modelViewProj)
{
  oPosition = mul(modelViewProj, position);
  objectPos = position.xyz;
  oNormal = normal;
}
```

Example 5-2. The **C5E2v_fragmentLighting** Vertex Program

5.3.3   The Fragment Program for Per-Fragment Lighting

The **C5E3f_basicLight** program is almost identical to the vertex program for per-vertex lighting, and so we will not go through it in detail. Example 5-3 shows the source code for the per-fragment lighting program.

It is common to assume that the object-space per-vertex normal is already normalized. In such a case, one operation that **C5E3f_basicLight** performs that the corresponding vertex program would not require is renormalizing the interpolated per-fragment normal:

```
float3 N = normalize(normal);
```

This **normalize** is necessary because linear interpolation of a texture coordinate set can cause the per-fragment normal vector to become denormalized.

The **C5E3f_basicLight** fragment program shows that Cg really does allow you to express your ideas the same way in both vertex and fragment programs (as long as your GPU is powerful enough to keep up—this program, as written, requires a fourth-generation GPU or better). But per-fragment calculations aren't free. In most cases, there will be more fragments in the frame than there are vertices, which means that the fragment program needs to run many more times than the vertex program. Therefore, longer fragment programs tend to have a more significant impact on performance than longer vertex programs. Chapter 10 discusses in more detail the trade-offs between using vertex and fragment programs.

```
void C5E3f_basicLight(float4 position   : TEXCOORD0,
                      float3 normal     : TEXCOORD1,

              out float4 color          : COLOR,

           uniform float3 globalAmbient,
           uniform float3 lightColor,
           uniform float3 lightPosition,
           uniform float3 eyePosition,
           uniform float3 Ke,
           uniform float3 Ka,
           uniform float3 Kd,
           uniform float3 Ks,
           uniform float  shininess)
{
  float3 P = position.xyz;
  float3 N = normalize(normal);

  // Compute the emissive term
  float3 emissive = Ke;

  // Compute the ambient term
  float3 ambient = Ka * globalAmbient;

  // Compute the diffuse term
  float3 L = normalize(lightPosition - P);
  float diffuseLight = max(dot(N, L), 0);
  float3 diffuse = Kd * lightColor * diffuseLight;

  // Compute the specular term
  float3 V = normalize(eyePosition - P);
  float3 H = normalize(L + V);
  float specularLight = pow(max(dot(N, H), 0),
                            shininess);
  if (diffuseLight <= 0) specularLight = 0;
  float3 specular = Ks * lightColor * specularLight;

  color.xyz = emissive + ambient + diffuse + specular;
  color.w = 1;
}
```

Example 5-3. The `C5E3f_basicLight` Fragment Program

In the rest of this chapter, and the remainder of this book, we avoid complex fragment programs where possible, to make the examples accessible to a broad range of GPU generations. But you can usually move a per-vertex computation to the fragment program if you want to.

5.4 Creating a Lighting Function

In the preceding section, we simply copied most of the code from the per-vertex example to the per-fragment example, but there's a better solution: encapsulating the key aspects of lighting in a function.

In a complex Cg program, lighting might be only one of several computations that the program performs. In the per-vertex lighting example, you saw the various steps that were necessary to calculate lighting. But you would not want to rewrite all this code whenever you wanted to compute lighting. Fortunately, you don't have to. As we mentioned in Chapter 2, you can write an internal function that encapsulates the lighting task and reuse the same lighting function in different entry functions.

Unlike functions in C or C++, functions in Cg are typically inlined (though this may depend on the profile—advanced profiles such as **vp30** can support function calls in addition to inlining). Inlining functions means that they have no associated function-call overhead. Therefore, you should use functions whenever possible, because they improve readability, simplify debugging, encourage reuse, and make future optimization easier.

Cg, like C, requires that you declare functions before using them.

5.4.1 Declaring a Function

In Cg, functions are declared just as in C. You can optionally specify parameters to pass to the function, as well as values that will be returned by the function. Here is a simple function declaration:

```
float getX(float3 v)
{
    return v.x;
}
```

This function takes a three-component vector **v** as a parameter and returns a **float** that is the *x* component of **v**. The **return** keyword is used to return the function's result. You call the **getX** function just as you would call any other Cg function:

```
// Declare a scratch vector
float3 myVector = float3(0.5, 1.0, -1.0);

// Get the x component of myVector
float x = getX(myVector);
// Now x = 0.5
```

Sometimes, you want a function to return several results instead of just one. In these situations, you can use the **out** modifier (as explained in Section 3.3.4) to specify that a particular parameter to a program be for output only. Here is an example that takes a vector and returns its *x*, *y*, and *z* components:

```
void getComponents(float3 vector,
                out float x,
                out float y,
                out float z)
{
  x = vector.x;
  y = vector.y;
  z = vector.z;
}
```

Note that this function is declared **void**, because it returns all its values through parameters. Here is a code sample that shows how **getComponents** would be used:

```
// Declare a scratch vector
float3 myVector = float3(0.5, 1.0, -1.0);

// Declare scratch variables
float x, y, z;

// Get the x, y, and z components of myVector
getComponents(myVector, x, y, z);
// Now x = 0.5, y = 1.0, z = -1.0
```

5.4.2 A Lighting Function

Because lighting is a complex process, you can write many different types of lighting functions, each of which can take different parameters. For now, take the Basic model that you implemented and create a function for it. Here is a first shot at this function:

```
float3 lighting(float3 Ke,
                float3 Ka,
                float3 Kd,
                float3 Ks,
                float  shininess,
                float3 lightPosition,
                float3 lightColor,
                float3 globalAmbient,
                float3 P,
                float3 N,
                float3 eyePosition)
{
   // Calculate lighting here
}
```

One major problem with this approach is that the function requires so many parameters. It would be far neater to group the parameters into "material parameters" and "light parameters," and then to pass each set as an individual variable. Fortunately, Cg supports structures, which provide exactly this functionality.

5.4.3 Structures

As we mentioned in Chapter 2, Cg structures are declared the same way they are in C or C++. The **struct** keyword is used, followed by the list of structure members. Here is an example of a structure that encapsulates all the properties of a particular material based on the Basic lighting model:

```
struct Material {
   float3 Ke;
   float3 Ka;
   float3 Kd;
   float3 Ks;
   float shininess;
};
```

Structure members are accessed using the period operator. The following code snippet shows how to declare and access a structure:

```
Material shiny;
shiny.Ke = float3(0.0, 0.0, 0.0);
shiny.Ka = float3(0.1, 0.1, 0.1);
shiny.Kd = float3(0.2, 0.4, 0.2);
shiny.Ks = float3(0.8, 0.8, 0.8);
shiny.shininess = 90.0;
```

You could create a second structure to hold light properties:

```
struct Light {
  float4 position;
  float3 color;
};
```

Now, you can redefine the lighting function using structures as parameters:

```
float3 lighting(Material material,
                Light light,
                float3 globalAmbient,
                float3 P,
                float3 N,
                float3 eyePosition)
{
   // Calculate lighting here
}
```

With this approach, you could later make your light or material model more complex, without having to add more parameters to the lighting function itself. Another advantage is that you can calculate the effects of multiple lights by using an array of **Light** structures instead of just one.

5.4.4 Arrays

Cg supports arrays much as C does. Because Cg currently does not support pointers, you must always use array syntax rather than pointer syntax when dealing with arrays. Here is an example of an array declaration and access in Cg:

```
// Declare a four-element array
float3 myArray[4];
int index = 2;

// Assign a vector to element 2 of the array
myArray[index] = float3(0.1, 0.2, 0.3);
```

An important difference from C is that arrays are first-class types in Cg. This means that array assignments actually copy the entire array, and arrays that are passed as parameters are passed by value (the entire array is copied before making any changes), rather than by reference.

You can also pass arrays as parameters to functions. We're going to use this feature to create a function that computes the lighting from two distinct light sources, as shown in Example 5-4.

As you look over the code for **C5E4v_twoLights**, you will notice that it starts by calculating the emissive and ambient terms, which are independent of the light sources. The function then loops over the two light sources using a **for** loop, accumulating the diffuse and specular contributions from the lights. These contributions are calculated using the **C5E5_computeLighting** helper function, which we will define shortly. First, let's learn a little more about **for** loops and other constructs that control the flow of Cg programs.

5.4.5 Flow Control

Cg offers a subset of C's flow-control capabilities. In particular, Cg supports:

- functions and the **return** statement
- **if-else**
- **for**
- **while** and **do-while**

These are identical to their C counterparts, except for profile-specific restrictions that may exist. For example, some profiles allow **for** or **while** loops only if the number of loop iterations can be determined ahead of time by the Cg compiler.

Cg reserves keywords for other C flow-control constructs, such as **goto** and **switch**. However, these constructs are not currently supported.

Chapter 5: Lighting

```
void C5E4v_twoLights(float4 position : POSITION,
                     float3 normal   : NORMAL,

              out float4 oPosition : POSITION,
              out float4 color     : COLOR,

          uniform float4x4 modelViewProj,
          uniform float3   eyePosition,
          uniform float3   globalAmbient,
          uniform Light     lights[2],
          uniform float     shininess,
          uniform Material material)
{
  oPosition = mul(modelViewProj, position);

  // Calculate emissive and ambient terms
  float3 emissive = material.Ke;
  float3 ambient = material.Ka * globalAmbient;

  // Loop over diffuse and specular contributions
  // for each light
  float3 diffuseLight;
  float3 specularLight;
  float3 diffuseSum  = 0;
  float3 specularSum = 0;
  for (int i = 0; i < 2; i++) {
    C5E5_computeLighting(lights[i], position.xyz, normal,
                         eyePosition, shininess, diffuseLight,
                         specularLight);
    diffuseSum += diffuseLight;
    specularSum += specularLight;
  }

  // Now modulate diffuse and specular by material color
  float3 diffuse = material.Kd * diffuseSum;
  float3 specular = material.Ks * specularSum;

  color.xyz = emissive + ambient + diffuse + specular;
  color.w = 1;
}
```

Example 5-4. The **C5E4v_twoLights** Vertex Program

5.4 Creating a Lighting Function

5.4.6 Computing the Diffuse and Specular Lighting

The final piece of the puzzle is the **C5E5_computeLighting** function, which is responsible for calculating the diffuse and specular contributions for a particular light source. Example 5-5 re-implements the diffuse and specular lighting code that we wrote earlier.

```
void C5E5_computeLighting(Light  light,
                          float3 P,
                          float3 N,
                          float3 eyePosition,
                          float  shininess,

                          out float3 diffuseResult,
                          out float3 specularResult)
{
  // Compute the diffuse lighting
  float3 L = normalize(light.position - P);
  float diffuseLight = max(dot(N, L), 0);
  diffuseResult = light.color * diffuseLight;

  // Compute the specular lighting
  float3 V = normalize(eyePosition - P);
  float3 H = normalize(L + V);
  float specularLight = pow(max(dot(N, H), 0),
                            shininess);
  if (diffuseLight <= 0) specularLight = 0;
  specularResult = light.color * specularLight;
}
```

Example 5-5. The **C5E5_computeLighting** Internal Function

5.5 Extending the Basic Model

Now that you have implemented a Basic lighting model, let's look at how we can make it a little more useful. The following sections present three enhancements: distance attenuation, spotlight effects, and directional lights. Each enhancement will work at both the vertex level and the fragment level.

Lighting is a very complicated topic, and there are a huge number of techniques to explore. Our goal is just to get you started.

5.5.1 Distance Attenuation

The Basic lighting model assumes that the intensity of the light source is always the same no matter how far the light is from the surface being shaded. Although that is a reasonable approximation for some light sources (such as when the Sun lights objects on Earth), we usually want to create lights for which intensity diminishes with distance. This property is called *distance attenuation*. In OpenGL or Direct3D, the attenuation at any particular point is modeled using the following formula:

$$attenuationFactor = \frac{1}{k_C + k_L d + k_Q d^2}$$

where:

- d is the distance from the light source and
- k_C, k_L, and k_Q are constants that control the amount of attenuation.

In this formulation of attenuation, k_C, k_L, and k_Q, respectively, are the constant, linear, and quadratic coefficients of attenuation. In the real world, the intensity of illumination from a point light source decays as $1/d^2$, but sometimes that might not give the effect you want. The idea behind having three attenuation parameters is to give you more control over the appearance of your scene's lighting.

The attenuation factor modulates the diffuse and specular terms of the lighting equation. So the equation becomes:

$$lighting = emissive + ambient + attenuationFactor \times (diffuse + specular)$$

Example 5-6 describes a Cg function that calculates attenuation, given the surface position and **Light** structure (to which we have now added **kC**, **kL**, and **kQ**).

```
float C5E6_attenuation(float3 P,
                       Light  light)
{
  float d = distance(P, light.position);
  return 1 / (light.kC + light.kL * d +
              light.kQ * d * d);
}
```

Example 5-6. The **C5E6_attenuation** Internal Function

We take advantage of the **distance** function that is yet another one of Cg's Standard Library functions. Here is the formal definition of **distance**:

---

distance(pt1, pt2) Euclidean distance between points **pt1** and **pt2**

The attenuation calculation needs to be added to the **C5E5_computeLighting** function, because it affects both the diffuse contribution and the specular contribution from the light source. You should calculate the attenuation first, so that you can use it to modulate the diffuse and specular contributions. The **C5E7_attenuate-Lighting** internal function in Example 5-7 shows the necessary modifications.

5.5.2   Adding a Spotlight Effect

Another commonly used extension for the Basic lighting model is making the light a spotlight instead of an omnidirectional light. A spotlight cut-off angle controls the spread of the spotlight cone, as shown in Figure 5-18. Only objects within the spotlight cone receive light.

To create the spotlight cone, you need to know the spotlight position, spotlight direction, and position of the point that you are trying to shade. With this information, you can compute the vectors V (the vector from the spotlight to the vertex) and D (the direction of the spotlight), as shown in Figure 5-19.

By taking the dot product of the two normalized vectors, you can find the cosine of the angle between them, and use that to find out if P lies within the spotlight cone. P is affected by the spotlight only if **dot(V, D)** is greater than the cosine of the spotlight's cut-off angle.

Based on this math, we can create a function for the spotlight calculation, as shown in Example 5-8. The function **C5E8_spotlight** returns 1 if P is within the spotlight cone, and 0 otherwise. Note that we have added **direction** (the spotlight direction—assumed to be normalized already) and **cosLightAngle** (the cosine of the spotlight's cut-off angle) to the **Light** structure from Example 5-6.

Intensity Variation

So far, we have assumed that the intensity of light given off by the spotlight is uniform within the spotlight's cone. Rarely, if ever, is a real spotlight so uniformly focused. To make things more interesting, we will divide the cone into two parts: an inner cone

```
void C5E7_attenuateLighting(Light  light,
                            float3 P,
                            float3 N,
                            float3 eyePosition,
                            float  shininess,

                       out float diffuseResult,
                       out float specularResult)
{
  // Compute attenuation
  float attenuation = C5E6_attenuation(P, light);

  // Compute the diffuse lighting
  float3 L = normalize(light.position - P);
  float diffuseLight = max(dot(N, L), 0);
  diffuseResult = attenuation *
                  light.color * diffuseLight;

  // Compute the specular lighting
  float3 V = normalize(eyePosition - P);
  float3 H = normalize(L + V);
  float specularLight = pow(max(dot(N, H), 0),
                           shininess);
  if (diffuseLight <= 0) specularLight = 0;
  specularResult = attenuation *
                   light.color * specularLight;
}
```

Example 5-7. The **C5E7_attenuateLighting** Internal Function

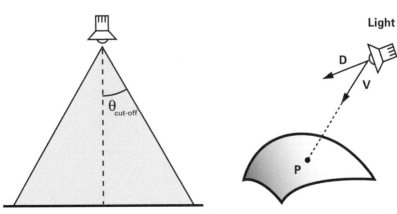

Figure 5-18. Specifying a Spotlight Cut-Off Angle

Figure 5-19. Vectors for Calculating the Spotlight Effect

```
float C5E8_spotlight(float3 P,
                     Light  light)
{
  float3 V = normalize(P - light.position);
  float cosCone = light.cosLightAngle;
  float cosDirection = dot(V, light.direction);
  if (cosCone <= cosDirection)
    return 1;
  else
    return 0;
}
```

Example 5-8. The `C5E8_spotlight` Internal Function

and an outer cone. The inner cone (or "hotspot") emits a constant intensity, and this intensity drops off smoothly outside the cone, as shown in Figure 5-20. This commonly used approach creates the more sophisticated effect demonstrated in the right side of Figure 5-21.

It's not hard to find out if a particular point *P* is in the inner cone or the outer cone. The only difference from the basic spotlight is that you now need to vary the intensity calculation based on which cone *P* lies.

If *P* lies in the inner cone, it receives the spotlight's full intensity. If *P* lies in between the inner and outer cones, you need to lower the intensity gradually based on how far *P* is from the inner cone. Cg's **lerp** function works well for this type of transition, but with advanced profiles, you can do better.

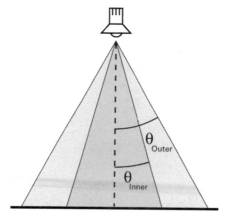

Figure 5-20. Specifying Inner and Outer Cones for a Spotlight

Chapter 5: Lighting

Figure 5-21. The Effect of Adding Inner and Outer Spotlight Cones

Cg has a **smoothstep** function that produces more visually appealing results than a simple **lerp**. Unfortunately, the **smoothstep** function might not work with some basic profiles, because of their limited capabilities. We'll use **smoothstep** in this example, though you could replace it with another function of your choice.

The **smoothstep** function interpolates between two values, using a smooth polynomial:

smoothstep(min, max, x)	Returns **0** if **x < min**;
	Returns **1** if **x >= max**;
	Otherwise, returns a smooth Hermite
	interpolation between 0 and 1 given by:
	$-2 * ((x - min)/(max - min))^3 +$
	$3 * ((x - min)/(max - min))^2$

Figure 5-22 graphs what the **smoothstep** function looks like. Use **smoothstep** when you want to create a visually pleasing transition between two values. Another convenient feature of **smoothstep** is that it clamps to the [0, 1] range. If you set up your parameters to **smoothstep** correctly, it will return 1.0 when P is in the inner cone, and 0.0 when P is outside the outer cone.

Once again, we can extend the **Light** structure to include the new spotlight parameters. The single cut-off angle is now replaced by an inner angle cosine and an outer angle cosine.

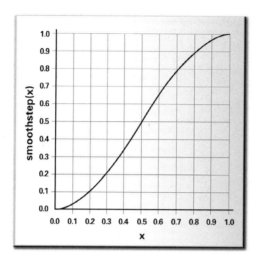

Figure 5-22. A Graph of the `smoothstep` Function

Here is how our further updated version of the **Light** structure looks:

```
struct Light {
  float4 position;
  float3 color;
  float  kC;
  float  kL;
  float  kQ;
  float  direction;
  float  cosInnerCone;    // New member
  float  cosOuterCone;    // New member
};
```

The **C5E9_dualConeSpotlight** internal function shown in Example 5-9 combines all this to create a spotlight with a hotspot.

The **C5E10_spotAttenLighting** internal function combines both the attenuation and the spotlight terms with specular and diffuse lighting, as shown in Example 5-10.

5.5.3   Directional Lights

Although computations such as the spotlight effect and attenuation add to the visual complexity of your scenes, the results are not always noticeable. Consider rays from the Sun that light objects on Earth. All the rays seem to come from the same direction

```
float C5E9_dualConeSpotlight(float3 P,
                             Light  light)
{
  float3 V = normalize(P - light.position);
  float cosOuterCone = light.cosOuterCone;
  float cosInnerCone = light.cosInnerCone;
  float cosDirection = dot(V, light.direction);
  return smoothstep(cosOuterCone,
                    cosInnerCone,
                    cosDirection);
}
```

Example 5-9. The `C5E9_dualConeSpotlight` Internal Function

```
void C5E10_spotAttenLighting(Light  light,
                             float3 P,
                             float3 N,
                             float3 eyePosition,
                             float  shininess,

                         out float diffuseResult,
                         out float specularResult)
{
  // Compute attenuation
  float attenuationFactor = C5E6_attenuation(P, light);

  // Compute spotlight effect
  float spotEffect = C5E9_dualConeSpotlight(P, light);

  // Compute the diffuse lighting
  float3 L = normalize(light.position - P);
  float diffuseLight = max(dot(N, L), 0);
  diffuseResult = attenuationFactor * spotEffect *
                  light.color * diffuseLight;

  // Compute the specular lighting
  float3 V = normalize(eyePosition - P);
  float3 H = normalize(L + V);
  float specularLight = pow(max(dot(N, H), 0),
                            shininess);
  if (diffuseLight <= 0) specularLight = 0;
  specularResult = attenuationFactor * spotEffect *
                   light.color * specularLight;
}
```

Example 5-10. The `C5E10_spotAttenLighting` Internal Function

5.5 Extending the Basic Model

because the Sun is so far away. In such a situation, it does not make sense to calculate a spotlight effect or to add attenuation, because all objects receive essentially the same amount of light. A light with this property is called a *directional light*. Directional lights do not exist in reality, but in computer graphics, it is often worthwhile to identify situations in which a directional light is sufficient. This allows you to avoid computations that will not produce perceptible results.

5.6   Exercises

1. **Answer this:** What visual differences distinguish surfaces rendered with a per-vertex lighting model from those rendered with a per-fragment lighting model? In particular, discuss specular highlights and spotlights.

2. **Try this yourself:** Modify the **C5E5_computeLighting** function to assume a directional light, as described in Section 5.5.3. You should be able to improve the function's performance by eliminating a vector difference and through normalization.

3. **Try this yourself:** The lighting examples in this chapter assume that your application specifies the light position in object space. You could also specify light positions in eye space. Using eye space to specify light positions is convenient because it avoids requiring the application to transform the light position from world or eye space into object space for each object's distinct object space. Also, the view vector for computing the specular contribution is simply the eye-space vertex position because the eye is at the origin. Lighting in eye space, however, requires transforming the object-space position and normal into eye space for every vertex. Transforming an object-space position and normal into eye space requires multiplying each by the modelview matrix and inverse transpose of the modelview matrix, respectively. If the modelview matrix scales vectors, you must normalize the eye-space normal, because the modelview matrix would denormalize the normal. Modify the **C5E5_computeLighting** function to assume that the position **P** and normal **N** are in eye space. Also, modify **C5E4v_twoLights** to transform the object-space position and normal into eye space prior to passing these vectors to your new **C5E5_computeLighting** function.

4. **Try this yourself:** Modify the eye-space version of the **C5E5_computeLighting** function you implemented for Exercise 3 to assume that the eye-space vector **V** is always in the direction (0, 0, 1). This is known as the *infinite viewer* specular optimization, and it eliminates the requirement to normalize **V** prior to computing **H**.

How much does this change your rendering results? Is this optimization possible when implementing object-space lighting?

5. **Answer this:** Which is more efficient: object-space or eye-space lighting? Also, which is more convenient for the application programmer?

6. **Try this yourself:** Write a pair of Cg vertex and fragment programs that mix per-vertex and per-fragment lighting. Compute the emissive, ambient, and diffuse contributions in the vertex program. Also, compute the half-angle and normal vectors in the vertex program, and then pass these vectors to your fragment program. In the fragment program, compute just the specular contribution using the interpolated half-angle and normal vectors. This partitioning of the lighting task means that most of the lighting math occurs at the per-vertex level, but the specular contribution that is the most subject to per-vertex artifacts is computed at the per-fragment level for better quality. Compare the quality and performance of this approach to a pure per-vertex and per-fragment lighting implementation.

7. **Try this yourself:** Brushed or grooved surfaces such as hair, vinyl records, satin Christmas ornaments, and brushed metal finishes reflect light differently than conventional materials do because the grooved microstructure of these surfaces creates anisotropic light scattering. Research the topic of anisotropic lighting as discussed in the "Further Reading" section. Create a vertex or fragment program that implements anisotropic lighting.

5.7   Further Reading

The lighting chapter of the *OpenGL Programming Guide: The Official Guide to Learning OpenGL, Third Edition* (Addison-Wesley, 1999), by Mason Woo, Jackie Neider, Tom Davis, and Dave Shreiner, presents the complete OpenGL fixed-function lighting model. Although the presentation is OpenGL-centric, the corresponding Direct3D fixed-function lighting model is almost identical. To find out more about Direct3D's lighting model, refer to "Mathematics of Lighting" in Microsoft's online DirectX documentation.

Eric Lengyel's book *Mathematics for 3D Game Programming and Computer Graphics* (Charles River Media, 2001) has a good chapter titled "Illumination" that discusses the practical math for implementing various lighting models.

David Banks published a SIGGRAPH paper titled "Illumination in Diverse Co-dimensions" (ACM Press) in 1994 that discussed anisotropic lighting. Wolfgang Heidrich and Hans-Peter Seidel published "Efficient Rendering of Anisotropic Surfaces Using Computer Graphics Hardware" in 1998; that paper, which applied anisotropic lighting to a surface in real time, provides the equations you will need for Exercise 7.

Robert Cook and Kenneth Torrance published a detailed, physically plausible lighting model in a paper titled "A Reflectance Model for Computer Graphics" in *ACM Transactions on Graphics* in 1982.

Andrew Glassner's two-volume *Principles of Digital Image Synthesis* (Morgan Kaufmann, 1995) is a detailed study of how light interacts with materials, approached from a computer graphics viewpoint.

Chapter 6

Animation

This chapter describes various ways to animate objects using Cg. It has the following five sections:

- **"Movement in Time"** introduces the concept of animation.
- **"A Pulsating Object"** shows a vertex program that periodically displaces an object's surface outward, in the direction of its normal vectors.
- **"Particle Systems"** describes how to use a physically based simulation to create a particle system, with all the calculations done by the GPU.
- **"Key-Frame Interpolation"** explains key-frame animation, in which a vertex program animates an object by interpolating between different object poses.
- **"Vertex Skinning"** explains how to displace vertices based on multiple weighted control matrices for more dynamic control in character animation.

6.1 Movement in Time

Animation is the result of an action that happens over time—for example, an object that pulsates, a light that fades, or a character that runs. Your application can create these types of animation using vertex programs written in Cg. The source of the animation is one or more program parameters that vary with the passing of time in your application.

To create animated rendering, your application must keep track of time at a level above Cg and even above OpenGL or Direct3D. Applications typically represent time with a global variable that is regularly incremented as your application's sense of time advances. Applications then update other variables as a function of time.

You could compute animation updates on the CPU and pass the animated data to the GPU. However, a more efficient approach is to perform as much of the animation computation as possible on the GPU with a vertex program, rather than require the CPU to do all the number-crunching. Offloading animation work from the CPU can help balance the CPU and GPU resources and free up the CPU for more involved computations, such as collision detection, artificial intelligence, and game play.

6.2 A Pulsating Object

In this first example, you will learn how to make an object deform periodically so that it appears to bulge. The goal is to take a time parameter as input and then modify the vertex positions of the object geometry based on the time. More specifically, you need to displace the surface position in the direction of the surface normal, as shown in Figure 6-1.

By varying the magnitude of the displacement over time, you create a bulging or pulsing effect. Figure 6-2 shows renderings of this effect as it is applied to a character. The pulsating animation takes place within a vertex program.

6.2.1 The Vertex Program

Example 6-1 shows the complete source code for the **C6E1v_bulge** vertex program, which is intended to be used with the **C2E2f_passthrough** fragment program from Chapter 2. Only the vertex position and normal are really needed for the bulging effect. However, lighting makes the effect look more interesting, so we have included material and light information as well. A helper function called **computeLighting** calculates just the diffuse and specular lighting (the specular material is assumed to be white for simplicity).

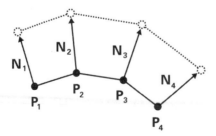

Figure 6-1. Making an Object Bulge

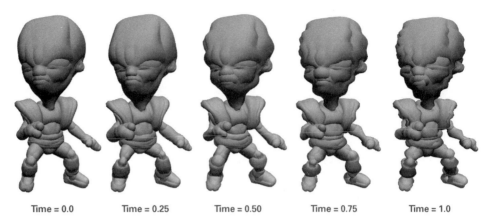

Time = 0.0   Time = 0.25   Time = 0.50   Time = 0.75   Time = 1.0

Figure 6-2. A Pulsating Alien

```
float3 computeLighting(float3 lightPosition,
                       float3 lightColor,
                       float3 Kd,
                       float  shininess,
                       float3 P,
                       float3 N,
                       float3 eyePosition)
{
  // Compute the diffuse lighting
  float3 L = normalize(lightPosition - P);
  float diffuseLight = max(dot(N, L), 0);
  float3 diffuseResult = Kd * lightColor * diffuseLight;

  // Compute the specular lighting
  float3 V = normalize(eyePosition - P);
  float3 H = normalize(L + V);
  float3 specularLight = lightColor * pow(max(dot(N, H), 0),
                                          shininess);
  if (diffuseLight <= 0) specularLight = 0;
  float3 specularResult = lightColor * specularLight;
  return diffuseResult + specularResult;
}
```

Example 6-1. The **C6E1v_bulge** Vertex Program

```
void C6E1v_bulge(float4 position   : POSITION,
                 float3 normal      : NORMAL,

             out float4 oPosition : POSITION,
             out float4 color     : COLOR,

         uniform float4x4 modelViewProj,
         uniform float    time,
         uniform float    frequency,
         uniform float    scaleFactor,
         uniform float3   Kd,
         uniform float    shininess,
         uniform float3   eyePosition,
         uniform float3   lightPosition,
         uniform float3   lightColor)
{
  float displacement = scaleFactor * 0.5 *
                         sin(position.y * frequency * time) + 1;
  float4 displacementDirection = float4(normal.x, normal.y,
                                        normal.z, 0);
  float4 newPosition = position +
                         displacement * displacementDirection;
  oPosition = mul(modelViewProj, newPosition);
  color.xyz = computeLighting(lightPosition, lightColor,
                       Kd, shininess,
                       newPosition.xyz, normal,
                       eyePosition);
  color.w = 1;
}
```

Example 6-1 (*continued*). The **C6E1v_bulge** Vertex Program

6.2.2 Displacement Calculation

Creating a Time-Based Function

The idea here is to calculate a quantity called **displacement** that moves the vertex position up or down in the direction of the surface normal. To animate the program's effect, **displacement** has to change over time. You can choose any function you like for this. For example, you could pick something like this:

```
float displacement = time;
```

Of course, this behavior doesn't make a lot of sense, because **displacement** would always increase, causing the object to get larger and larger endlessly over time. Instead, we want a pulsating effect in which the object oscillates between bulging larger and returning to its normal shape. The sine function provides such a smoothly oscillating behavior.

A useful property of the sine function is that its result is always between −1 and 1. In some cases, such as in this example, you don't want any negative numbers, so you can scale and bias the results into a more convenient range, such as from 0 to 1:

```
float displacement = 0.5 * (sin(time) + 1);
```

 Did you know that the **sin** function is just as efficient as addition or multiplication in the CineFX architecture? In fact, the **cos** function, which calculates the cosine function, is equally fast. Take advantage of these features to add visual complexity to your programs without slowing down their execution.

Adding Controls to the Program

To allow finer control of your program, you can add a uniform parameter that controls the frequency of the sine wave. Folding this uniform parameter, **frequency**, into the displacement equation gives:

```
float displacement = 0.5 * (sin(frequency * time) + 1);
```

You may also want to control the amplitude of the bulging, so it's useful to have a uniform parameter for that as well. Throwing that factor into the mix, here's what we get:

```
float displacement = scaleFactor * 0.5 *
                     (sin(frequency * time) + 1);
```

As it is now, this equation produces the same amount of protrusion all over the model. You might use it to show a character catching his breath after a long chase. To do this, you would apply the program to the character's chest. Alternatively, you could provide additional uniform parameters to indicate how rapidly the character is breathing, so that over time, the breathing could return to normal. These animation effects are inexpensive to implement in a game, and they help to immerse players in the game's universe.

Varying the Magnitude of Bulging

But what if you want the magnitude of bulging to vary at different locations on the model? To do this, you have to add a dependency on a per-vertex varying parameter. One idea might be to pass in **scaleFactor** as a varying parameter, rather than as a uniform parameter. Here we show you an even easier way to add some variation to the pulsing, based on the vertex position:

```
float displacement = scaleFactor * 0.5 *
                     sin(position.y * frequency * time) + 1;
```

This code uses the *y* coordinate of the position to vary the bulging, but you could use a combination of coordinates, if you prefer. It all depends on the type of effect you are after.

Updating the Vertex Position

In our example, the displacement scales the object-space surface normal. Then, by adding the result to the object-space vertex position, you get a displaced object-space vertex position:

```
float4 displacementDirection = float4(normal.x, normal.y,
                                      normal.z, 0);
float4 newPosition = position +
                     displacement * displacementDirection;
```

Precompute Uniform Parameters When Possible

The preceding example demonstrates an important point. Take another look at this line of code from Example 6-1:

```
float displacement = scaleFactor * 0.5 *
                     sin(position.y * frequency * time) + 1;
```

If you were to use this equation for the displacement, all the terms would be the same for each vertex, because they all depend only on uniform parameters. This means that you would be computing this displacement on the GPU for *each vertex,* when in fact you could simply calculate the displacement on the CPU just once for the entire mesh and pass the displacement as a uniform parameter. However, when the vertex position is part of the displacement equation, the sine function must be evaluated for each vertex. And as you might expect, if the value of the displacement varies for every vertex like this, such a per-vertex computation can be performed far more efficiently on the GPU than on the CPU.

 If a computed value is a constant value for an entire object, optimize your program by precomputing that value on a per-object basis with the CPU. Then pass the precomputed value to your Cg program as a uniform parameter. This approach is more efficient than recomputing the value for every fragment or vertex processed.

6.3 Particle Systems

Sometimes, instead of animating vertices in a mesh, you want to treat each vertex as a small object, or *particle*. A collection of particles that behave according to specific rules is known as a *particle system*. This example implements a simple particle system in a vertex program. For now, focus on how the system works; don't worry about its simplistic appearance. At the end of this section, we will mention one easy method to enhance your particle system's appearance. Figure 6-3 shows the particle system example progressing in time.

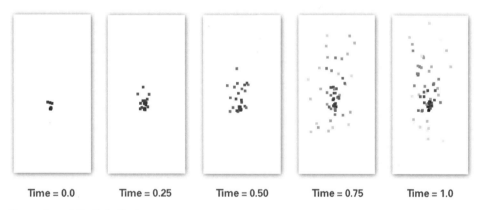

Time = 0.0   Time = 0.25   Time = 0.50   Time = 0.75   Time = 1.0

Figure 6-3. A Particle System

The example particle system behaves according to a simple vector kinematic equation from physics. The equation gives the *x, y,* and *z* positions of each particle for any time. The basic equation from which you will start is shown in Equation 6-1.

$$p_{final} = p_{initial} + vt + \tfrac{1}{2}at^2$$

Equation 6-1. Particle Trajectory

where:

- p_{final} is the particle's final position,
- $p_{initial}$ is the particle's initial position,
- v is the particle's initial velocity,
- a is the particle's acceleration, and
- t is the time taken.

The equation models the trajectory of a particle set in initial motion and under the influence of gravity, but not otherwise interacting with other particles. This equation gives the position of a particle for any value of time, assuming that you provide its initial position, initial velocity, and constant acceleration, such as gravity.

6.3.1 Initial Conditions

The application must supply the initial position and initial velocity of each particle as varying parameters. These two parameter values are known as *initial conditions* because they describe the particle at the beginning of the simulation.

In this particular simulation, the acceleration due to gravity is the same for every particle. Therefore, gravity is a uniform parameter.

To make the simulation more accurate, you could factor in effects such as drag and even spin—we leave that as an exercise for you.

6.3.2 Vectorized Computations

Modern GPUs have powerful vector-processing capabilities, particularly for addition and multiplication; they are well suited for processing vectors with up to four components. Therefore, it is often just as efficient to work with such vector quantities as it is to work with scalar (single-component) quantities.

Equation 6-1 is a vector equation because the initial position, initial velocity, constant acceleration, and computed position are all three-component vectors. By implementing the particle system equation as a vector expression when writing the Cg vertex program, you help the compiler translate your program to a form that executes efficiently on your GPU.

 Vectorize your calculations whenever possible, to take full advantage of the GPU's powerful vector-processing capabilities.

6.3.3 The Particle System Parameters

Table 6-1 lists the variables used by the vertex program presented in the next section.

Each variable is a parameter to the vertex program, except for the relative time (**t**) and final position (**pFinal**), which are calculated inside the vertex program. Note that the y component of the acceleration is negative—because gravity acts downward, in the negative y direction. The constant 9.8 meters per second squared is the acceleration of gravity on Earth. The initial position, initial velocity, and uniform acceleration are object-space vectors.

Table 6-1. Variables in the Particle Equation

Variable	Type	Description	Source (Type)
pInitial	**float3**	Initial position	Application (Varying)
vInitial	**float3**	Initial velocity	Application (Varying)
tInitial	**float3**	Time at which particle was created	Application (Varying)
acceleration	**float3**	Acceleration (0.0, -9.8, 0.0)	Application (Uniform)
globalTime	**float**	Global time	Application (Uniform)
pFinal	**float3**	Current position	Internal
t	**float**	Relative time	Internal

```
void C6E2v_particle(float4 pInitial  : POSITION,
                    float4 vInitial  : TEXCOORD0,
                    float  tInitial  : TEXCOORD1,

                out float4 oPosition : POSITION,
                out float4 color     : TEXCOORD0,
                out float  pointSize : PSIZE,

            uniform float    globalTime,
            uniform float4   acceleration,
            uniform float4x4 modelViewProj)
{
  float t = globalTime - tInitial;
  float4 pFinal = pInitial +
                  vInitial * t +
                  0.5 * acceleration * t * t;

  oPosition = mul(modelViewProj, pFinal);

  color = float4(t, t, t, 1);

  pointSize = -8.0 * t * t +
               8.0 * t +
               0.1 * pFinal.y + 1;

}
```

Example 6-2. The **C6E2v_particle** Vertex Program

6.3.4   The Vertex Program

Example 6-2 shows the source code for the **C6E2v_particle** vertex program. This program is meant to work in conjunction with the **C2E2f_passthrough** fragment program.

Computing the Particle Positions

In this program, the application keeps track of a "global time" and passes it to the vertex program as the uniform parameter **globalTime**. The global time starts at zero when the application initializes and is continuously incremented. As each particle is created, the particle's time of creation is passed to the vertex program as the varying

Plate 13.
Bump Mapping a Textured Polygonal Mesh

The same triangle exists in 2D texture space *(left)* and 3D object space *(center and right).*
See Chapter 8 for a full description.

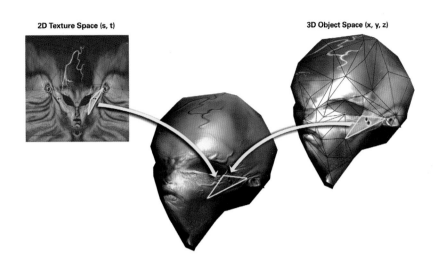

2D Texture Space (s, t)   3D Object Space (x, y, z)

Plate 14.
Nonphotorealistic Rendering

A cartoon-shaded ray gun and the corresponding image with diffuse and specular shading applied.
See Chapter 9 for a full description.

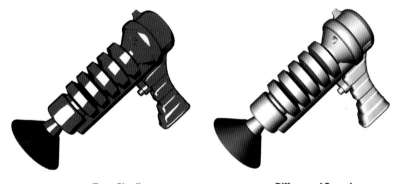

Toon Shading   **Diffuse and Specular**

Plate 15.
The Dawn Character, Driven by Shaders for the Skin's Surface, Skeletal Skinning, and Shape Blending

The skin shader uses a combination of color, specular, and blood characteristic maps to produce very realistic skin. In addition, a series of cube maps— for diffuse specular and "highlight" skin lighting—produce the subtleties of the scene's lighting. For the wings, a translucent shader modifies both the color reflected off them and the amount of light passing through them, based on viewing and light angles. Shaders also manipulate vertex positions to compute skeletal skinning and shape blending animation.

Plate 16.
NVIDIA Time Machine Demo

Each of the aging materials in the scene has a single shader associated with it. Each shader procedurally controls the application of color, normal, specular, reflection, reflectivity, and reveal maps.

Plate 17.
NVIDIA Dancing Ogre Demo

In a GeForce FX demo, vertex and fragment programs drive animated real-time characters created by Spellcraft Studios. An advanced skin shader uses true Blinn bump mapping with a combination of color, bump, and specular texture maps. Lighting effects include shadow-map shadows and object self-occlusion.

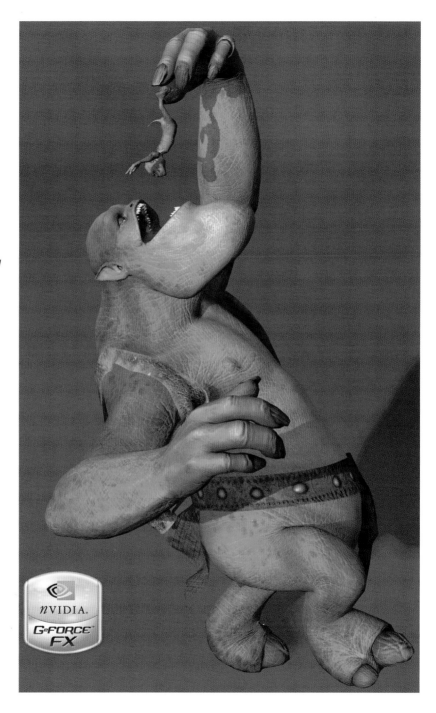

Plate 18.
Yeti's Gun Metal Game, Using Cg for Advanced Visual Effects

Copyright © 2002. Gun Metal is a registered trademark of Yeti Studios Limited.

Plate 19.
Iritor Online, Using Cg Shaders

Copyright © 2002 Wootsoft Entertainment. Iritor Online and the Iritor Online logo are registered trademarks of Wootsoft Entertainment. All Rights Reserved.

Plate 20.
Procedural Wood Shader

Cg program by Arkadiusz Waliszewski implements per-pixel correct lighting on a procedurally generated, three-dimensional wood texture. *See **www.cgshaders.org** for more details about shaders in Plates 20 to 23.*

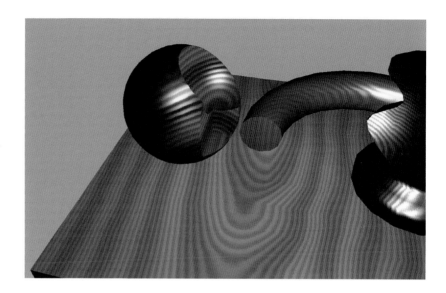

Plate 21.
Depth of Field

Depth-of-field effect with dynamic per-pixel lighting is implemented in a Cg program by Arkadiusz Waliszewski.

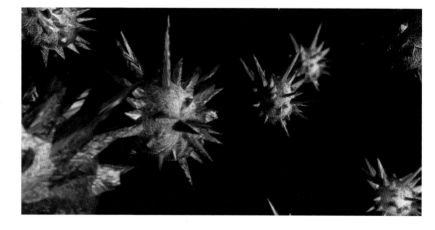

Plate 22.
Dynamic Reaction Diffusion Textures

Sequential images from a simulation produced with a Cg program by Mark Harris illustrate the reaction and subsequent diffusion of two reacting chemicals.

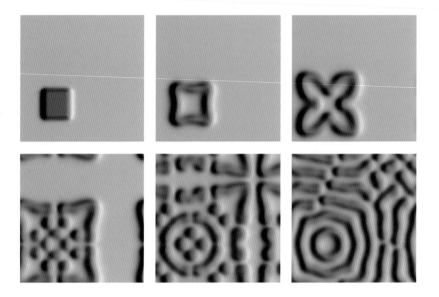

Plate 23.
Relief Texture Mapping

Implemented with a Cg program by Fabio Policarpo, this image-based rendering technique uses object normals and depth values from a pre-generated cubic texture map to represent large, dense meshes with a simple bounding box.

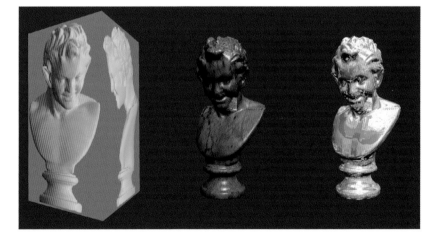

Plate 24.
Bump Reflection Mapping

Cg program from the NVIDIA Cg Browser uses normal maps and a cubic environment map to make the surface of the flying saucers appear bumpy and reflective.

Plate 25.
Detail Normal Maps

The underlying wireframe of a simple polygonal mesh highlights the result of layering two normal maps to create both a fine and a coarse bump mapping effect. Generated with a Cg program from the NVIDIA Cg Browser.

Plate 26.
Water Interaction

Cg vertex and pixel programs are used to animate the water height and convert the height values into a surface normal map for reflective shading. On the GPU, the Cg shaders compute a physics simulation of water, which is then used to generate the surface normal map. Produced with a Cg program from the NVIDIA Cg Browser.

Plate 27.
A Procedural Terrain Demo

To conserve constant memory, this vertex program combines the permutation and gradient tables into one array of **float4**s. Produced with a program from the NVIDIA Cg Browser implementing Cg noise, based on Ken Perlin's original code.

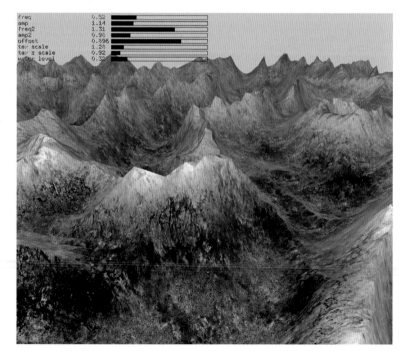

Plate 28.
Realistic Fresnel Reflection Effects

Several distinct textured objects are shaded to look like polished glass using a single Cg shader. Each object uses slightly different parameters, including varying indices of refraction.

Plate 29.
The NVIDIA Cg Browser Interface

The screen shows three views of the Cg Browser application: a hierarchical tree of examples *(left)*, the Cg source code for an anisotropic lighting example *(middle)*, and an interactive display of the anisotropic lighting shader applied to a flying saucer model *(right)*.

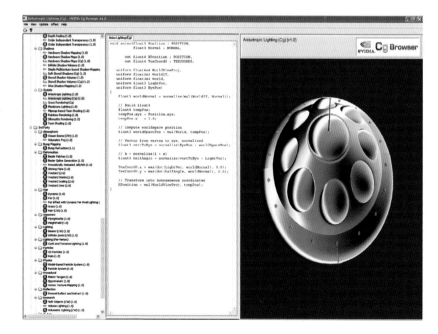

Plate 30.
A Mechanical Model with a Gooch Cg Shader Applied

Gooch shading replaces light-to-dark transitions with warm and cool tones, in this case enabling engineers to see form and curvature in all areas of a complex machine part.

Plate 31.
Using CgFX to Apply Multiple Shaders to a Ray Gun Model

The same CgFX file is applied to the barrel and to the body of the gun, with different specular and color parameters. Additional parameters are visible in the connection editor of the Cg Viewer.

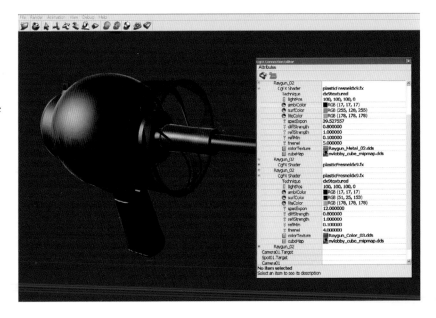

parameter **tInitial**. To find out how long a particle has been active, you simply have to subtract **tInitial** from **globalTime**:

```
float t = globalTime - tInitial;
```

Now you can plug **t** into Equation 6-1 to find the particle's current position:

```
float4 pFinal = pInitial +
                vInitial * t +
                0.5 * acceleration * t * t;
```

This position is in object space, so it needs to be transformed into clip space, as usual:

```
oPosition = mul(modelViewProj, pFinal);
```

Computing the Particle Color

In this example, time controls the particle color:

```
color = float4(t, t, t, 1);
```

This is a simple idea, but it produces an interesting visual variation. The color increases with time linearly. Note that colors saturate to pure white (1, 1, 1, 1). You can try your own alternatives, such as varying the color based on the particle's position, or varying the color based on a combination of position and time.

Computing the Particle Size

C6E2v_particle uses a new vertex program output semantic called **PSIZE**. When you render a point to the screen, an output parameter with this semantic specifies the width (and height) of the point in pixels. This gives your vertex program programmatic control of the point size used by the rasterizer.

The point size of each particle varies as time passes. The particles start out small, increase in size, and then gradually shrink. This variation adds to the fireworks-like effect. As an extra touch, we added a slight dependence on the particles' height, so that they get a little larger on their way up. To accomplish all this, we use the following function for the point size:

```
pointSize = -8.0 * t * t +
             8.0 * t +
             0.1 * pFinal.y + 1;
```

153

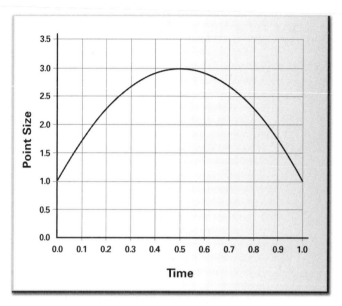

Figure 6-4. A Point Size Function

Figure 6-4 shows what the function looks like.

This function is nothing special—we merely created the formula to achieve the effect that we wanted. In other words, the formula does not have any real physical meaning, aside from attempting to mimic the effect we had in mind.

6.3.5 Dressing Up Your Particle System

Although the **C6E2v_particle** program produces interesting particle motion, the particles themselves do not look very appealing—they are just solid-colored squares of different sizes.

However, you can improve the particle appearance by using *point sprites*. With point sprites, the hardware takes each rendered point and, instead of drawing it as a single vertex, draws it as a square made up of four vertices, as shown in Figure 6-5. Point sprites are automatically assigned texture coordinates for each corner vertex. This allows you to alter the appearance of the particles from a square to any texture image you want.

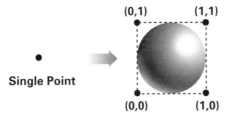

Figure 6-5. Converting Points to Point Sprites

By rendering the points as point sprites, you can use the assigned texture coordinates to sample a texture that supplies the shape and appearance of each point vertex, instead of simply rendering each point vertex as a square point. Point sprites can create the impression of added geometric complexity without actually drawing extra triangles. Figure 6-6 shows a more visually interesting example of a particle system, using point sprites. Both OpenGL and Direct3D have standard interfaces for rendering point sprites.

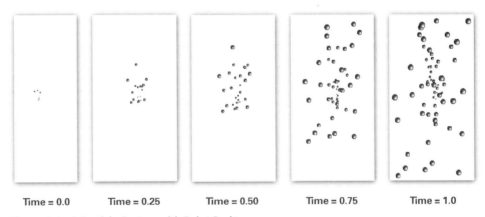

Figure 6-6. A Particle System with Point Sprites

6.4 Key-Frame Interpolation

3D games often use a sequence of key frames to represent an animated human or creature in various poses. For example, a creature may have animation sequences for standing, running, kneeling, ducking, attacking, and dying. Artists call each particular pose that they create for a given 3D model a key frame.

6.4.1 Key-Framing Background

The term *key frame* comes from cartoon animation. To produce a cartoon, an artist first quickly sketches a rough sequence of frames for animating a character. Rather than draw every frame required for the final animation, the artist draws only the important, or "key," frames. Later, the artist goes back and fills in the missing frames. These in-between frames are then easier to draw, because the prior and subsequent key frames serve as before-and-after references.

Computer animators use a similar technique. A 3D artist makes a key frame for each pose of an animated character. Even a standing character may require a sequence of key frames that show the character shifting weight from one foot to the other. Every key frame for a model must use the exact same number of vertices, and every key frame must share the same vertex connectivity. A vertex used in a given key frame corresponds to the same point on the model in every other key frame of the model. The entire animation sequence maintains this correspondence. However, the position of a particular vertex may change from frame to frame, due to the model's animation.

Given such a key-framed model, a game animates the model by picking two key frames and then blending together each corresponding pair of vertex positions. The blend is a weighted average in which the sum of the weights equals 100 percent. Figure 6-7 shows an alien character with several key frames. The figure includes two key frames, marked A and B, to be blended into an intermediate pose by a Cg program.

An application can use a Cg vertex program to blend the two vertices together. This blending may include further operations to illuminate the blended character appropriately for more realism. Usually, an application specifies a single position for each vertex, but for key-frame blending, each vertex has two positions, which are combined with a uniform weighting factor.

Key-frame interpolation assumes that the number and order of vertices are the same in all the key frames for a given model. This assumption ensures that the vertex program is always blending the correct pairs of vertices. The following Cg code fragment blends key-frame positions:

```
blendedPosition = (1 - weight) * keyFrameA + weight * keyFrameB;
```

The **keyFrameA** and **keyFrameB** variables contain the (*x*, *y*, *z*) positions of the vertex being processed at key frames A and B, respectively. Note that **weight** and **(1 – weight)** sum to 1. If **weight** is 0.53, the Cg program adds 47 percent (1.0 – 0.53) of the position of key frame A to 53 percent of the position of key frame B. Figure 6-8 shows an example of this type of animation.

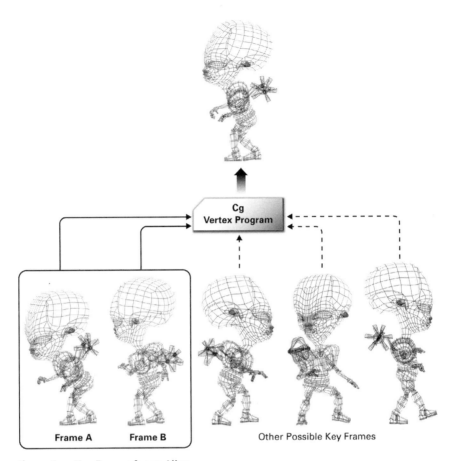

Figure 6-7. Key Frames for an Alien

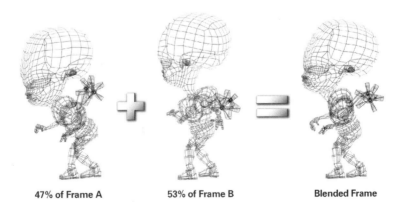

47% of Frame A   53% of Frame B   Blended Frame

Figure 6-8. An Example of Key-Frame Blending

6.4 Key-Frame Interpolation

To maintain the appearance of continuous animation, the key-frame weight increases with each rendered frame until it reaches 1.0 (100 percent). At this point, the existing key frame B becomes the new key frame A, the weight resets to 0, and the game selects a new key frame B to continue the animation. Animation sequences, such as walking, may loop repeatedly over the set of key frames that define the character's walking motion. The game can switch from a walking animation to a running animation just by changing over to the sequence of key frames that define the running animation.

It is up to the game engine to use the key frames to generate convincing animated motion. Many existing 3D games use this style of key-frame animation. When an application uses a Cg vertex program to perform the key-frame blending operations, the CPU can spend time improving the gameplay rather than continuously blending key frames. By using a Cg vertex program, the GPU takes over the task of key-frame blending.

6.4.2   Interpolation Approaches

There are many types of interpolation. Two common forms for key-frame interpolation are *linear interpolation* and *quadratic interpolation*.

Linear Interpolation

With linear interpolation, the transition between positions happens at a constant rate. Equation 6-2 shows the definition of linear interpolation:

$$blendedPosition = positionA \times (1 - f) + positionB \times f$$

Equation 6-2. Linear Interpolation

As f varies from 0 to 1 in this equation, the intermediate position varies between *positionA* and *positionB*. When f is equal to 0, the intermediate position is exactly *positionA*, the starting position. When f is equal to 1, the intermediate position is *positionB*, the ending position. Once again, you can use Cg's **lerp** function to accomplish the interpolation.

Using **lerp**, the interpolation between two positions can be written concisely as:

```
intermediatePosition = lerp(positionA, positionB, f);
```

Quadratic Interpolation

Linear interpolation is good for many situations, but sometimes you want the rate of transition to change over time. For example, you might want the transition from

Chapter 6: Animation

positionA to *positionB* to start out slowly and get faster as time passes. For this, you might use quadratic interpolation, as in the following code fragment:

```
intermediatePosition = position1 * (1 - f * f) +
                       position2 * f * f
```

Other functions that you might use are step functions, spline functions, and exponential functions. Figure 6-9 (on page 160) shows several common types of interpolation functions.

6.4.3 Basic Key-Frame Interpolation

Example 6-3 shows the **C6E3v_keyFrame** vertex program. This program performs the object-space blending of two positions, each from a different key frame. The **lerp** Standard Library function linearly interpolates the two positions, and then the program transforms the blended position into clip space. The program passes through a texture coordinate set and a color.

As indicated by the input semantics for **positionA** and **positionB**, the application is responsible for configuring key frame A's position as the conventional position (**POSITION**) and key frame B's position as texture coordinate set 1 (**TEXCOORD1**).

```
void C6E3v_keyFrame(float3 positionA : POSITION,
                    float3 positionB : TEXCOORD1,
                    float4 color     : COLOR,
                    float2 texCoord  : TEXCOORD0,

                out float4 oPosition : POSITION,
                out float2 oTexCoord : TEXCOORD0,
                out float4 oColor    : COLOR,

            uniform float    keyFrameBlend,
            uniform float4x4 modelViewProj)
{
  float3 position = lerp(positionA, positionB,
                         keyFrameBlend);
  oPosition = mul(modelViewProj, float4(position, 1));
  oTexCoord = texCoord;
  oColor = color;
}
```

Example 6-3. The **C6E3v_keyFrame** Vertex Program

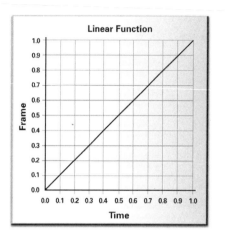

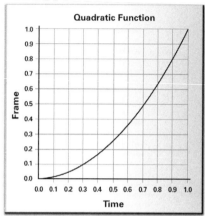

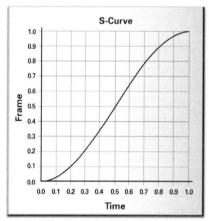

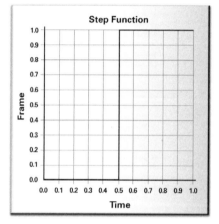

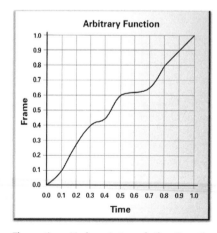

Figure 6-9. Various Interpolation Functions

Chapter 6: Animation

The application is also responsible for determining the key-frame blending factor via the uniform parameter **keyFrameBlend**. The value of **keyFrameBlend** should transition from 0 to 1. Once 1 is reached, the application chooses another key frame in the animation sequence, the old key frame B position input is then configured as the key frame A position input, and the new key-frame position data feeds the key frame B position input.

6.4.4 Key-Frame Interpolation with Lighting

You often want to light a key-framed model. This involves not merely blending two positions (the vertex in two different key frames), but also blending the two corresponding surface normals. Then you can calculate lighting computations with the blended normal. Blending two normals may change the length of the resulting normal, so you must normalize the blended normal prior to lighting.

Example 6-4 shows the **C6E4v_litKeyFrame** vertex program that adds per-vertex

```
struct Light {
  float3 eyePosition;   // In object space
  float3 lightPosition; // In object space
  float4 lightColor;
  float  specularExponent;
  float  ambient;
};


float4 computeLighting(Light light,
                       float3 position,  // In object space
                       float3 normal)    // In object space
{
  float3 lightDirection = light.lightPosition - position;
  float3 lightDirNorm = normalize(lightDirection);
  float3 eyeDirection = light.eyePosition - position;
  float3 eyeDirNorm = normalize(eyeDirection);
  float3 halfAngle = normalize(lightDirNorm + eyeDirNorm);
  float diffuse = max(0, dot(lightDirNorm, normal));
  float specular = pow(max(0, dot(halfAngle, normal)),
                   light.specularExponent);
  return light.lightColor * (light.ambient +
                             diffuse + specular);
}
```

Example 6-4. The **C6E4v_litKeyFrame** Vertex Program

```
void C6E4v_litKeyFrame(float3 positionA : POSITION,
                       float3 normalA   : NORMAL,
                       float3 positionB : TEXCOORD1,
                       float3 normalB   : TEXCOORD2,
                       float2 texCoord  : TEXCOORD0,

                   out float4 oPosition : POSITION,
                   out float2 oTexCoord : TEXCOORD0,
                   out float4 color     : COLOR,

               uniform float     keyFrameBlend,
               uniform Light     light,
               uniform float4x4  modelViewProj)
{
  float3 position = lerp(positionA, positionB,
                    keyFrameBlend);
  float3 blendNormal = lerp(normalA, normalB,
                       keyFrameBlend);
  float3 normal = normalize(blendNormal);
  oPosition = mul(modelViewProj, float4(position, 1));
  oTexCoord = texCoord;
  color = computeLighting(light, position, normal);
}
```

Example 6-4 (*continued*). The **C6E4v_litKeyFrame** Vertex Program

lighting to the **C6E3v_keyFrame** example. In the updated example, each key frame also supplies its own corresponding per-vertex surface normal.

The **computeLighting** internal function computes a conventional lighting model using object-space lighting.

6.5   Vertex Skinning

Another approach to animating characters is *vertex skinning*. Many 3D modeling packages author 3D content suitable for vertex skinning. The technique is also known as *matrix palette blending*.

6.5.1   The Theory of Vertex Skinning

Rather than have key frames for each pose of a character, vertex skinning maintains a single default pose and a large set of matrices that appropriately rotate and translate various subregions of the default pose's polygonal mesh. For reasons that will become apparent, these various matrix transforms are often called "bones."

One or more of these matrices control each vertex in the default pose's polygonal mesh. Each matrix is assigned a weighting factor (from 0 to 100 percent), which indicates how much that matrix affects each vertex. Only a small number of matrices usually control each vertex, meaning that only these few matrices have positive and significant weighting factors for a given vertex. We call this small set of matrices the *bone set* for each vertex. We assume that the weighting factors for all the matrices in a vertex's bone set always sum to 100 percent.

When rendering this type of model, you first transform every vertex by each matrix in the vertex's bone set, then weight the results of each matrix transform according to the matrix's corresponding weighting factor, and finally sum the results. This new position is the *skinned vertex position*.

When all the matrices are identity matrices (no rotation, no translation), the mesh is in the default pose. 3D artists often pick a default pose in which the character is standing and facing forward, with legs apart and arms outstretched.

Constructing Poses from Matrices

By controlling the matrices, you can create novel poses. For example, a vertex on a character's forearm close to the elbow might use 67 percent of the forearm matrix, 21 percent of the elbow matrix, and 12 percent of the upper arm matrix. The animator who creates a model for vertex skinning must appropriately localize each matrix so that, for example, the matrix that controls the left shoulder has no effect on vertices near the ankle. Often, the number of matrices affecting any given vertex is limited to no more than four. For the 3D artist, once all the weights and matrices are assigned to the model's default pose, constructing a new pose is a matter of manipulating the matrices appropriately, rather than attempting to position each individual vertex. Posing and animating the model is much simpler when it is authored for vertex skinning.

For a character model, the most significant matrices represent the way rigid bones in the character's body move and rotate; hence, the vertex-skinning matrices are called *bones.* The vertices represent points on the skin. Vertex skinning simulates how bones, represented as matrices, tug and reposition various points, represented as vertices, on the character's skin.

Lighting

For correct lighting, you can compute the same sort of transformed and weighted average used for positions, except that you transform normals by the inverse transpose of each matrix rather than by the matrix itself. Weighted normals may no longer be unit length, so normalization is required.

Assuming that the bone matrices are merely rotations and translations simplifies the transformation of the normals for lighting, because the inverse transpose of a matrix without scaling or projection is the matrix itself.

Storage Requirements Compared with Key Frames

With the key frame approach, every pose requires a distinct set of vertex positions and normals. This becomes unwieldy if huge numbers of poses are required.

However, with vertex skinning, each pose requires just the default pose—shared by all poses—and the matrix values for the given pose. There are generally substantially fewer matrices per character than vertices, so representing a pose as a set of bone matrices is more compact than representing the pose with a key frame. With vertex skinning, you can also create novel poses dynamically, either by blending existing bone matrices from different poses or by controlling matrices directly. For example, if you know what matrices control an arm, you can wave the arm by controlling those matrices.

In addition to requiring the matrices for each pose, the model's default pose needs each vertex to have a default position, a default normal, some number of matrix indices to identify which subset of matrices control the vertex, and the same number of weighting factors, corresponding to each respective matrix.

This data for the default pose is constant for all other poses. Generating a new pose requires only new matrices, not any changes to the default pose data. If the GPU can perform all the vertex-skinning computations, this means that the CPU needs to update only the bone matrices for each new pose, but not otherwise manipulate or access the default pose data.

Vertex skinning is quite amenable to storing and replaying motion-capture sequences. You can represent each motion-capture frame as a set of bone matrices that you can

Chapter 6: Animation

then apply to different models that share the same default pose and matrix associations. Inverse kinematics solvers can also generate bone matrices procedurally. An inverse kinematics solver attempts to find an incremental sequence of bone matrices that transition from one given pose to another given pose in a realistic, natural manner.

6.5.2 Vertex Skinning in a Vertex Program

The **C6E5v_skin4m** vertex program in Example 6-5 implements vertex skinning, assuming that no more than four bone matrices affect each vertex (a common assumption).

An array of 24 bone matrices, each a 3×4 matrix, represents each pose. The entire array is a uniform parameter to the program. The program assumes that each bone matrix consists of a translation and a rotation (no scaling or projection).

The per-vertex **matrixIndex** input vector provides a set of four bone-matrix indices for accessing the **boneMatrix** array. The per-vertex **weight** input vector provides the four weighting factors for each respective bone matrix. The program assumes that the weighting factors for each vertex sum to 100 percent.

 For performance reasons, the program treats **boneMatrix** as an array of **float4** vectors rather than an array of **float3x4** matrices. The **matrixIndex** array contains floating-point values instead of integers, and so the addressing of a single array of vectors is more efficient than accessing an array of matrices. The implication of this is that the indices in the **matrixIndex** vector should be three times the actual matrix index. So, the program assumes 0 is the first matrix in the array, 3 is the second matrix, and so on. The indices are fixed for each vertex, so you improve performance by moving this "multiply by 3" outside the vertex program.

A **for** loop, looping four times, transforms the default pose position and normal by each bone matrix. Each result is weighted and summed.

The program computes both the weighted position and normal for the pose. The same **computeLighting** internal function from Example 6-4 computes per-vertex object-space lighting with the weighted position and normal.

Although this example is rather limited, you could generalize it to handle more bone matrices, general bone matrices (for example, allowing scaling), and matrices influencing each vertex—and to compute a better lighting model.

```
void C6E5v_skin4m(float3 position    : POSITION,
                  float3 normal      : NORMAL,
                  float2 texCoord    : TEXCOORD0,
                  float4 weight      : TEXCOORD1,
                  float4 matrixIndex : TEXCOORD2,

              out float4 oPosition : POSITION,
              out float2 oTexCoord : TEXCOORD0,
              out float4 color     : COLOR,

          uniform Light light,
          uniform float4    boneMatrix[72], // 24 matrices
          uniform float4x4  modelViewProj)
{
  float3 netPosition = 0, netNormal = 0;

  for (int i = 0; i < 4; i++) {
    float index = matrixIndex[i];
    float3x4 model = float3x4(boneMatrix[index + 0],
                              boneMatrix[index + 1],
                              boneMatrix[index + 2]);
    float3 bonePosition = mul(model, float4(position, 1));
    // Assume no scaling in matrix, just rotate & translate
    float3x3 rotate = float3x3(model[0].xyz,
                               model[1].xyz,
                               model[2].xyz);
    float3 boneNormal = mul(rotate, normal);
    netPosition += weight[i] * bonePosition;
    netNormal   += weight[i] * boneNormal;
  }
  netNormal = normalize(netNormal);

  oPosition = mul(modelViewProj, float4(netPosition, 1));
  oTexCoord = texCoord;
  color = computeLighting(light, netPosition, netNormal);
}
```

Example 6-5. The **C6E5v_skin4m** Vertex Program

6.6   Exercises

1. **Answer this:** What are some common types of interpolation functions for key-frame interpolation? Describe situations in which you might use each one.

2. **Try this yourself:** Make the bulging program also glow periodically by adding an emissive term that varies with the time. As a further step, base the emissive term at each vertex on the vertex's diffuse material color.

3. **Try this yourself:** Optimize the `C6E2v_particle` program by passing `t`, `0.5*t*t`, and `-0.8*t*t+0.8*t` as uniform parameters.

4. **Try this yourself:** The particle system you implemented used specific functions for the particle size and color. Try replacing these with functions of your own. One interesting idea for the particle size is to make it dependent on the distance from the eye position. To do this, modify the application to pass the eye position as a uniform parameter to the vertex program. You can then compute the distance from any particle to the eye position and scale based on *1/distance²* or some similar function that you prefer.

5. **Try this yourself:** If you vary the twisting angle temporally, the `C3E4v_twist` example in Chapter 3 becomes a procedural 2D animation. Write a 3D version of animated twisting and apply it to 3D models.

6. **Try this yourself:** Modify the `C6E5v_skin4m` example to handle bone matrices that include scaling. Keep in mind that the inverse transpose matrix required for transforming normals is distinct from the matrix required to transform positions if that matrix includes scaling.

7. **Try this yourself:** Modify the `C6E5v_skin4m` example to handle six bone matrices per vertex instead of just four. This means that you may need to split the weights and matrix indices into multiple input parameters.

6.7   Further Reading

If you are interested in the physics behind the particle system you created, you can learn more by reviewing kinematics in any high school or college physics textbook.

Jeff Lander wrote a series of articles in 1998 and 1999 for *Game Developer Magazine* about various animation techniques. You can find these articles on the **www.darwin3d.com** Web site. For particle systems, read "The Ocean Spray in Your

Face." For vertex skinning, check out "Skin Them Bones: Game Programming for the Web Generation."

The original volume of *Game Programming Gems* (Charles River Media, 2000), edited by Mark DeLoura, contains several gems related to key-frame animation and vertex skinning. Check out these articles: "Interpolated 3D Keyframe Animation," by Herbert Marselas; "A Fast and Simple Skinning Technique," by Torgeir Hagland; and "Filling the Gaps—Advanced Animation Using Stitching and Skinning," by Ryan Woodland.

John Vince's book *3-D Computer Animation* (Addison-Wesley, 1992) covers many of the techniques described in this chapter, as well as others, such as free-form deformation (FFD).

DirectX 8 added point sprites to Direct3D. OpenGL implementations from multiple hardware vendors support the **NV_point_sprite** extension. The specification for this OpenGL extension is available at the **www.opengl.org** Web site.

Chapter 7

Environment Mapping Techniques

This chapter explains environment mapping and presents several applications of the technique. The chapter has the following four sections:

- **"Environment Mapping"** introduces the technique and explains its key assumptions and limitations.

- **"Reflective Environment Mapping"** explains the physics of reflection and how to simulate reflective materials with environment mapping.

- **"Refractive Environment Mapping"** describes Snell's Law and shows how to use environment maps to implement an effect that approximates refraction.

- **"The Fresnel Effect and Chromatic Dispersion"** combines reflection, refraction, the Fresnel effect, and the chromatic properties of light to produce a more complex effect called chromatic dispersion.

7.1   Environment Mapping

The preceding chapters showed some basic shading techniques. By now, you know how to light, transform, texture, and animate objects with Cg. However, your renderings are probably not quite what you envisioned. The next few chapters describe a few simple techniques that can dramatically improve your images.

This chapter presents several techniques based on *environment mapping*. Environment mapping simulates an object reflecting its surroundings. In its simplest form, environment mapping gives rendered objects a chrome-like appearance.

Environment mapping assumes that an object's environment (that is, everything surrounding it) is infinitely distant from the object and, therefore, can be encoded in an omnidirectional image known as an environment map.

7.1.1 Cube Map Textures

All recent GPUs support a type of texture known as a *cube map*. A cube map consists of not one, but six square texture images that fit together like the faces of a cube. Together, these six images form an omnidirectional image that we use to encode environment maps. Figure 7-1 shows an example of a cube map that captures an environment consisting of a cloudy sky and foggy mountainous terrain.

Figure 7-1. Texture Images for a Cube Map

A 2D texture maps a 2D texture coordinate set to a color in a single texture image. In contrast, you access a cube map texture with a three-component texture coordinate set that represents a 3D direction vector.

Think of this vector as a ray originating from the center of the cube. As the ray shoots outward, it will intersect one of the six cube map faces. The result of a cube map texture access is the filtered color at that point of intersection with one of the six texture images.

Cube map textures are ideal for environment mapping. Each face of the cube map encodes one-sixth of the panoramic environment around an object. A cube map texture provides a quick way to determine what the object centered within that environment would "see" in any particular direction.

7.1.2   Generating Cube Maps

To generate a cube map, replace the object you want to put reflections on with a camera at the object's position and take snapshots in six directions (positive *x*, negative *x*, positive *y*, negative *y*, positive *z*, and negative *z*). Each snapshot should have a 90-degree field of view and a square aspect ratio, so that the six cube faces seam up tightly—with no gaps or overlap—to create an omnidirectional panorama. Use these images as the six faces of your cube map.

You can either render the six views with a computer, or capture an actual environment with a set of photographs and then warp them together to create an environment map. The electronic material that supplements this book contains pregenerated cube maps that you can use as well.

7.1.3   The Environment Mapping Concept

When you look at a highly reflective object such as a chrome sphere, what you see is not the object itself but how the object reflects its environment. When you gaze at some point on a highly reflective surface, the surface at that point reflects the *view ray*—that is, the ray that travels from your eye to the point on the surface—into the environment. The characteristics of the reflected ray depend on the original view ray and on the surface normal at the point where the view ray reaches the surface. What you see is not the surface itself but what the environment looks like in the direction of the reflected ray.

When you use a cube map to encode what the environment looks like in all directions, rendering a point on a reflective surface is a matter of computing the reflected view direction for that point on the surface. Then you can access the cube map, based on the reflected view direction, to determine the color of the environment for the point on the surface.

7.1.4 Computing Reflection Vectors

Figure 7-2 illustrates an object, an eye position, and a cube map texture that captures the environment surrounding the object. Because Figure 7-2 is, of course, depicting a 3D scene in 2D, the object is shown as a trapezoid and the environment is shown as the surrounding square, rather than an actual cube

The vector I—called the *incident ray*—goes from the eye to the object's surface. When I reaches the surface, it is reflected in the direction R based on the surface normal N. This second ray is the *reflected ray*. Figure 7-3 shows the geometry of the situation.

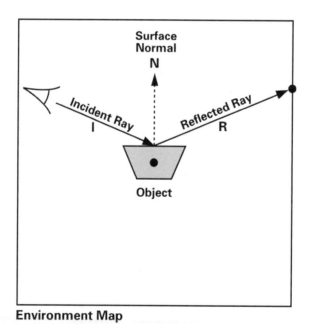

Environment Map

Figure 7-2. Environment Mapping

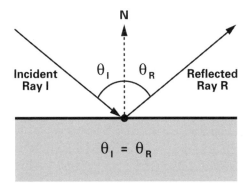

Figure 7-3. Calculating the Reflected Ray

The angle of incidence (θ_I) is the same as the angle of reflection (θ_R) for a perfect reflector such as a mirror. You can compute the reflected vector R in terms of the vectors I and N with Equation 7-1.

$$R = I - 2N(N \cdot I)$$

Equation 7-1. Vector Reflection

Calculating a reflected vector is a common operation in computer graphics, so Cg provides the **reflect** Standard Library function. This function takes in the incident vector and the surface normal and returns the reflected vector.

reflect(I, N)	Returns the reflected vector for the incident ray **I** and the surface normal **N**. The vector **N** should be normalized. The reflected vector's length is equal to the length of **I**. This function is valid only for three-component vectors.

Though you are better off using the Cg Standard Library routine because of its efficiency, the straightforward implementation of **reflect** is as follows:

```
float3 reflect(float3 I, float3 N)
{
  return I - 2.0 * N * dot(N, I);
}
```

We will be putting the **reflect** function to work later.

7.1.5   Assumptions for Environment Mapping

The preceding discussion mentioned that environment mapping assumes that the environment is infinitely distant from the object. Now we explore the implications of this assumption.

The reason for the assumption is that environment maps are accessed solely based on a 3D direction. Environment mapping has no allowance for variations in position to affect the reflected appearance of surfaces. If everything in the environment is sufficiently far away from the surface, then this assumption is approximately true.

In practice, the visual artifacts that result when the environment is not sufficiently distant typically go completely unnoticed. Reflections, particularly on curved surfaces, are subtle enough that most people fail to notice when a reflection is not physically accurate. As long as reflections match the coarse coloration of the environment and change appropriately with the curvature of the surface, surfaces rendered with environment mapping appear believable.

You'll be surprised at what you can get away with.

Ideally, every environment-mapped object in a scene should have its own environment map. In practice, objects can often share environment maps with no one noticing.

In theory, you should regenerate an environment map when objects in the environment move or when the reflective object using the environment map moves significantly relative to the environment. In practice, convincing reflections are possible with static environment maps.

With an environment map, an object can reflect only the environment; it cannot reflect itself. Similarly, do not expect multiple reflections, such as when two shiny objects reflect each other. Because an environment-mapped object can reflect only its environment and not itself, environment mapping works best on convex or mostly convex objects—rather than more concave objects.

Because environment mapping depends solely on direction and not on position, it works poorly on flat reflective surfaces such as mirrors, where the reflections depend heavily on position. In contrast, environment mapping works best on curved surfaces.

7.2 Reflective Environment Mapping

Let's start with the most common use of environment mapping: creating a chrome-like reflective object. This is the bare-bones application of the technique, yet it already produces nice results, as shown in Figure 7-4.

In this example, the vertex program computes the incident and reflected rays. It then passes the reflected ray to the fragment program, which looks up the environment map and uses it to add a reflection to the fragment's final color. To make things more interesting, and to make our example more like a real application, we blend the reflection with a decal texture. A uniform parameter called **reflectivity** allows the application to control how reflective the material is.

You might wonder why we don't use the fragment program to calculate the reflection vector. A reflection vector computed per-fragment by the fragment program would deliver higher image quality, but it wouldn't work on basic fragment profiles. Therefore, we leave the per-fragment implementation as an exercise for you. Later in this chapter, we discuss the trade-offs and implications of using the vertex program versus using the fragment program.

Figure 7-4. Reflective Environment Mapping

7.2.1 Application-Specified Parameters

Table 7-1 lists the data that the application needs to provide to the graphics pipeline.

Table 7-1. Application-Specified Parameters for Per-Vertex Environment Mapping

Parameter	Variable Name	Type
VERTEX PROGRAM VARYING PARAMETERS		
Object-space vertex position	`position`	`float4`
Object-space vertex normal	`normal`	`float3`
Texture coordinates	`texCoord`	`float2`
VERTEX PROGRAM UNIFORM PARAMETERS		
Concatenated modelview and projection matrices	`modelViewProj`	`float4x4`
Object space to world space transform	`modelToWorld`	`float4x4`
FRAGMENT PROGRAM UNIFORM PARAMETERS		
Decal texture	`decalMap`	`sampler2D`
Environment map	`environmentMap`	`samplerCUBE`
Eye position (in world space)	`eyePositionW`	`float3`
Reflectivity	`reflectivity`	`float`

7.2.2 The Vertex Program

Example 7-1 gives the vertex program that performs the per-vertex reflection vector computation for environment mapping.

Basic Operations

The vertex program starts with the mundane operations: transforming the position into clip space and passing through the texture coordinate set for the decal texture.

```
oPosition = mul(modelViewProj, position);
oTexCoord = texCoord;
```

```
void C7E1v_reflection(float4 position : POSITION,
                      float2 texCoord : TEXCOORD0,
                      float3 normal   : NORMAL,

                  out float4 oPosition  : POSITION,
                  out float2 oTexCoord  : TEXCOORD0,
                  out float3 R          : TEXCOORD1,

              uniform float3   eyePositionW,
              uniform float4x4 modelViewProj,
              uniform float4x4 modelToWorld)
{
  oPosition = mul(modelViewProj, position);
  oTexCoord = texCoord;

  // Compute position and normal in world space
  float3 positionW = mul(modelToWorld, position).xyz;
  float3 N = mul((float3x3)modelToWorld, normal);
  N = normalize(N);

  // Compute the incident and reflected vectors
  float3 I = positionW - eyePositionW;
  R = reflect(I, N);
}
```

Example 7-1. The **C7E1v_reflection** Vertex Program

Transforming the Vectors into World Space

Environment maps are typically oriented relative to world space, so you need to calculate the reflection vector in world space (or whatever coordinate system orients the environment map). To do that, you must transform the rest of the vertex data into world space. In particular, you need to transform the vertex position and normal by multiplying them by the **modelToWorld** matrix:

```
float3 positionW = mul(modelToWorld, position).xyz;
float3 N = mul((float3x3)modelToWorld, normal);
```

The **modelToWorld** matrix is of type **float4x4**, but we require only the upper 3×3 section of the matrix when transforming a normal. Cg allows you to cast larger matrices to smaller matrices, as in the previous code. When you cast a larger matrix to a smaller matrix type, such as a **float4x4** matrix cast to a **float3x3** matrix, the upper left portion of the larger matrix fills in the matrix of the smaller type. For example, if you had a **float4x4** matrix M:

$$M = \begin{bmatrix} 1.0 & 2.0 & 3.0 & 4.0 \\ 5.0 & 6.0 & 7.0 & 8.0 \\ 9.0 & 10.0 & 11.0 & 12.0 \\ 13.0 & 14.0 & 15.0 & 16.0 \end{bmatrix}$$

and you cast it to a **float3x3** matrix, you would end up with the matrix N:

$$N = \begin{bmatrix} 1.0 & 2.0 & 3.0 \\ 5.0 & 6.0 & 7.0 \\ 9.0 & 10.0 & 11.0 \end{bmatrix}$$

 Recall from Chapter 4 (Section 4.1.3) that the modeling transform converts object-space coordinates to world-space coordinates. In this example, we assume that the modeling transform is *affine* (rather than projective) and uniform in its scaling (rather than nonuniformly scaling *x, y,* and *z*). We also assume that the *w* component of **position** is 1, even though **position** is defined to be a **float4** in the prototype for **C7E1v_reflection**.

These assumptions are commonly true, but if they do not hold for your case, here is what you need to do.

If the modeling transform scales positions nonuniformly, you must multiply **normal** by the inverse transpose of the modeling matrix (**modelToWorldInvTrans**), rather than simply by **modelToWorld**. That is:

```
float3 N = mul((float3x3)modelToWorldInvTrans, normal);
```

If the modeling transform is projective or the *w* component of the object-space **position** is not 1, you must divide **positionW** by its *w* component. That is:

```
positionW /= positionW.w;
```

The **/=** operator is an assignment operator, like the one in C and C++, which in this case divides **positionW** by **positionW.w** and then assigns the result to **positionW**.

Normalizing the Normal

The vertex normal needs to be normalized:

```
N = normalize(N);
```

 In certain cases, we can skip this **normalize** function call. If we know that the upper 3×3 portion of the **modelToWorld** matrix causes no nonuniform scaling *and* the object-space normal parameter is guaranteed to be already normalized, the **normalize** call is unnecessary.

Calculating the Incident Vector

The incident vector is the opposite of the view vector used in Chapter 5 for specular lighting. The *incident vector* is the vector from the eye to the vertex (whereas the view vector is from the vertex to the eye). With the world-space eye position (**eyePositionW**) available as a uniform parameter and the world-space vertex position (**positionW**) available from the previous step, calculating the incident vector is a simple subtraction:

```
float3 I = positionW - eyePositionW;
```

Calculating the Reflection Vector

You now have the vectors you need—the position and normal, both in world space—so you can calculate the reflection vector:

```
float3 R = reflect(I, N);
```

Next, the program outputs the reflected world-space vector **R** as a three-component texture coordinate set. The fragment program example that follows will use this texture coordinate set to access a cube map texture containing an environment map.

Normalizing Vectors

You might be wondering why we did not normalize **I** or **R**. Normalization is not needed here because the reflected vector is used to query a cube map. The direction of the reflected vector is all that matters when accessing a cube map. Regardless of its length, the reflected ray will intersect the cube map at exactly the same location.

And because the **reflect** function outputs a reflected vector that has the same length as the incident vector as long as **N** is normalized, the incident vector's length doesn't matter either in this case.

There is one more reason not to normalize **R**. The rasterizer interpolates **R** prior to use by the fragment program in the next example. This interpolation is more accurate if the per-vertex reflection vector is not normalized.

7.2.3   The Fragment Program

Example 7-2 shows a fragment program that is quite short, because the **C7E1v_reflection** vertex program already took care of the major calculations. All that's left are the cube map lookup and the final color calculation.

```
void C7E2f_reflection(float2 texCoord : TEXCOORD0,
                      float3 R         : TEXCOORD1,

                  out float4 color : COLOR,

              uniform float reflectivity,
              uniform sampler2D decalMap,
              uniform samplerCUBE environmentMap)
{
  // Fetch reflected environment color
  float4 reflectedColor = texCUBE(environmentMap, R);

  // Fetch the decal base color
  float4 decalColor = tex2D(decalMap, texCoord);

  color = lerp(decalColor, reflectedColor, reflectivity);
}
```

Example 7-2. The **C7E2f_reflection** Fragment Program

The fragment program receives the interpolated reflected vector that it uses to obtain the reflected color from the environment map:

```
float4 reflectedColor = texCUBE(environmentMap, R);
```

Notice the new texture lookup function **texCUBE**. This function is used specifically for accessing cube maps, and so it interprets the second parameter (which is a three-component texture coordinate set) as a direction.

At this point, you could assign **reflectedColor** to **color**, making the rendered object completely reflective. However, no real material is a perfect reflector, so to make things more interesting, the program adds a decal texture lookup, and then mixes the decal color with the reflected color:

```
float4 decalColor = tex2D(decalMap, texCoord);
color = lerp(decalColor, reflectedColor, reflectivity);
```

The **lerp** function performs linear interpolation, as you have seen before in Section 3.3.5. The parameters to **lerp** are **decalColor**, **reflectedColor**, and **reflectivity**. So, when **reflectivity** is 0, your program writes out just the decal color and shows no reflection. In contrast, when **reflectivity** is 1, the program writes out just the reflected color, producing a completely reflective, chrome-like appearance. Intermediate values of **reflectivity** result in a decaled model that has some reflective qualities.

7.2.4 Control Maps

In this example, **reflectivity** is a uniform parameter. The assumption is that each piece of geometry in the scene has the same reflectivity over its entire surface. But this doesn't necessarily have to be the case! You can create more interesting effects by encoding reflectivity in a texture. This approach allows you to vary the amount of reflectivity at each fragment, which makes it easy to create objects with both reflective and nonreflective parts.

Because the idea of using a texture to control shading parameters is so powerful, we call such a texture a *control map*. Control maps are especially important because they leverage the GPU's efficient texture manipulation capabilities. In addition, control maps give artists increased control over effects without having to have a deep understanding of the underlying programs. For example, an artist could paint a "reflectivity map" without understanding how environment mapping works.

Control maps are an excellent way to add detail and complexity to almost any program.

7.2.5   Vertex Program vs. Fragment Program

We mentioned previously that you could achieve higher image quality by using the fragment program (instead of the vertex program) to calculate the reflected vector. Why is this? It is for the same reason that per-fragment lighting looks better than per-vertex lighting.

As with specular lighting, the reflection vector for environment mapping varies in a nonlinear way from fragment to fragment. This means that linearly interpolated per-vertex values will be insufficient to capture accurately the variation in the reflection vector. In particular, subtle per-vertex artifacts tend to appear near the silhouettes of objects, where the reflection vector changes rapidly within each triangle. To obtain more accurate reflections, move the reflection vector calculation to the fragment program. This way, you explicitly calculate the reflection vector for each fragment instead of interpolating it.

Despite this additional accuracy, per-fragment environment mapping may not improve image quality enough to justify the additional expense. As explained earlier in the chapter, most people are unlikely to notice or appreciate the more correct reflections at glancing angles. Keep in mind that environment mapping does not generate physically correct reflections to begin with.

7.3   Refractive Environment Mapping

Now that you have learned how to implement basic environment mapping, you can use it to simulate some related physical phenomena. The techniques you will learn in the following sections illustrate how easy it is to put theory into practice when you are using a high-level language like Cg. The same techniques could be implemented without Cg, but they would require a great deal of assembly-level coding skill. As a result, the techniques and resulting image quality would be out of reach for most developers, even though the effects would be supported by the underlying graphics hardware.

In this section, you are going to learn how to implement refraction using a little physics and a little environment mapping. Figure 7-5 illustrates the effect you will be trying to achieve.

Figure 7-5. Refractive Environment Mapping

7.3.1 The Physics of Refraction

When light passes through a boundary between two materials of different density (air and water, for example), the light's direction changes. This change in direction happens because light travels more slowly in denser materials (or *media*, as materials are called in the context of refraction). For example, light travels quickly in air, but more slowly in water. The classic example of refraction is the "bend" that appears in a straw when you place it in a glass of water.

Snell's Law

Snell's Law describes what happens to light at a boundary (or *interface*, as such boundaries are called in the context of refraction) between two media, as shown in Figure 7-6. The refracted vector is represented by *T*, which stands for "transmitted." Snell's Law is expressed mathematically by Equation 7-2. The equation has four variables: the

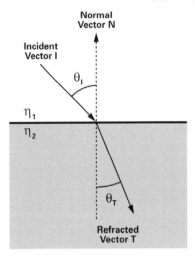

Figure 7-6. Snell's Law

Table 7-2. Indices of Refraction

Material	Index of Refraction
Vacuum	1.0
Air	1.0003
Water	1.3333
Glass	1.5
Plastic	1.5
Diamond	2.417

Note
Different types of glass have different indices of refraction, but 1.5 is a reasonable value for ordinary window glass. It is also a decent approximation for most plastics.

incident angle θ_I, the refracted angle θ_T, and an index of refraction for each medium, η_1 and η_2.

$$\eta_1 \sin\theta_I = \eta_2 \sin\theta_T$$

Equation 7-2. Snell's Law

A medium's index of refraction measures how the medium affects the speed of light. The higher the index of refraction for a medium, the slower light travels in it. Table 7-2 lists a few common materials and their approximate indices of refraction. (The index of refraction for a material actually depends not only on the material, but also on the wavelength of the incoming light, but we ignore this complexity for the moment.)

In this example, you will simulate refraction, as shown in Figure 7-7. Each incident ray from the eye is refracted, and each refracted ray is used to look up the environment map (just as each reflected ray was used to look up the environment map in the reflection mapping example).

Notice that we only simulate the first refracted ray. Figure 7-8 shows the difference for a simple object between our approach and a more accurate approach. The incident ray should really be refracted twice—once as it enters the object, and again as it leaves (as the vector T'). However, we do not simulate the second refraction, so we use T in-

Chapter 7: Environment Mapping Techniques

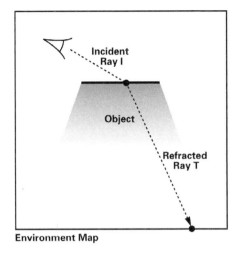

Figure 7-7. Refraction into an
Environment Map

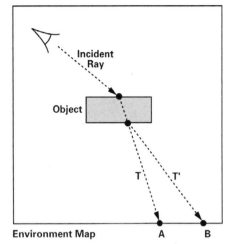

Figure 7-8. Multiple Refractions vs. One
Refraction

stead of T' as the transmitted ray. The two rays end up intersecting the environment in different locations (labeled A and B in Figure 7-8). Fortunately, refraction is complicated enough that the resulting images are hard to distinguish in most cases. Especially for a casual viewer, it will be hard to tell that the generated refraction is not truly correct.

This type of simplification occurs routinely in real-time computer graphics. The thing to remember is that the result is what matters. If your images look convincing, it often doesn't matter that they might be physically inaccurate. In many cases, if you were to compute a complete physical simulation, your frame rate would drop significantly. This is why, from its early days, real-time computer graphics has focused on finding new, efficient techniques to make images look good. Of course, the goal is still to find techniques that are both accurate and fast, but in most cases, the programmer must still make an appropriate trade-off between accuracy and performance.

The Ratio of Indices of Refraction

To calculate refraction, one of the key values you need is the ratio between the index of refraction of each medium. For the next example, the application needs to pass **etaRatio**, the ratio of indices of refraction of the two media, to the vertex program. Conventionally, the Greek letter η ("eta") is used for a single material's index of refraction. However, the ratio of indices of refraction is more efficient in practice, because it saves the vertex program from having to calculate the ratio for each vertex (when it needs to be calculated only once per mesh).

7.3.2 The Vertex Program

Refraction is, in many ways, similar to reflection. In both cases, an incident ray hits a surface and something happens to it (it bounces off in the case of reflection, and it changes direction inside the surface in the case of refraction). These similarities hint that the Cg code for refraction is similar to the code for reflection. And indeed, it is.

The vertex program **C7E3v_refraction** in Example 7-3 for refraction needs to compute and output the refracted ray, rather than the reflected ray as in **C7E1v_reflection**. You do not need to apply Snell's Law yourself, because Cg has a **refract** function that will do it for you. Here is the function definition:

refract(I, N, etaRatio)	Given incident ray direction **I**, surface normal **N**, and relative index of refraction **etaRatio**, this function computes refraction vector T, as illustrated in Figure 7-6. The vector **N** should be normalized. The refracted vector's length is equal to the length of **I**. **etaRatio** is the ratio of the index of refraction in the medium containing the incident ray to that of the medium being entered. This function is valid only for three-component vectors.

Here is a sample implementation of the **refract** Standard Library routine:

```
float3 refract(float3 I, float3 N, float etaRatio)
{
  float cosI = dot(-I, N);
  float cosT2 = 1.0f - etaRatio * etaRatio *
                      (1.0f - cosI * cosI);
  float3 T = etaRatio * I +
             ((etaRatio * cosI - sqrt(abs(cosT2))) * N);
  return T * (float3)(cosT2 > 0);
}
```

```
void C7E3v_refraction(float4 position : POSITION,
                      float2 texCoord : TEXCOORD0,
                      float3 normal   : NORMAL,

                  out float4 oPosition : POSITION,
                  out float2 oTexCoord : TEXCOORD0,
                  out float3 T         : TEXCOORD1,

              uniform float etaRatio,
              uniform float3 eyePositionW,
              uniform float4x4 modelViewProj,
              uniform float4x4 modelToWorld)
{
  oPosition = mul(modelViewProj, position);
  oTexCoord = texCoord;

  // Compute position and normal in world space
  float3 positionW = mul(modelToWorld, position).xyz;
  float3 N = mul((float3x3)modelToWorld, normal);
  N = normalize(N);

  // Compute the incident and refracted vectors
  float3 I = positionW - eyePositionW;
  T = refract(I, N, etaRatio);
}
```

Example 7-3. The **C7E3v_refraction** Vertex Program

 When light passes from a dense medium to a less dense medium, the light can refract so much that total internal reflection occurs. For example, if you are under water in a pool and the surface of the water is smooth enough, the surface of the water will look like a mirror when viewed at a glancing angle. In this case, **cosT2** is less than or equal to zero and the **refract** routine returns a zero vector.

The key difference between the earlier **C7E1v_reflection** example and the **C7E3v_refraction** example is the use of the **refract** function (rather than the **reflect** function) to calculate the refracted vector **T**.

The Fragment Program

The fragment program does not have to be changed because its role remains the same: it looks up the environment map based on the incoming vector. The incoming vector is now the refracted vector instead of the reflected vector, but the fragment program still behaves exactly the same way that it did in the reflection mapping example. The fragment program looks up the environment map, mixes the result with the decal texture color, and returns the result. For correctness, the fragment program **C7E4f_refraction** in Example 7-4 renames **reflectedColor** to **refractedColor** and **reflectivity** to **transmittance**, but those are only cosmetic changes from the earlier **C7E2f_reflection** program.

```
void C7E4f_refraction(float2 texCoord : TEXCOORD0,
                      float3 T        : TEXCOORD1,

                  out float4 color : COLOR,

              uniform float       transmittance,
              uniform sampler2D   decalMap,
              uniform samplerCUBE environmentMap)
{
  // Fetch the decal base color
  float4 decalColor = tex2D(decalMap, texCoord);

  // Fetch refracted environment color
  float4 refractedColor = texCUBE(environmentMap, T);

  // Compute the final color
  color = lerp(decalColor, refractedColor, transmittance);
}
```

Example 7-4. The **C7E4f_refraction** Fragment Program

7.4 The Fresnel Effect and Chromatic Dispersion

You now know how to implement reflection and refraction. The next example combines them and throws in a few other extensions. You will learn about two new effects: the Fresnel effect and chromatic dispersion.

7.4.1 The Fresnel Effect

In general, when light reaches an interface between two materials, some light reflects off the surface at the interface, and some refracts through the surface. This phenomenon is known as the *Fresnel effect* (pronounced "freh-'nell"). The Fresnel equations describe how much light is reflected and how much is refracted. If you have ever wondered why you can see fish in a pond only when you're looking practically straight down, it's because of the Fresnel effect. At shallow angles, there is a lot of reflection and almost no refraction, so it is hard to see through the water's surface.

The Fresnel effect adds realism to your images, because it allows you to create objects that exhibit a mix of reflection and refraction, more like real-world objects.

The Fresnel equations, which quantify the Fresnel effect, are complicated. (You can learn more about them in most optics textbooks.) Once again, the idea here is to create images that look plausible, not necessarily to describe accurately the intricacies of the underlying physics. So, instead of using the equations themselves, we are going to use the empirical approximation in Equation 7-3, which gives good results with significantly less complication:

$$reflectionCoefficient = \max(0, \min(1, bias + scale \times (1 + I \bullet N)^{power}))$$

Equation 7-3. An Approximation of the Fresnel Equation

The concept underlying this equation is that when I and N are nearly coincident, the reflection coefficient should be 0 or nearly 0, indicating that most of the light should be refracted. As I and N diverge, the reflection coefficient should gradually increase and eventually abruptly increase (due to the exponentiation) to 1. When I and N are sufficiently divergent, almost all the light should be reflected, with little or none of it being refracted.

The range of the reflection coefficient is clamped to the range [0, 1], because we use the reflection coefficient to mix the reflected and refracted contributions according to the following formula (where C stands for color):

$$C_{Final} = reflectionCoefficient \times C_{Reflected} + (1 - reflectionCoefficient) \times C_{Refracted}$$

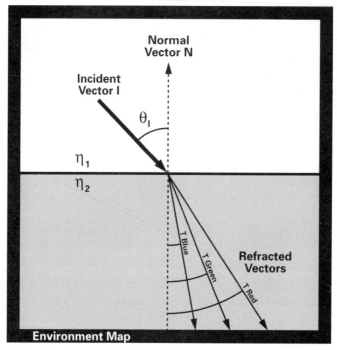

Figure 7-9. Understanding Chromatic Dispersion

7.4.2   Chromatic Dispersion

The earlier discussion of refraction was somewhat simplified. We mentioned that re-fraction depends on the surface normal, incident angle, and ratio of indices of refrac-tion. In addition to these factors, the amount of refraction also depends on the wavelength of the incident light. For example, red light gets refracted more than blue light. This phenomenon is known as *chromatic dispersion*, and it is what happens when white light enters a prism and emerges as a rainbow.

Figure 7-9 illustrates chromatic dispersion conceptually. The incident illumination (assumed to be white) is split into several refracted rays. You will simulate what hap-pens to the red, green, and blue components of the light, because these are the stan-dard components of colors in computer graphics. You will use the refracted red, green, and blue rays to look up into the environment map, just as you did for a single ray in the refraction example.

Keep in mind that real light is a band of wavelengths rather than three particular and discrete wavelengths. Still, this approximation is effective enough to be useful.

Chapter 7: Environment Mapping Techniques

Figure 7-10. The Fresnel Effect and Chromatic Dispersion

Combining the Fresnel effect with chromatic dispersion creates a rainbow effect, as if the rendered object were made of crystal, as shown in Figure 7-10. Plate 11, in the book's center insert, shows this image in color.

7.4.3 Application-Specified Parameters

Because we are now using a more complicated lighting model for our object's surface, the application needs to send extra uniform parameters to the vertex and fragment programs. These additional parameters are listed in Table 7-3.

The **x**, **y**, and **z** components in **etaRatio**, respectively, store the ratio of indices of refraction for red, green, and blue light. The **fresnelPower**, **fresnelScale**, and **fresnelBias** variables provide a way to shape the function that we use to approximate the Fresnel equations. Together, all the application-specified parameters define the material properties of your object.

Table 7-3. The `C7E5v_dispersion` Program Parameters

Parameter	Variable Name	Type
Ratio of indices of refraction for red, green, and blue light (packed into one **float3**)	`etaRatio`	`float3`
Fresnel power	`fresnelPower`	`float`
Fresnel scale	`fresnelScale`	`float`
Fresnel bias	`fresnelBias`	`float`

7.4.4   The Vertex Program

The `C7E5v_dispersion` vertex program in Example 7-5 calculates the reflected vector, along with red, green, and blue refracted vectors. In addition, you will use the approximation of Fresnel's formula to compute the reflection coefficient. All this information is then interpolated and received by the fragment program.

Calculating the Reflected Vector

The reflected vector calculation stays the same:

```
R = reflect(I, N);
```

Calculating the Refracted Vectors

You compute refracted vectors using an approach that is similar to the one that you used in the earlier refraction example. The difference is that now you have to calculate a refraction vector for each color component, instead of just one that applies equally to red, green, and blue:

```
TRed   = refract(I, N, etaRatio.x);
TGreen = refract(I, N, etaRatio.y);
TBlue  = refract(I, N, etaRatio.z);
```

Recall that the **x**, **y**, and **z** components in **etaRatio** respectively store the ratio of indices of refraction for red, green, and blue light.

```
void C7E5v_dispersion(float4 position : POSITION,
                      float3 normal   : NORMAL,

             out float4 oPosition         : POSITION,
             out float  reflectionFactor  : COLOR,
             out float3 R                 : TEXCOORD0,
             out float3 TRed              : TEXCOORD1,
             out float3 TGreen            : TEXCOORD2,
             out float3 TBlue             : TEXCOORD3,

         uniform float fresnelBias,
         uniform float fresnelScale,
         uniform float fresnelPower,
         uniform float3 etaRatio,
         uniform float3 eyePositionW,
         uniform float4x4 modelViewProj,
         uniform float4x4 modelToWorld)
{
  oPosition = mul(modelViewProj, position);

  // Compute position and normal in world space
  float3 positionW = mul(modelToWorld, position).xyz;
  float3 N = mul((float3x3)modelToWorld, normal);
  N = normalize(N);

  // Compute the incident, reflected, and refracted vectors
  float3 I = positionW - eyePositionW;
  R = reflect(I, N);
  I = normalize(I);
  TRed   = refract(I, N, etaRatio.x);
  TGreen = refract(I, N, etaRatio.y);
  TBlue  = refract(I, N, etaRatio.z);

  // Compute the reflection factor
  reflectionFactor = fresnelBias +
                     fresnelScale * pow(1 + dot(I, N),
                                        fresnelPower);
}
```

Example 7-5. The **C7E5v_dispersion** Vertex Program

Calculating the Reflection Coefficient

Translating Equation 7-3 into Cg code is straightforward. Use the **dot** and **pow** functions. The program outputs **reflectionFactor** as an interpolated color, as indicated by its associated **COLOR** semantic. Interpolated colors are automatically clamped to the range [0, 1], so there is no need to perform this clamping explicitly.

```
reflectionFactor = fresnelBias +
                   fresnelScale * pow(1 + dot(I, N),
                                      fresnelPower);
```

7.4.5 The Fragment Program

The **C7E6f_dispersion** fragment program in Example 7-6 receives all the interpolated data for the reflected and refracted vectors, along with the reflection coefficient that is clamped to [0, 1]. The fragment program looks up the various reflected and refracted vectors in an environment map and blends the results appropriately. Notice that the program expects the same environment cube map texture for each of the four texture units. The application must bind the environment map to each of these four texture units, because the program is written to run on both basic and advanced fragment profiles. Recall that basic fragment profiles can only sample a given texture unit with that texture unit's corresponding texture coordinate set, so the environment map must be replicated. Advanced fragment profiles do not have this limitation, so a single **environmentMap** cube map sampler would suffice.

Performing the Texture Lookups

First, the program performs four cube map lookups—one for the reflected color, and one for each component of the three refracted colors:

```
// Fetch the reflected environment color
float4 reflectedColor = texCUBE(environmentMap0, R);

// Compute the refracted environment color
float4 refractedColor;
refractedColor.r = texCUBE(environmentMap1, TRed).r;
refractedColor.g = texCUBE(environmentMap2, TGreen).g;
refractedColor.b = texCUBE(environmentMap3, TBlue).b;
```

For each of the three refracted texture lookups, the program uses swizzling to extract only the matching color component. That is, you extract the red component of the texture value sampled at **TRed**, the green component of the texture value sampled at

```
void C7E6f_dispersion(float   reflectionFactor : COLOR,
                      float3 R                  : TEXCOORD0,
                      float3 TRed               : TEXCOORD1,
                      float3 TGreen             : TEXCOORD2,
                      float3 TBlue              : TEXCOORD3,

                  out float4 color : COLOR,

              uniform samplerCUBE environmentMap0,
              uniform samplerCUBE environmentMap1,
              uniform samplerCUBE environmentMap2,
              uniform samplerCUBE environmentMap3)
{
  // Fetch the reflected environment color
  float4 reflectedColor = texCUBE(environmentMap0, R);

  // Compute the refracted environment color
  float4 refractedColor;
  refractedColor.r = texCUBE(environmentMap1, TRed).r;
  refractedColor.g = texCUBE(environmentMap2, TGreen).g;
  refractedColor.b = texCUBE(environmentMap3, TBlue).b;
  refractedColor.a = 1;

  // Compute the final color
  color = lerp(refractedColor,
               reflectedColor,
               reflectionFactor);
}
```

Example 7-6. The `C7E6f_dispersion` Fragment Program

TGreen, and the blue component of the texture value sampled at **TBlue**. The program then combines the respective *r*, *g*, and *b* components of **refractedColor**.

Computing the Final Result

Finally, the program blends the reflected and refracted colors according to the fraction given by the reflection factor:

```
color = lerp(refractedColor,
             reflectedColor,
             reflectionFactor);
```

And there you have it: the Fresnel effect with chromatic dispersion.

7.5   Exercises

1. **Answer this:** What are the key assumptions behind environment mapping? For what situations does it break down?

2. **Try this yourself:** How would Figure 7-10 look if the value for the **etaRatio** index of refraction vector in **C7E5v_dispersion** were (1, 1, 1)?

3. **Try this yourself:** Try reimplementing the **C7E1v_reflection** vertex program to perform the reflection vector computation in object space and then transforming the resulting object-space reflection vector into world space.

4. **Answer this:** What is the Fresnel effect?

5. **Try this yourself:** When mipmapping is enabled, both OpenGL and Direct3D support a texture mapping feature known as texture *level-of-detail* (LOD) bias. Texture LOD bias can be useful to avoid unnaturally crisp reflections. Modify one of this chapter's examples to provide a positive bias for the cube map texture used as the environment map. This creates blurry reflections.

6. **Answer this:** Prior to hardware support for cube map textures, a technique known as *sphere mapping* was used to project 3D vectors onto a 2D texture. Research this technique and explain why everyone uses cube map textures now.

7.6   Further Reading

Jim Blinn and Martin Newell introduced environment mapping in a 1976 paper titled "Texture and Reflection in Computer Generated Images," which appeared in the *Communications of the ACM*.

Ned Greene published an important paper titled "Environment Mapping and Other Applications of World Projections," which appeared in a 1986 issue of *IEEE Computer Graphics and Applications*. Greene proposed the idea of storing environment maps as cube maps.

RenderMan uses cube map textures for its environment mapping support. See *The RenderMan Companion: A Programmer's Guide to Realistic Computer Graphics* (Addison-Wesley, 1989), by Steve Upstill, for more details.

Doug Voorhies and Jim Foran published a SIGGRAPH paper titled "Reflection Vector Shading Hardware" (ACM Press) in 1994. The paper proposed a dedicated hardware approach for computing per-fragment reflection vectors that were used to sample an environment map stored in a cube map texture.

OpenGL 1.3 and DirectX 7 introduced hardware support for cube map textures. The OpenGL 1.3 or later specification provides the mathematics for how texture coordinates map to particular cube faces.

Matthias Wloka's 2002 paper "Fresnel Reflection" (available on NVIDIA's Developer Web site, **developer.nvidia.com**) discusses the Fresnel effect in further detail. The paper explains various implementations and trade-offs between them.

Chapter 8

Bump Mapping

This chapter enhances the per-fragment lighting discussion in Chapter 5 with texture-encoded normals to create an effect known as bump mapping. This chapter has the following five sections:

- **"Bump Mapping a Brick Wall"** introduces bump mapping of a single rectangle.

- **"Bump Mapping a Brick Floor"** explains how to make bump mapping consistent for two planes.

- **"Bump Mapping a Torus"** shows how to bump map curved surfaces that have mathematical representations, such as the torus.

- **"Bump Mapping Textured Polygonal Meshes"** shows how to apply bump mapping to textured polygonal models.

- **"Combining Bump Mapping with Other Effects"** combines bump mapping techniques with other textures, such as decals and gloss maps, for more sophisticated shading.

8.1   Bump Mapping a Brick Wall

The earlier presentation of lighting in Chapter 5 discussed per-vertex and per-fragment light computations. This chapter introduces an advanced lighting approach commonly called *bump mapping*. Bump mapping combines per-fragment lighting with surface normal perturbations supplied by a texture, in order to simulate lighting interactions on bumpy surfaces. This effect is achieved without requiring excessive geometric tessellation of the surface.

As an example, you can use bump mapping to make surfaces appear as if they have bricks protruding from them, and mortar between the bricks.

Most real-world surfaces such as brick walls or cobblestones have small-scale bumpy features that are too fine to represent with highly tessellated geometry. There are two reasons to avoid representing this kind of fine detail using geometry. The first is that representing the model with sufficient geometric detail to capture the bumpy nature of the surface would be too large and cumbersome for interactive rendering. The second is that the surface features may well be smaller than the size of a pixel, meaning that the rasterizer could not accurately render the full geometric detail.

With bump mapping, you can capture the detailed surface features that influence an object's lit appearance in a texture instead of actually increasing the object's geometric complexity. Done well, bump mapping convinces viewers that a bump-mapped scene has more geometry and surface richness than is actually present. Bump mapping is most compelling when lights move in relation to a surface, affecting the bump-mapped surface's illuminated appearance.

Benefits of bump mapping include:

- A higher level of visual complexity in a scene, without adding more geometry.
- Simplified content authoring, because you can encode surface detail in textures as opposed to requiring artists to design highly detailed 3D models.
- The ability to apply different bump maps to different instances of the same model to give each instance a distinct surface appearance. For example, a building model could be rendered once with a brick bump map and a second time with a stucco bump map.

8.1.1   The Brick Wall Normal Map

Consider a wall made of bricks of varying texture stacked on top of each other in a regular pattern. Between the bricks is mortar that holds the bricks together. The mortar is set into the wall. Though a brick wall may look flat from a distance, on closer inspection, the brickwork pattern is not flat at all. When the wall is illuminated, the gaps between bricks, cracks, and other features of the brick surface scatter light quite differently than a truly flat surface.

One approach to rendering a brick wall would be to model every brick, mortar gap, and even individual cracks in the wall with polygons, each with varying surface normals used for lighting. During lighting, the surface normals at each vertex would alter the illuminated surface appearance appropriately. However, this approach may require a tremendous number of polygons.

At a sufficiently coarse scale, a brick wall is more or less flat. Aside from all the surface variations that we've mentioned, a wall's geometry is quite simple. A single rectangle can adequately represent a roughly flat rectangular section of brick wall.

8.1.2 Storing Bump Maps As Normal Map Textures

Before you encounter your first Cg program that lights surfaces with bump mapping, you should understand how textures for bump mapping are created and what they represent.

Conventional Color Textures

Conventional textures typically contain RGB or RGBA color values, though other formats are also available. As you know, each texel in an RGB texture consists of three components, one each for red, green, and blue. Each component is typically a single unsigned byte.

Because programmable GPUs allow arbitrary math and other operations to be performed on the results of texture lookups, you can use textures to store other types of data, encoded as colors.

Storing Normals in Conventional Color Textures

Bump maps can take a variety of forms. All the bump mapping examples in this book represent surface variations as surface normals. This type of bump map is commonly called a *normal map,* because normals, rather than colors, are stored in the texture. Each normal is a direction vector that points away from the surface and is usually stored as a three-component vector.

Conventional RGB texture formats are typically used to store normal maps. Unlike colors that are unsigned, direction vectors require signed values. In addition to being unsigned, color values in textures are typically constrained to the [0, 1] range. Because the normals are normalized vectors, each component has a [-1, 1] range.

To allow texture-filtering hardware for unsigned colors to operate correctly, signed texture values in the [-1, 1] range are range-compressed to the unsigned [0, 1] range with a simple scale and bias.

Signed normals are range-compressed this way:

```
colorComponent = 0.5 * normalComponent + 0.5;
```

After conventional unsigned texture filtering, range-compressed normals are expanded back to their signed range this way:

```
normalComponent = 2 * (colorComponent - 0.5);
```

By using the red, green, and blue components of an RGB texture to store the *x*, *y*, and *z* components of a normal, and range-compressing the signed values to the [0, 1] unsigned range, normals may be stored in RGB textures.

Recent GPUs support signed floating-point color formats, but normal maps are still often stored in unsigned color textures because existing image file formats for unsigned colors can store normal maps. Recent GPUs have no performance penalty for expanding range-compressed normals from textures. So whether you store normals in a range-compressed form (using an unsigned texture format) or use a signed texture format is up to you.

Generating Normal Maps from Height Fields

Authoring normal maps raises another issue. Painting direction vectors in a computer paint program is very unintuitive. However, most normal maps are derived from what is known as a *height field*. Rather than encoding vectors, a height field texture encodes the height, or elevation, of each texel. A height field stores a single unsigned component per texel rather than using three components to store a vector. Figure 8-1 shows an example of a brick wall height field. (See Plate 12 in the book's center insert for a color version of the normal map.) Darker regions of the height field are lower; lighter regions are higher. Solid white bricks are smooth. Bricks with uneven coloring are bumpy. The mortar is recessed, so it is the darkest region of the height field.

Converting a height field to a normal map is an automatic process, and it is typically done as a preprocessing step along with range compression. For each texel in the height field, you sample the height at the given texel, as well as the texels immediately above and to the right of the given texel. The normal vector is the normalized version of the cross product of two difference vectors. The first difference vector is $(1, 0, H_a - H_g)$,

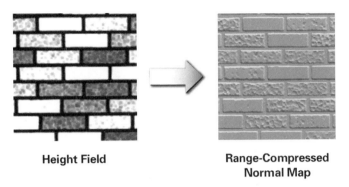

Height Field

**Range-Compressed
Normal Map**

Figure 8-1. A Height Field Image for a Brick Bump Map

where H_g is the height of the given texel and H_a is the height of the texel directly above the given texel. The second difference vector is $(0, 1, H_r - H_g)$, where H_r is the height of the texel directly to the right of the given texel.

The cross product of these two vectors is a third vector pointing away from the height field surface. Normalizing this vector creates a normal suitable for bump mapping. The resulting normal is:

$$normal = \frac{\langle H_g - H_a, H_g - H_r, 1 \rangle}{\sqrt{(H_g - H_a)^2 + (H_g - H_r)^2 + 1}}$$

This normal is signed and must be range-compressed to be stored in an unsigned RGB texture. Other approaches exist for converting height fields to normal maps, but this approach is typically adequate.

The normal $(0, 0, 1)$ is computed in regions of the height field that are flat. Think of the normal as a direction vector pointing up and away from the surface. In bumpy or uneven regions of the height field, an otherwise straight-up normal tilts appropriately.

As we've already mentioned, range-compressed normal maps are commonly stored in an unsigned RGB texture, where red, green, and blue correspond to x, y, and z. Due to the nature of the conversion process from height field to normal map, the z component is always positive and often either 1.0 or nearly 1.0. The z component is stored in the blue component conventionally, and range compression converts positive z values to the $[0.5, 1]$ range. Thus, the predominant color of range-compressed normal maps stored in an RGB texture is blue. Figure 8-1 also shows the brick wall height field converted into a normal map. Because the coloration is important, you should refer to the color version of Figure 8-1 shown in Plate 12.

8.1.3 Simple Bump Mapping for a Brick Wall

Now that you know what a normal map is, you're ready for your first bump mapping example. The example will show how to use the brick wall normal map in Figure 8-1 to render a single bump-mapped rectangle to look like a brick wall. When you interactively move a single light source, you will change the appearance of the wall due to the brick pattern in the normal map, as shown in Figure 8-2. The figure shows the effect of three different light positions. In the left image, the light is at the lower left of the wall. In the center image, the light is directly in front of the wall. And in the right image, the light is at the upper right of the wall.

To keep things simple, this first example is quite constrained. We position the rendered wall rectangle in the *x-y* plane, with *z* equal to 0 everywhere on the wall. Without bump mapping, the surface normal for the wall would be (0, 0, 1) at every point on the wall.

The Vertex Program

The **C8E1v_bumpWall** vertex program in Example 8-1 computes the object-space vector from a vertex to a single light source. The program also transforms the vertex position into clip space using a conventional modelview-projection matrix, and it passes through a 2D texture coordinate set intended to sample the normal map texture.

Figure 8-2. A Bump-Mapped Brick Wall with Different Light Positions

```
void C8E1v_bumpWall(float4 position : POSITION,
                    float2 texCoord : TEXCOORD0,

                out float4 oPosition      : POSITION,
                out float2 oTexCoord      : TEXCOORD0,
                out float3 lightDirection : TEXCOORD1,

            uniform float3   lightPosition,  // Object space
            uniform float4x4 modelViewProj)
{
  oPosition = mul(modelViewProj, position);
  oTexCoord = texCoord;
  // Compute object-space light direction
  lightDirection = lightPosition - position.xyz;
}
```

Example 8-1. The **C8E1v_bumpWall** Vertex Program

The Fragment Program

The dot product of the light vector and the normal vector for diffuse lighting requires a unit-length light vector. Rather than implement the normalization directly with math operations, the **C8E2f_bumpSurf** fragment program in Example 8-2 normalizes the interpolated light direction vector using a *normalization cube map,* which will be explained shortly. For now, think of a normalization cube map as a way to take an unnormalized vector that is interpolated as a texture coordinate set and generate a normalized and range-compressed version of it. Because the program implements normalization with a cube map texture access, this style of per-fragment vector normalization is fast and well suited for the broadest range of GPUs.

In addition to normalizing the interpolated light vector, the **C8E2f_bumpSurf** program samples the normal map with conventional 2D texture coordinates. The result of the normal map access is another range-compressed normal.

Next, the program's helper function, named **expand**, converts both the range-compressed normalized light direction and the range-compressed normal into signed vectors. Then the program computes the final fragment color with a dot product to simulate diffuse lighting.

Example 8-2 illustrates how the appearance of the brick wall changes with different light positions. The wall's surface, rendered with the **C8E1v_bumpWall** and **C8E2f_bumpSurf** programs, really looks like it has the texture of a brick wall.

```
float3 expand(float3 v)
{
  return (v - 0.5) * 2;   // Expand a range-compressed vector
}


void C8E2f_bumpSurf(float2 normalMapTexCoord : TEXCOORD0,
                    float3 lightDir          : TEXCOORD1,

              out float4 color : COLOR,

          uniform sampler2D   normalMap,
          uniform samplerCUBE normalizeCube)
{
  // Normalizes light vector with normalization cube map
  float3 lightTex = texCUBE(normalizeCube, lightDir).xyz;
  float3 light = expand(lightTex);
  // Sample and expand the normal map texture
  float3 normalTex = tex2D(normalMap, normalMapTexCoord).xyz;
  float3 normal = expand(normalTex);
  // Compute diffuse lighting
  color = dot(normal, light);
}
```

Example 8-2. The **C8E2f_bumpSurf** Fragment Program

Constructing a Normalization Cube Map

Chapter 7 explained how you could use cube maps for encoding environment maps as a way to give objects a reflective appearance. To simulate surface reflections, the 3D texture coordinate vector used for accessing the environment cube map represents a reflection vector. But cube map textures can encode other functions of direction vectors as well. Vector normalization is one such function.

The Cg Standard Library includes a routine called **normalize** for normalizing vectors. The routine has several overloaded variants, but the three-component version is most commonly used. The standard implementation of **normalize** is this:

```
float3 normalize(float3 v)
{
  float d = dot(v, v);   // x*x + y*y + z*z
  return d / sqrt(d);
}
```

The problem with this implementation of **normalize** is that basic fragment profiles provided by second-generation and third-generation GPUs cannot directly compile the **normalize** routine that we just presented. This is because these GPUs lack arbitrary floating-point math operations at the fragment level.

The normalization cube map—a fast way to normalize vectors supplied as texture coordinates—works on all GPUs, whether or not they support advanced fragment programmability.

 Even on GPUs supporting advanced fragment profiles, using normalization cube maps is often faster than implementing normalization with math operations, because GPU designers highly optimize texture accesses.

Figure 8-3 shows how a cube map normalizes a vector. The vector (3, 1.5, 0.9) pierces the cube map on the positive *x* face of the cube map, as shown. The faces of the normalization cube map are constructed such that the texel pierced by any given direction vector contains the normalized version of that vector. When signed texture components are unavailable, the normalized version of the vector may be stored range-compressed and then expanded prior to use as a normalized vector. This is what the examples in this chapter assume. So the range-compressed texel pierced by (3, 1.5, 0.9) is approximately (0.93, 0.72, 0.63). When this vector is expanded, it is (0.86, 0.43, 0.26), which is the approximate normalized version of (3, 1.5, 0.9).

A resolution of 32×32 texels is typically sufficient for a normalization cube map face with 8-bit color components. A resolution of 16×16, and even 8×8, can also generate acceptable results.

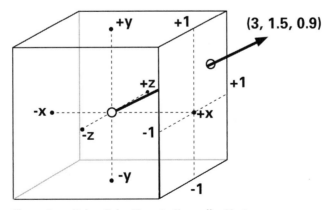

Figure 8-3. Using Cube Maps to Normalize Vectors

8.1 Bump Mapping a Brick Wall

The electronic material accompanying this book includes a normalization cube map, as well as source code for constructing normalization cube maps. All of your Cg programs can share just one normalization cube map.

8.1.4 Specular Bump Mapping

You can further enhance the preceding programs by adding specular and ambient lighting terms and by adding control over the diffuse material, specular material, and light color. The next pair of programs illustrate this.

The Vertex Program

Example 8-3 extends the earlier **C8E1v_bumpWall** example to compute the half-angle vector, which the rasterizer interpolates as an additional texture coordinate set. The **C8E3v_specWall** program computes the half-angle vector by normalizing the sum of the vertex's normalized light and eye vectors.

```
void C8E3v_specWall(float4 position : POSITION,
                    float2 texCoord : TEXCOORD0,

            out float4 oPosition      : POSITION,
            out float2 oTexCoord      : TEXCOORD0,
            out float3 lightDirection : TEXCOORD1,
            out float3 halfAngle      : TEXCOORD2,

          uniform float3   lightPosition,  // Object space
          uniform float3   eyePosition,    // Object space
          uniform float4x4 modelViewProj)
{
  oPosition = mul(modelViewProj, position);
  oTexCoord = texCoord;
  lightDirection = lightPosition - position.xyz;
  // Add the computation of a per-vertex half-angle vector
  float3 eyeDirection = eyePosition - position.xyz;
  halfAngle = normalize(normalize(lightDirection) +
                        normalize(eyeDirection));
}
```

Example 8-3. The **C8E3v_specWall** Vertex Program

The Fragment Program

The corresponding fragment program, shown in Example 8-4, requires more modifications. In addition to normalizing the light vector with a normalization cube map as

```
float3 expand(float3 v) { return (v - 0.5) * 2; }

void C8E4f_specSurf(float2 normalMapTexCoord : TEXCOORD0,
                    float3 lightDirection    : TEXCOORD1,
                    float3 halfAngle         : TEXCOORD2,

            out float4 color : COLOR,

        uniform float  ambient,
        uniform float4 LMd, // Light-material diffuse
        uniform float4 LMs, // Light-material specular
        uniform sampler2D normalMap,
        uniform samplerCUBE normalizeCube,
        uniform samplerCUBE normalizeCube2)
{
  // Fetch and expand range-compressed normal
  float3 normalTex = tex2D(normalMap, normalMapTexCoord).xyz;
  float3 normal = expand(normalTex);
  // Fetch and expand normalized light vector
  float3 normLightDirTex = texCUBE(normalizeCube,
                                  lightDirection).xyz;
  float3 normLightDir = expand(normLightDirTex);
  // Fetch and expand normalized half-angle vector
  float3 normHalfAngleTex = texCUBE(normalizeCube2,
                                  halfAngle).xyz;
  float3 normHalfAngle = expand(normHalfAngleTex);

  // Compute diffuse and specular lighting dot products
  float diffuse = saturate(dot(normal, normLightDir));
  float specular = saturate(dot(normal, normHalfAngle));
  // Successive multiplies to raise specular to 8th power
  float specular2 = specular * specular;
  float specular4 = specular2 * specular2;
  float specular8 = specular4 * specular4;

  color = LMd * (ambient + diffuse) + LMs * specular8;
}
```

Example 8-4. The **C8E4f_specSurf** Fragment Program

before, the updated fragment program also normalizes the half-angle vector with a second normalization cube map. Then, the program computes the dot product of the normalized half-angle vector with the perturbed normal obtained from the normal map.

In the original **C8E2f_bumpSurf** program, the program outputs the diffuse dot product as the final color. The final color's **COLOR** output semantic implicitly clamps any negative dot product results to zero. This clamping is required by the diffuse lighting equation, because negative illumination is physically impossible. The **C8E4f_specSurf** program combines the diffuse and specular dot products, so the program explicitly clamps negative values to zero with the **saturate** Standard Library function:

---

saturate(x)   Clamps a scalar or all the components of a vector to the range [0, 1].

Basic fragment profiles such as **fp20** and **ps_1_3** lack support for true exponentiation. To simulate specular exponentiation and support a broad range of fragment profiles, the program uses three successive multiplications to raise the specular dot product to the eighth power. Advanced profiles could use the **pow** or **lit** Standard Library functions for more generality.

Finally, the output color is computed by modulating the ambient and diffuse terms by a uniform parameter, **LMd**. The application supplies **LMd**, which represents the light color premultiplied by the material's diffuse color. Similarly, the **LMs** uniform parameter modulates the specular illumination and represents the light color premultiplied by the material's specular color.

 ## Further Improvements

The **C8E4f_specSurf** program compiles under basic and advanced fragment profiles. Although this makes the bump mapping effect portable to a wider variety of GPUs, various improvements are possible if you target an advanced fragment profile. Following are a few examples.

C8E4f_specSurf binds the same normalization cube map texture into two texture units. As you saw in Chapter 7, this duplicate binding is required because basic fragment profiles can only sample a given texture unit with that texture unit's corresponding texture coordinate set. Advanced fragment profiles do not have this limitation, so a single **normalizeCube** cube map sampler can normalize both the light vector and half-angle vector.

C8E4f_specSurf also computes the specular exponent by raising the specular dot product to the eighth power using successive multiplies, because basic fragment profiles do not support arbitrary exponentiation. An advanced profile version could use the following code:

```
color = Kd * (ambient + diffuse) +
        Ks * pow(specular, specularExponent);
```

where **specularExponent** is a uniform parameter, or even a value from a texture.

C8E3v_specWall computes a per-vertex half-angle vector. Ideally, you should compute the half-angle vector from the light and view vectors at every fragment. You could modify the vertex program to output the **eyeDirection** value rather than the half-angle vector. Then you could modify **C8E4f_specSurf** to compute the half-angle vector at each fragment, as shown:

```
// Fetch and expand normalized eye vector
float3 normEyeDirTex = texCUBE(normalizeCube,
                                    eyeDirection).xyz;
float3 normEyeDir = expand(normEyeDirTex);
// Sum light and eye vectors and normalize with cube map
float3 normHalfAngle = texCUBE(normalizeCube,
                                    normLightDir + normEyeDir);
normHalfAngle = expand(normHalfAngle);
```

As explained in Chapter 5, computing the half-angle vector at every fragment creates more realistic specular highlights than computing the half-angle vector per-vertex, but it is more expensive.

8.1.5 Bump Mapping Other Geometry

You have learned how to bump map a brick wall, and the results in Figure 8-2 are quite promising. However, bump mapping is not as simple as these first examples might have you believe.

The wall rectangle rendered in Figure 8-2 happens to be flat and has a surface normal that is uniformly (0, 0, 1). Additionally, the texture coordinates assigned to the rectangle are related to the vertex positions by a uniform linear mapping. At every point on the wall rectangle, the *s* texture coordinate is different from the *x* position by only a positive scale factor. The same is true of the *t* texture coordinate and the *y* position.

Under these considerably constrained circumstances, you can directly replace the surface normal with the normal sampled from the normal map. This is exactly what the prior examples do, and the bump mapping looks fine.

However, what happens when you bump map arbitrary geometry with the **C8E1v_bumpWall** and **C8E2f_bumpSurf** programs? What if the surface normal for the geometry is not uniformly (0, 0, 1)? What if the *s* and *t* texture coordinates used to access the normal map are not linearly related to the geometry's *x* and *y* object-space positions?

In these situations, your rendering results may resemble correct bump mapping, but a closer inspection will show that the lighting in the scene is not consistent with the actual light and eye positions. What happens is that the object-space light vector and half-angle vectors used in the per-fragment bump mapping math no longer share a consistent coordinate system with the normals in the normal map. The lighting results are therefore noticeably wrong.

Object-Space Bump Mapping

One solution is to make sure that the normals stored in your normal map are oriented so that they directly replace the object-space surface normals for the geometry rendered. This means that the normal map effectively stores object-space normals, an approach known as *object-space bump mapping*. This approach does work, which is why our earlier bump-mapped wall example (Figure 8-2) is correct, though only for the particular wall rectangle shown.

Unfortunately, object-space bump mapping ties your normal map textures to the specific geometry that you are bump mapping. Creating a normal map requires knowing the exact geometry to which you will apply the normal map. This means that you cannot use a single brick-pattern normal map texture to bump map all the different possible brick walls in a scene. Instead, you end up needing a different normal map for every different brick wall you render. If the object animates its object-space vertex positions, every different pose potentially requires its own object-space normal map. For these reasons, object-space bump mapping is very limiting.

Texture-Space Bump Mapping

Correct bump mapping requires that the light vector and half-angle vector share a consistent coordinate system with the normal vectors in the normal map. It does not matter what coordinate system you choose, as long as you choose it consistently for all vectors in the lighting equations. Object space is one consistent coordinate system, but it is not the only choice.

You do not need to make all the normals in the normal map match up with the object-space coordinate system of the object to be bump mapped. Instead, you can rotate the object-space light vectors and half-angle vectors into the normal map's coordinate system. It is a lot less work to rotate two direction vectors into an alternative coordinate system than to adjust every normal in a normal map. The coordinate system used by the normal map texture is called *texture space*, so this approach is known as *texture-space bump mapping* (sometimes called *tangent-space bump mapping*).

Vertex programs are efficient at transforming vectors from one coordinate system to another. The vector transformations required for texture-space bump mapping are akin to transforming positions from object space to clip space with the modelview-projection matrix.

You can program your GPU to transform each object-space light and half-angle vector into the coordinate system that matches your normal map texture.

However, a modelview-projection matrix is fixed for a given rendered object. In contrast, the transformation required to rotate object-space light and half-angle vectors into the coordinate system that matches your normal map typically varies over the surface you render. Every vertex you render may require a distinct rotation matrix!

Although it may require a distinct rotation matrix for each vertex, texture-space bump mapping has one chief advantage. It allows you to apply a single normal map texture to multiple models—or to a single model being animated—while keeping the per-fragment mathematics required for bump mapping simple and efficient enough for GPUs that support only basic fragment profiles.

8.2   Bump Mapping a Brick Floor

Before we consider bump mapping polygonal meshes, consider an only slightly more complicated case. Instead of rendering a bump-mapped brick wall that has an object-space surface normal (0, 0, 1), consider rendering the same brick-textured rectangle repositioned so it becomes a brick floor rather than a wall. The surface normal for the floor is (0, 1, 0), straight up in the y direction.

In this floor example, apply the same brick normal map to the floor that you applied to the wall in the last example. However, "straight up" in the normal map is the (0, 0, 1) vector, while "straight up" for the floor in object space is (0, 1, 0). These two coordinate systems are not consistent.

What does it take to make these two coordinate systems consistent? The floor has the same normal at every point, so the following rotation matrix transforms the floor's object-space "straight up" vector to the normal map's corresponding "straight up" vector:

$$\begin{bmatrix} 0 & 0 & 1 \end{bmatrix} = \begin{bmatrix} 0 & 1 & 0 \end{bmatrix} \begin{bmatrix} 1 & 0 & 0 \\ 0 & 0 & 1 \\ 0 & -1 & 0 \end{bmatrix}$$

Sections 8.3 and 8.4 will explain the details of how to construct this 3×3 matrix for arbitrary textured rectangles and triangles. For now, the important thing is that such a matrix exists and provides a way to transform vectors from object space to the normal map's texture space.

We can use this matrix to rotate the object-space light and half-angle vectors for the floor rectangle so they match the coordinate system of the normal map. For example, if L is the light vector in object space (written as a row vector), then L' in the normal map coordinate system can be computed as follows:

$$L' = \begin{bmatrix} L_x' & L_y' & L_z' \end{bmatrix} = \begin{bmatrix} L_x & -L_z & L_y \end{bmatrix} = \begin{bmatrix} L_x & L_y & L_z \end{bmatrix} \begin{bmatrix} 1 & 0 & 0 \\ 0 & 0 & 1 \\ 0 & -1 & 0 \end{bmatrix}$$

To perform specular texture-space bump mapping, you must also rotate the half-angle vector in object space into texture space the same way. Although this example's rotation matrix is trivial, the same principle applies to an arbitrary rotation matrix.

About Rotation Matrices

You can always represent a 3D rotation as a 3×3 matrix. Each column and each row of a rotation matrix must be a unit-length vector. Moreover, each column vector is mutually orthogonal to the other two column vectors, and the same applies to the row vectors. The length of a vector transformed by a rotation matrix does not change after transformation. A 3D rotation matrix can act as the bridge between direction vectors in two 3D coordinate systems.

The columns of a rotation matrix used to transform object-space direction vectors into a normal map's texture space are named *tangent* (T), *binormal* (B), and *normal* (N), respectively. So rotation matrix entries can be labeled as in Equation 8-1.

$$\begin{bmatrix} T_x & B_x & N_x \\ T_y & B_y & N_y \\ T_z & B_z & N_z \end{bmatrix}$$

Equation 8-1. A Rotation Matrix Formed by Tangent, Binormal, and Normal Column Vectors

Given two columns (or rows) of a rotation matrix, the third column (or row) is the cross product of the two known columns (or rows). For the columns, this means that the relationship in Equation 8-2 exists.

$$B = N \times T$$
$$N = T \times B$$
$$T = B \times N$$

Equation 8-2. Cross-Product Relationships Between Tangent, Binormal, and Normal Vectors

8.2.1 The Vertex Program for Rendering a Brick Floor

You can enhance the **C8E1v_bumpWall** example so that it can bump map using texture-space bump mapping. To do this, pass the tangent and normal vectors of the rotation matrix needed to transform object-space vectors into texture-space vectors.

Example 8-5's **C8E5v_bumpAny** vertex program, in conjunction with the earlier **C8E2f_bumpSurf** fragment program, can bump map the brick wall and brick floor with the same normal map texture. But to do this, you must supply the proper normal and tangent vectors of the rotation matrix that maps between object space and texture space. You must specify these two vectors for each vertex. The program computes the binormal with a cross product. Rather than requiring the binormal to be passed as yet another per-vertex parameter, the program computes the binormal in order to reduce the amount of dynamic data that the GPU must read for each vertex processed. Computing the binormal also avoids having to precompute and devote memory to storing binormals.

```
void C8E5v_bumpAny(float3 position  : POSITION,
                   float3 normal    : NORMAL,
                   float3 tangent   : TEXCOORD1,
                   float2 texCoord  : TEXCOORD0,

              out float4 oPosition          : POSITION,
              out float2 normalMapCoord      : TEXCOORD0,
              out float3 lightDirection      : TEXCOORD1,

          uniform float3    lightPosition,  // Object space
          uniform float3    eyePosition,    // Object space
          uniform float4x4  modelViewProj)
{
  oPosition = mul(modelViewProj, float4(position, 1));

  // Compute the object-space light vector
  lightDirection = lightPosition - position;

  // Construct object-space-to-texture-space 3x3 matrix
  float3 binormal = cross(tangent, normal);
  float3x3 rotation = float3x3(tangent,
                               binormal,
                               normal);
  // Rotate the light vector using the matrix
  lightDirection = mul(rotation, lightDirection);

  normalMapCoord = texCoord;
}
```

Example 8-5. The **C8E5v_bumpAny** Vertex Program

Texture-space bump mapping is also known as tangent-space bump mapping because
a tangent vector to the surface, in conjunction with the surface normal, establishes the
required rotation matrix.

Figure 8-4 compares two images of a simple scene with the same bump-mapped wall
and floor arrangement, the same normal map texture, the same light position, and the
same **C8E2f_bumpSurf** fragment program. But each image uses a different vertex
program. The lighting in the left image is consistent and correct because it uses the
C8E5v_bumpAny vertex program with the correct object-space-to-texture-space rotation for correct texture-space bump mapping. However, the lighting in the right image
is inconsistent. The lighting on the wall is correct, but the lighting on the floor is

C8E5v_bumpAny &
C8E2f_bumpSurf

Wall and Floor Lit
Consistently and Correctly

C8E1v_bumpWall &
C8E2f_bumpSurf

Wall Lit Correctly
Floor Lit Incorrectly (Too Dark)
and Inconsistently

Figure 8-4. Consistent Texture-Space Bump Mapping vs. Inconsistent Object-Space Bump Mapping

wrong. The inconsistent lighting arises because the image on the right uses the **C8E1v_bumpWall** vertex program for both the wall and the floor.

Conventionally, we write position vectors as column vectors and direction vectors as row vectors. Using Equation 8-2, **C8E5v_bumpAny** computes the binormal as a cross product of the per-vertex tangent and normal vectors:

```
float3 binormal = cross(tangent, normal);
```

The **cross** routine for computing the cross product of two vectors is part of Cg's Standard Library.

The program then constructs a rotation matrix with the **float3x3** matrix constructor:

```
float3x3 rotation = float3x3(tangent,
                             binormal,
                             normal);
```

The rows of the constructed rotation matrix are the tangent, binormal, and normal, so the constructed matrix is the transpose of the matrix shown in Equation 8-1. Multiplying a row vector by a matrix is the same as multiplying the transpose of a matrix by a column vector. The **C8E5v_bumpAny** example's multiply is a matrix-by-vector multiply because the rotation matrix is really the transpose of the intended matrix, as shown:

```
lightDirection = mul(rotation, lightDirection);
```

Enhancing the **C8E3v_specWall** program in the same way requires also rotating the half-angle vector, as shown:

8.2 Bump Mapping a Brick Floor

```
eyeDirection = mul(rotation, eyeDirection);
halfAngle = normalize(normalize(lightDirection) +
                      normalize(eyeDirection));
```

The scene in Figure 8-4 has only flat surfaces. This means that the rotation matrix required for the wall, and the other rotation matrix required for the floor, are uniform across each flat surface. The **C8E5v_bumpAny** program permits distinct tangent and normal vectors for every vertex. A curved surface or a mesh of polygons would require this support for varying the tangent and normal vectors that define the rotation from object space to texture space at every vertex. Figure 8-5 shows how a curved triangular shape requires distinct normal, tangent, and binormal vectors at each vertex. These vectors define distinct rotation matrices at each vertex that rotate the light vector properly into texture space. In the figure, the light vectors are shown in gray.

The next two sections explain how to generalize texture-space bump mapping to support curved surfaces and polygonal meshes.

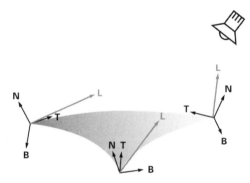

Figure 8-5. Per-Vertex Texture Space Bases

8.3   Bump Mapping a Torus

 This section and the next are for readers who want a more mathematically based understanding of texture space. In particular, these sections explain the mathematics of how to construct the rotation matrices for transforming object-space vectors to and from texture space. These topics are not essential if you are content to rely on 3D authoring tools or other software to generate the rotation matrices for texture-space bump mapping. If you are not interested in this level of detail, you are encouraged to skip ahead to Section 8.5.

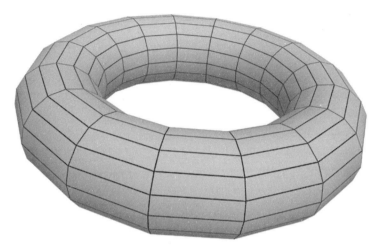

Figure 8-6. A Tessellated Torus

In this section, we describe how to bump map a tessellated torus, as depicted in Figure 8-6. Bump mapping a torus is more involved than bump mapping a brick wall because the surface of a torus curves. That curvature means that there isn't a single, fixed rotation from object space to texture space for the entire torus.

8.3.1 The Mathematics of the Torus

For bump mapping, the torus provides a well-behaved surface with which to develop your mathematical intuition before you apply these ideas to the more general case of an arbitrary polygonal model in Section 8.4.

Bump mapping a torus is more straightforward than bump mapping an arbitrary polygonal model, because a single set of parametric mathematical equations, shown in Equation 8-3, defines the surface of a torus.

$$x = (M + N\cos(2\pi t))\cos(2\pi s)$$
$$y = (M + N\cos(2\pi t))\sin(2\pi s)$$
$$z = N\sin(2\pi t)$$

Equation 8-3. Parametric Equations for a Torus

The parametric variables $(s, t) \in [0, 1]$ map to 3D positions (x, y, z) on the torus, where M is the radius from the center of the hole to the center of the torus tube, and N is the radius of the tube. The torus lies in the $z=0$ plane and is centered at the origin.

By defining the surface of a torus with a set of parametric equations, you can determine the exact curvature of a torus analytically, using partial differential equations.

The analytic definition of the torus in Equation 8-3 lets you determine an oriented surface-local coordinate system, the texture space we seek for bump mapping, in terms of the parametric variables (s, t) used to define the torus. These same parametric variables also serve as texture coordinates to access a normal map texture for bump mapping.

In practical terms, this provides a way to convert an object-space light vector and an object-space view vector into a surface-local coordinate system that is consistently oriented for normals stored in a normal map texture. Once you have a set of normal, light, and view vectors in this consistent coordinate system, the lighting equations explained in Chapter 5 work correctly. As discussed in Section 8.1.5, the trick to bump mapping is finding a consistent coordinate system and properly transforming all vectors required for lighting into that space.

If we assume that a surface is reasonably tessellated, we need to compute only the light and view vectors required for lighting at each vertex, and then interpolate these vectors for computing the lighting equations for every rasterized fragment. This assumption holds well for a uniformly tessellated torus.

As with the flat brick wall, we seek a rotation, in the form of a 3×3 matrix, that we can use to convert object-space vectors to a surface-local coordinate system oriented according to the (s, t) parameterization of the torus. Because of the curvature of the torus, the 3×3 matrix must be different for every vertex of the torus.

Constructing the rotation matrices requires the partial derivatives of the parametric equations that define the torus. These are shown in Equation 8-4.

$$\frac{\partial x}{\partial s} = -2\pi(M + N\cos(2\pi t))\sin(2\pi s) \qquad \frac{\partial x}{\partial t} = -2N\pi\sin(2\pi t)\cos(2\pi s)$$

$$\frac{\partial y}{\partial s} = 2\pi(M + N\cos(2\pi t))\cos(2\pi s) \qquad \frac{\partial y}{\partial t} = -2N\pi\cos(2\pi t)\sin(2\pi s)$$

$$\frac{\partial z}{\partial s} = 0 \qquad \frac{\partial z}{\partial t} = 2N\pi\cos(2\pi t)$$

Equation 8-4. Partial Derivatives of the Parametric Torus

We call the three-component vector formed from the partial derivatives in terms of either *s* or *t* an *inverse gradient* because it resembles the per-component reciprocal of a conventional gradient. An inverse gradient indicates the instantaneous direction and magnitude of change in surface position in terms of a single parametric variable.

You can use these inverse gradients to define a surface-local coordinate system. Forming a 3D coordinate system takes two orthogonal vectors. One vector that is essential for any surface-local coordinate system is the surface normal. By definition, the surface normal points away from the surface. You can construct the surface normal at a point on a surface by computing the cross product of two noncoincident inverse gradients to the surface at that point.

For our torus example, the surface normal *N* is given by Equation 8-5.

$$N = \left\langle \frac{\partial x}{\partial s}, \frac{\partial y}{\partial s}, \frac{\partial z}{\partial s} \right\rangle \times \left\langle \frac{\partial x}{\partial t}, \frac{\partial y}{\partial t}, \frac{\partial z}{\partial t} \right\rangle$$

Equation 8-5. The Normal of a Surface Expressed in Terms of Its Parametric Inverse Gradients

By picking the inverse gradient in terms of *s* as your tangent vector, in conjunction with the surface normal, you fashion a surface-local coordinate system.

The rotation matrix required to transform object-space vectors into the texture-space coordinate system for any particular torus vertex is

$$\begin{bmatrix} \hat{T}_x & \hat{B}_x & \hat{N}_x \\ \hat{T}_y & \hat{B}_y & \hat{N}_y \\ \hat{T}_z & \hat{B}_z & \hat{N}_z \end{bmatrix}$$

where the $\hat{V}$ notation indicates a normalized vector, and given the equations shown in Equation 8-6.

$$T = \left\langle \frac{\partial x}{\partial s}, \frac{\partial y}{\partial s}, \frac{\partial z}{\partial s} \right\rangle$$

$$B = N \times T$$

$$N = \left\langle \frac{\partial x}{\partial s}, \frac{\partial y}{\partial s}, \frac{\partial z}{\partial s} \right\rangle \times \left\langle \frac{\partial x}{\partial t}, \frac{\partial y}{\partial t}, \frac{\partial z}{\partial t} \right\rangle$$

Equation 8-6. The Tangent, Binormal, and Normal on a Surface

You form the rotation matrix entirely of normalized vectors. This means that you can ignore the constant scale factors 2π and $2N\pi$ in Equation 8-4 for the inverse gradients in terms of s and t, respectively.

Furthermore, the normalized surface normal N of the torus based on Equation 8-5 simplifies to

$$N = \langle \cos(s)\cos(t), \sin(s)\cos(t), \sin(t) \rangle$$

8.3.2   The Bump-Mapped Torus Vertex Program

Example 8-6 shows the vertex program **C8E6v_torus** for rendering a bump-mapped torus. This program procedurally generates a torus from a 2D grid specified over (s, t) $\in [0, 1]$, as shown in Figure 8-7. Besides generating the torus, the program constructs the correct per-vertex rotation matrix, as described in Section 8.3.1. The program also rotates the uniform object-space light vector and half-angle vector parameters into texture space for consistent texture-space bump mapping.

Figure 8-8 (on page 224) shows two bump-mapped tori rendered with the **C8E6v_torus** vertex program and the **C8E4f_specSurf** fragment program. The example applies the brick normal map from Figure 8-1. The bricks bump outward consistently, and a specular highlight is visible in each case.

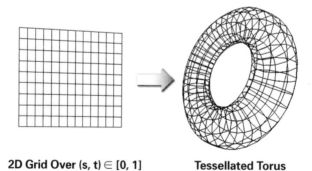

2D Grid Over (s, t) $\in$ [0, 1]   **Tessellated Torus**

Figure 8-7. Procedural Generation of a Torus from a 2D Grid

```
void C8E6v_torus(float2 parametric : POSITION,

            out float4 position      : POSITION,
            out float2 oTexCoord      : TEXCOORD0,
            out float3 lightDirection : TEXCOORD1,
            out float3 halfAngle      : TEXCOORD2,

        uniform float3 lightPosition,  // Object space
        uniform float3 eyePosition,    // Object space
        uniform float4x4 modelViewProj,
        uniform float2 torusInfo)
{
  const float pi2 = 6.28318530;  // 2 times Pi
  // Stretch texture coordinates counterclockwise
  // over torus to repeat normal map in 6 by 2 pattern
  float M = torusInfo[0];
  float N = torusInfo[1];
  oTexCoord = parametric * float2(-6, 2);
  // Compute torus position from its parametric equation
  float cosS, sinS;
  sincos(pi2 * parametric.x, sinS, cosS);
  float cosT, sinT;
  sincos(pi2 * parametric.y, sinT, cosT);
  float3 torusPosition = float3((M + N * cosT) * cosS,
                                (M + N * cosT) * sinS,
                                N * sinT);
  position = mul(modelViewProj, float4(torusPosition, 1));
  // Compute per-vertex rotation matrix
  float3 dPds = float3(-sinS * (M + N * cosT), cosS *
                       (M + N * cosT), 0);
  float3 norm_dPds = normalize(dPds);
  float3 normal = float3(cosS * cosT, sinS * cosT, sinT);
  float3 dPdt = cross(normal, norm_dPds);
  float3x3 rotation = float3x3(norm_dPds,
                               dPdt,
                               normal);
  // Rotate object-space vectors to texture space
  float3 eyeDirection = eyePosition - torusPosition;
  lightDirection = lightPosition - torusPosition;
  lightDirection = mul(rotation, lightDirection);
  eyeDirection = mul(rotation, eyeDirection);
  halfAngle = normalize(normalize(lightDirection) +
                        normalize(eyeDirection));
}
```

Example 8-6. The **C8E6v_torus** Vertex Program

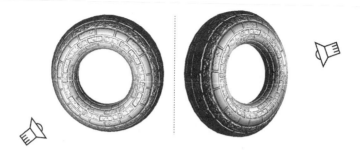

Figure 8-8. Two Bump-Mapped Brick Tori Rendered with `C8E6v_torus` and `C8E4f_specSurf`

8.4 Bump Mapping Textured Polygonal Meshes

Now consider the more general case of a textured polygonal model, such as the kind used for characters and other objects in 3D computer games. In general, objects are not strictly flat like a brick wall, nor easily described with a convenient mathematical expression, like a torus. Instead, an artist models such objects as a mesh of textured triangles.

Our approach is to explain how to bump map a single triangle from a textured polygonal mesh and then generalize this method to the entire mesh.

8.4.1 Examining a Single Triangle

Figure 8-9 shows a wireframe model of an alien head, along with a height-field texture for constructing the head's normal map. The figure shows the same triangle three times. The version of the triangle on the left lies in 2D on the height-field texture. The version of the triangle on the right is shown in 3D object space in relation to other triangles forming the head. The middle version of the triangle appears on the head as rendered with bump mapping.

Each vertex of this textured triangle has a 3D object-space position and a 2D texture coordinate set. Think of the combination of these five coordinates as a 5D vertex. You can then describe the triangle's vertices v_0, v_1, and v_2 this way:

$$v_0 = \langle x_0, y_0, z_0, s_0, t_0 \rangle$$
$$v_1 = \langle x_1, y_1, z_1, s_1, t_1 \rangle$$
$$v_2 = \langle x_2, y_2, z_2, s_2, t_2 \rangle$$

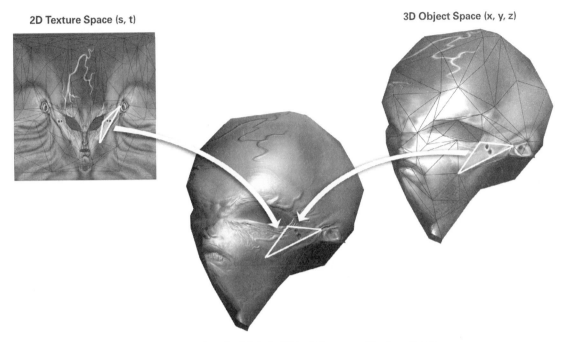

Figure 8-9. The Same Triangle Exists in Object Space and Texture Space

Because all these coordinates lie in the plane of the same triangle, it is possible to derive plane equations for x, y, and z in terms of s and t:

$$A_0 x + B_0 s + C_0 t + D_0 = 0$$
$$A_1 y + B_1 s + C_1 t + D_1 = 0$$
$$A_2 z + B_2 s + C_2 t + D_2 = 0$$

For each of these three equations, you can compute the values of the coefficients A, B, C, and D using the triangle's vertex coordinates. For example, A_0, B_0, C_0, and D_0 would be computed as shown in Equation 8-7.

$$\langle A_0, B_0, C_0 \rangle = \langle\langle x_0, s_0, t_0 \rangle - \langle x_1, s_1, t_1 \rangle\rangle \times \langle\langle x_0, s_0, t_0 \rangle - \langle x_2, s_2, t_2 \rangle\rangle$$
$$D_0 = -\langle A_0, B_0, C_0 \rangle \cdot \langle x_0, s_0, t_0 \rangle$$

Equation 8-7. Plane Equation Coefficients for (x, s, t) Plane for a Single-Textured Triangle

Rewriting the plane equations allows you to express x, y, and z in terms of s and t:

8.4 Bump Mapping Textured Polygonal Meshes

$$x = \frac{-B_0 s - C_0 t - D_0}{A_0}$$

$$y = \frac{-B_1 s - C_1 t - D_1}{A_1}$$

$$z = \frac{-B_2 s - C_2 t - D_2}{A_2}$$

These three equations provide a means to translate texture-space 2D positions on the triangle to their corresponding 3D positions in object space. These are simple linear functions of s and t that provide x, y, and z. The equations are similar to Equation 8-3 for the torus. As in the case of the torus, we are interested in the partial derivatives of the vector $\langle x, y, z \rangle$ in terms of s and t:

$$\left\langle \frac{\partial x}{\partial s}, \frac{\partial y}{\partial s}, \frac{\partial z}{\partial s} \right\rangle = \left\langle -\frac{B_0}{A_0}, -\frac{B_1}{A_1}, -\frac{B_2}{A_2} \right\rangle$$

$$\left\langle \frac{\partial x}{\partial t}, \frac{\partial y}{\partial t}, \frac{\partial z}{\partial t} \right\rangle = \left\langle -\frac{C_0}{A_0}, -\frac{C_1}{A_1}, -\frac{C_2}{A_2} \right\rangle$$

Equation 8-8. Object-Space Partial Derivatives for a Texture-Space Triangle in Terms of the Texture Coordinates

This equation provides inverse gradients analogous to those in Equation 8-4, but these inverse gradients are much simpler. Indeed, every term is a constant. That makes sense because a single triangle is uniformly flat, having none of the curvature of a torus.

Normalized versions of these inverse gradients form a rotation matrix in the same manner as the torus. Use the normalized inverse gradient in terms of s as the tangent vector, and use the normalized inverse gradient in terms of t as the binormal vector. You can use the cross product of these two inverse gradients as the normal vector, but if the model supplies a per-vertex normal for the vertices of the triangle, it is best to use the model's per-vertex normals instead. That's because the per-vertex normals ensure that your bump map lighting of the model is consistent with non-bump-mapped per-vertex lighting.

Normalizing the cross product of the two inverse gradients would give each triangle a uniform normal. This would create a faceted appearance.

8.4.2 Caveats

The Orthogonality of Texture Space with Object Space

There is no guarantee that the inverse gradient in terms of s will be orthogonal to the inverse gradient in terms of t. This happened to be true for every point on the torus (another reason the torus was used in Section 8.3), but it is not generally true. In practice, the two inverse gradients tend to be nearly orthogonal, because otherwise the artist who designed the model would have had to paint the associated texture accounting for a skew. Artists naturally choose to apply textures to models by using nearly orthogonal inverse gradients.

Beware of Zero-Area Triangles in Texture Space

It is possible that two vertices of the triangle will share the same (s, t) position in texture space (or very nearly the same position), or the three texture-space positions may all be collinear. This creates a degenerate triangle with zero area in texture space (or nearly zero area). This triangle may still have area in object space; it may only be degenerate in texture space. Artists should avoid authoring such triangles if the texture coordinates are intended for bump mapping.

If zero-area triangles in texture space are present on a bump-mapped model, they have a single perturbed normal for the entire triangle, leading to inappropriate lighting.

Negative-Area Triangles in Texture Space

Artists often mirror regions of a texture when applying texture coordinates to a polygonal model. For example, a texture may contain just the right half of a face. The artist can then apply the face's texture region to both the right *and* the left half of the face. The same half-face image applies to both sides of the face because faces are typically symmetric. This optimization more efficiently uses the available texture resolution.

Because decals have no sense of what direction they face, this technique works fine when applying a decal texture. However, normal maps encode direction vectors that flip when polygons mirror regions of the normal map in this manner.

This issue can be avoided either by requiring artists to forgo mirroring while applying texture coordinates to models, or by automatically identifying when a triangle is mirrored in texture space and appropriately flipping the per-vertex normal direction. The latter approach is preferable, because you can use software tools to flip (negate) the normal whenever a triangle has a negative area in texture space, and adjust the mesh appropriately (for example, using NVIDIA's NVMeshMender software, which is freely available from NVIDIA's Developer Web site, **developer.nvidia.com**).

Nonuniform Stretching of Bump Map Texture Coordinates

Artists can sometimes stretch a texture when assigning the texture coordinates for a model in a nonuniform manner. Again, this is usually fine for decals, but stretching creates issues for bump mapping. Nonuniform scaling of textures means that the inverse gradient in terms of s may have a much larger magnitude than the inverse gradient in terms of t. Typically, you automatically generate normal maps from height fields without reference to a particular model. Implicitly, you are assuming that any stretching of the normal map, when it applies to the model, is uniform.

You can avoid this issue either by requiring artists to avoid nonuniform stretching, or by accounting for the stretching when converting the height-field texture to a normal map.

8.4.3   Generalizing to a Polygonal Mesh

You can apply the approach described in the previous section on a polygon-by-polygon basis to every polygon in your polygonal mesh. You compute the tangent, binormal, and normal for every triangle in the mesh.

Blending Bases at Shared Vertices

However, in a mesh, more than one triangle may share a given vertex in the mesh. Typically, each triangle that shares a particular vertex will have its own distinct tangent, binormal, and normal vectors. Consequently, the basis—formed by the tangent, binormal, and normal vectors—for each triangle sharing the particular vertex is likewise distinct.

However, if the tangents, binormals, and normals for different triangles at a shared vertex are similar enough (and they often are), you can blend these vectors together without creating noticeable artifacts. The alternative is to create a copy of each vertex for each triangle shared by the original vertex. Generally, blending the bases at such vertices is the best approach if the vectors are not too divergent. This approach also helps to avoid a faceted appearance when a model is not optimally tessellated.

Mirroring, as discussed previously, is a situation in which the vectors are necessarily divergent. If mirroring occurs, you need to assign each triangle a distinct vertex with the appropriate tangent, binormal, and normal for each differently mirrored triangle.

8.5 Combining Bump Mapping with Other Effects

8.5.1 Decal Maps

The same texture coordinates used for your bump map are typically shared with decal map textures. Indeed, the discussion in Section 8.4 presumes that the texture coordinates assigned for applying a decal texture are used to derive the tangent and binormal vectors for bump mapping.

Often, when a game engine doesn't support bump mapping, artists are forced to enhance decal textures by painting lighting variations into the textures. When you bump map a surface, the bump mapping should supply these lighting variations. Artists constructing bump maps and decals must be careful to encode diffuse material variations alone, without lighting variations, in the decal map. Artists should encode geometrical surface variations in the height field from which the normal map is generated.

For example, an artist should paint a green solid shirt as solid green in the decal map. In contrast, the artist should paint the folds in the fabric of the shirt that account for the lighting variations in the height field, rather than in the decal. If artists are not careful about this, they can inadvertently create double lighting effects that make bump-mapped surfaces too dark.

8.5.2 Gloss Maps

It's common for some regions of an object to be shiny (such as belt buckles and armor) and other regions to be duller (such as fabric and flesh). A *gloss map* texture is a type of control map that encodes how specularity varies over a model. As with the decal map and normal map, the gloss map can share the same texture coordinate parameterization with these other texture maps. The gloss map can often be stored in the alpha component of the decal map (or even the bump map), because RGBA textures are often nearly as efficient as RGB textures.

This fragment of Cg code shows how a decal texture can provide both the decal material and a gloss map:

```
float4 decalTexture = tex2D(decal, texCoord);
color = lightColor * (decal.rgb * (ambient + diffuse) +
                      decal.a  * specular);
```

8.5.3 Geometric Self-Shadowing

Geometric self-shadowing accounts for the fact that a surface should not reflect a light if the light source is below the plane of the surface. For diffuse illumination, this occurs when the dot product of the light vector and the normal vector is negative. In this case, the dot product's result is clamped to zero. You can implement this in Cg as follows:

```
diffuse = max(dot(normal, light), 0);
```

Chapter 5 explained how the specular term should also account for geometric self-shadowing by clamping the specular term to zero *either* when the dot product of the half-angle vector and the normal vector is negative *or* when the diffuse contribution is clamped to zero. You can implement this in Cg as follows:

```
specular = dot(normal, light) > 0 ?
           max(dot(normal, halfAngle), 0) : 0;
```

When you bump map, there are actually two surface normals: the conventional interpolated normal *and* the perturbed surface normal supplied by the normal map. One way to think about these two normals is that the interpolated normal is a large-scale approximation of the surface orientation, and the perturbed normal is a small-scale approximation of the surface orientation.

If *either* normal faces away from the incoming light direction, then there should be no illumination from the light. When you're lighting in texture space for bump mapping, the light vector's z component indicates whether the light is above or below the horizon of the geometric (or large-scale) normal. If the z component is negative, the geometric orientation of the surface faces away from the light and there should be no illumination from the light on the surface. You can implement this in Cg as follows:

```
diffuse = light.z > 0 ? max(dot(normal, light), 0) : 0;
```

The **?:** test enforces geometric self-shadowing for the large-scale surface orientation; the **max** function enforces geometric self-shadowing for the small-scale surface orientation. You can implement the geometric self-shadowing for specular bump mapping in Cg this way:

```
specular = dot(normal, light) > 0 && light.z > 0 ?
           max(dot(normal, halfAngle), 0) : 0;
```

Whether or not you account for geometric self-shadowing in your bump mapping is a matter of personal preference and a performance trade-off. Accounting for geometric self-shadowing caused by the large-scale surface orientation means that a light source will not illuminate some fragments that might otherwise be illuminated. However, if you do not account for geometric self-shadowing caused by the large-scale surface orientation, then lights on bump-mapped surfaces (particularly surfaces with considerable variation of surface normals) do not provide a clear cue for the direction of the incoming light.

An abrupt cut-off might cause illumination on a bump-mapped surface to flicker unnaturally because of large-scale geometric self-shadowing when the scene is animating. To avoid this problem, use a function such as **lerp** or **smoothstep** to provide a more gradual transition.

8.6   Exercises

1. **Try this yourself:** Use an image-editing program to replace the normal map used in Example 8-6 with a cobblestone pattern. *Hint:* You can edit the file that contains the normal map. You should not need to modify any code.

2. **Try this yourself:** When generating a normal map from a height field, you can scale the difference vectors by some scalar factor s as shown:

$$normal = \frac{\left\langle s(H_g - H_a), s(H_g - H_r), 1 \right\rangle}{\sqrt{(s(H_g - H_a))^2 + (s(H_g - H_r))^2 + 1}}$$

What happens visually when you regenerate a normal map from its height field with an increased value for the s scale factor? What happens when you decrease the scale factor? What happens if you use one scale factor to scale $H_g - H_a$ and another scale factor to scale $H_g - H_r$?

3. **Try this yourself:** Implement bump mapping for multiple light sources by using a rendering pass per light contribution. Use "depth equal" depth testing and additive blending to combine contributions from multiple lights for a bump-mapped surface.

8.7   Further Reading

Jim Blinn invented bump mapping in 1978. Blinn's "Simulation of Wrinkled Surfaces" (ACM Press) is a seminal SIGGRAPH computer graphics paper.

Mark Peercy, John Airey, and Brian Cabral published a SIGGRAPH paper in 1997 titled "Efficient Bump Mapping Hardware" (ACM Press), which explains tangent space and its application to hardware bump mapping.

In 2000, Mark Kilgard published "A Practical and Robust Bump-Mapping Technique for Today's GPUs." The white paper explains the mathematics of bump mapping and presents a technique appropriate for third-generation GPUs. You can find this white paper on NVIDIA's Developer Web site (**developer.nvidia.com**).

Sim Dietrich published an article titled "Hardware Bump Mapping," in *Game Programming Gems* (Charles River Media, 2000), that introduced the idea of using the texture coordinates of polygonal models for texture-space bump mapping.

Chapter 9

Advanced Topics

This chapter covers advanced Cg usage and has the following five sections:

- **"Fog"** describes how to simulate a common atmospheric effect that looks like fog.
- **"Nonphotorealistic Rendering"** describes a field of rendering that focuses on stylized images, and it gives an example in the form of cartoon shading.
- **"Projective Texturing"** explains the theory and practice of projecting textures onto geometry.
- **"Shadow Mapping"** shows a common way to add shadows to your scenes, based on projective texturing.
- **"Compositing"** describes how to leverage the GPU's powerful texture mapping capabilities to combine images.

9.1 Fog

Fog, an atmospheric effect created by condensed water vapor, obscures visibility. Haze, mist, and smoke are similar phenomena created by particles suspended in the air. Our treatment of these effects is similar, so we will use the blanket term *fog* to refer to this broad range of atmospheric effects.

Computer graphics scenes, particularly outdoor environments, look abnormally sharp and clear without fog. Fog adds realism and character to renderings. Plus, it improves performance when it's combined with application-driven culling of fully fogged distant

Figure 9-1. Adding Uniform Fog to a Scene

features, such as mountains. If an object is sufficiently distant, it is totally obscured by the fog and does not need to be rendered.

In this section, you will learn how to implement one version of fog called *uniform fog*, which is illustrated in Figure 9-1. The left panel of the figure shows a basic city model without fog. In the right panel, uniform fog has been added to the scene, making the distant buildings look faded. In fact, one building is far enough away that the fog completely hides it. In such a situation, you could improve performance by using a lower level of detail for the distant buildings and leaving out the totally obscured building.

9.1.1   Uniform Fog

Along a particular ray from some object to your eye, fog particles suspended in the air "scatter" some of the light that would otherwise reach your eye. Pollutants, smoke, and other airborne particles can also absorb light, rather than scattering the light, thereby reducing the intensity of the light that reaches your eye.

Whereas some light that travels along the ray is absorbed or scattered away, fog particles can redirect other scattered light, so that *extra* light reaches your eye along the same ray. This redirected light comes from the aggregate scattering of light by the fog particles. Figure 9-2 shows the different ways that light travels from one point to another, depending on the presence of fog. If no fog particles intervene, the light rays go directly from point A to point B. If, however, there are fog particles in the air, then

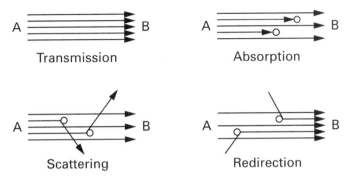

Figure 9-2. Fog Particles May Affect Light Traveling from Point A to Point B

they may absorb or scatter some of the light, and additionally redirect random light rays from aggregate scattering toward point B.

When the light is scattered by water vapor, the color of this aggregate scattered and redirected light tends to be dull white. When the scattering is due to pollution or smoke suspended in the air, the color can vary from gray for haze to black for thick smoke.

The farther the light travels along the ray from the viewed object to your eye, the greater the possibility that fog particles will scatter or extinguish light. At the same time, there is a greater opportunity to redirect extra light along the ray toward the eye. This is why fog is more apparent in the distance.

9.1.2 The Attributes of Fog

- The aggregate color of the scattered light that reaches your eye is the *fog color*.
- The measure of how much light is scattered or extinguished by fog over a given unit of distance on a view ray is the *fog density*. The greater the fog density, the thicker the fog appears.
- The distance along the view ray from an object to the eye is the *fog distance*. The larger the fog distance, the foggier an object appears.

For now, assume that the fog density and fog color are uniform and constant, but let the fog distance from the eye to a visible object vary. What we want to know, and what we want to compute with Cg, is how fog affects the apparent color of distant objects under these foggy conditions.

9.1.3　The Mathematics of Fog

Absorption, Scattering, and Redirection over a Unit Distance

If light travels a unit of distance along some ray through a uniformly foggy atmosphere, you can reason mathematically that the fog reduces the intensity of the light by some constant percentage because of absorption and scattering. At the same time, light redirected in the direction of the ray increases the intensity of the light. The following equation expresses this:

$$C_{leave} = C_{enter} - C_{reduction} + C_{increase}$$

where:

- C_{leave} is the color intensity of the light leaving a unit segment along a ray,
- C_{enter} is the color intensity of the light entering a unit segment along a ray,
- $C_{reduction}$ is the color intensity of all the light absorbed or scattered away along the unit segment, and
- $C_{increase}$ is the color intensity of additional light redirected by the fog in the direction of the ray along the unit segment.

The intensity of light absorbed or scattered away cannot be greater than the intensity of incoming light. Assuming a uniform fog density, there must be a fixed ratio between the color of incoming light and the color of light scattered away. So we have:

$$0 \leq C_{reduction} \leq C_{enter}$$
$$C_{reduction} = h \times C_{enter}$$
$$0 \leq h \leq 1$$

where:

- h is a constant scale factor dependent on the fog density.

Assuming a uniform fog color, the color of additional light scattered by the fog in the direction of the ray is:

$$C_{increase} = h \times C_{fog}$$

where:

- C_{fog} is the constant fog color.

Now you can express the color of the light leaving the fogged unit distance in terms of the color of the entering light, a constant percentage of light scattering and extinction, and a constant fog color. This relationship is:

$$C_{leave} = (1-h) \times C_{enter} + h \times C_{fog}$$

Expressing Fog As a Linear Blend

You can rearrange this equation as a linear blend, where $g = 1 - h$, so it then reads:

$$C_{leave} = g \times C_{enter} + (1-g) \times C_{fog}$$

This means that the intensity of the light at the end of the unit distance "fogged ray segment" is equal to the initial intensity of the light at the beginning of the segment, reduced by some fraction g of the initial light intensity, but increased by the fraction $(1 - g)$ of the fog color.

Applying Fog over Multiple Units of Distance

We can apply the formula recursively if the fog travels multiple units of distance, assuming that the fog density and color are uniform over all those units of distance. When the light travels three unit distances, the intensity of the light at the end of the three-unit ray is:

$$C_{leave} = g \times (g \times (g \times C_{enter} + (1-g) \times C_{fog}) + (1-g) \times C_{fog}) + (1-g) \times C_{fog}$$

This simplifies to the following:

$$C_{leave} = g^3 \times C_{enter} + (1-g^3) \times C_{fog}$$

Notice how we raise g to the third power in the course of applying fog over three units of distance. We generalize this function for an arbitrary fog distance z as:

$$C_{eye} = g^z \times C_{object} + (1-g^z) \times C_{fog}$$

Our true interest is the color of an object as seen by the eye looking through the fog, rather than merely two points at the beginning and end of an arbitrary ray, so we have relabeled C_{leave} as C_{eye} and C_{enter} as C_{object}.

Recall that you can rewrite an exponential such as g^z in terms of exponential and logarithmic functions, so:

$$g^z = \exp_2(\log_2(g) \times z)$$

Expressing C_{eye} in terms of exponential and logarithmic functions results in Equation 9-1.

$$C_{eye} = f \times C_{object} + (1-f) \times C_{fog}$$
$$f = \exp_2(-d \times z)$$
$$d = -\log_2(g)$$

Equation 9-1. Uniform Fog

We call z the fog distance, d the fog density, and f the fog factor. What base you choose for the exponential and logarithmic functions does not matter as long as the base is the same for both.

CineFX GPUs efficiently compute the base 2 exponential and logarithmic functions ($\exp_2$ and $\log_2$). For optimal performance, use the **exp2** and **log2** Cg Standard Library routines to compute these functions.

The exponential nature of the equation for computing the fog factor makes sense when you consider that for every unit of distance that light travels through fog, a certain percentage of the incoming intensity is scattered. This is similar to the process of radioactive decay of an isotope that is modeled by an exponential decay function.

We assume that the fog density d and fog distance z (an absolute distance) are non-negative. The negation of d in the computation of the fog factor ensures exponential decay, rather than growth.

9.1.4   Intuiting the Equations

To make sure that the previous equations match our intuition about how fog works, consider what happens when the fog distance z is 0, or very close to 0. In this case, the object is very close to the eye and we expect zero, or very little, fog. If $z = 0$, then:

$$f = \exp_2(-d \times 0) = 1$$

Chapter 9: Advanced Topics

and therefore the eye sees all (100 percent) of the object color and none (0 percent) of the fog color, as expected.

If the fog distance z is very large, then:

$$f = \exp_2(-d \times \infty) \approx \exp(-\infty) = 0$$

so the eye sees none of the object color and all of the fog color. This makes sense because fog obscures distant objects.

The larger the magnitude of the fog density d, the thicker the fog becomes. Likewise, small values of d reduce the fog. If d is 0, then:

$$f = \exp_2(-0 \times z) = 1$$

which means that the color of the object is 100 percent of the object color and 0 percent of the fog color.

9.1.5 Creating Uniform Fog with Cg

The Cg programs that follow implement the theory of fog as we've explained it in the preceding discussion.

Example 9-1's **C9E1f_fog** fragment program implements the fog equation presented in Section 9.1.3, specifically. The program samples a decal texture; modulates the decal color with the interpolated color; and fogs the textured fragment color, assuming an interpolated fog exponent and a uniform fog color.

The **C9E1f_fog** program is a good example of a situation in which the **fixed** data type improves performance on CineFX GPUs. Math operations such as three-component and four-component multiplies and **lerp** functions are more efficient when performed on **fixed** quantities on CineFX GPUs. Also, the **C9E1f_fog** fragment program relies on the **exp2** Standard Library routine, supported only by advanced fragment profiles.

The **C9E1f_fog** fragment program is meant to be combined with the vertex program shown in Example 9-2. The **C9E2v_fog** program computes a fog exponent from the shortest distance to the eye (computed with the **length** Standard Library function) and the uniform **fogDensity** parameter.

Other quality improvements and performance optimizations are possible.

```
void C9E1f_fog(float2 texCoord      : TEXCOORD0,
               float   fogExponent : TEXCOORD1,
               float4 color         : COLOR,

           out float4 oColor : COLOR,

       uniform sampler2D decal,
       uniform float3 fogColor)
{
  float fogFactor   = exp2(-abs(fogExponent));
  float4 decalColor = tex2D(decal, texCoord);
  float4 texColor   = color * decalColor;

  oColor.xyz = lerp(fogColor, texColor.xyz,
                    fogFactor);
  oColor.w   = color.w;
}
```

Example 9-1. The **C9E1f_fog** Fragment Program

```
void C9E2v_fog(float4 position     : POSITION,
               float4 color         : COLOR,
               float2 decalCoords : TEXCOORD0,

           out float4 oPosition      : POSITION,
           out float4 oColor         : COLOR,
           out float2 oDecalCoords : TEXCOORD0,
           out float  fogExponent  : TEXCOORD1,

       uniform float    fogDensity,  // Based on log2
       uniform float4x4 modelViewProj,
       uniform float4x4 modelView)
{
  // Assume nonprojective modelview matrix
  float3 eyePosition = mul(modelView, position).xyz;
  float fogDistance  = length(eyePosition);
  fogExponent = fogDistance * fogDensity;
  oPosition     = mul(modelViewProj, position);
  oDecalCoords = decalCoords;
  oColor        = color;
}
```

Example 9-2. The **C9E2v_fog** Vertex Program

Planar Fog Distance

Computing the planar eye distance, rather than the Euclidean eye distance, requires fewer vertex program operations. Instead of using the **length** routine to compute the **fogDistance**, use the following planar fog distance alternative, which is often acceptable:

```
float fogDistance = eyePosition.z;
```

For very wide angles of view, this approximation can lead to an inadequate amount of fog in the far edges of the field of view, but it usually works quite well.

Per-Fragment Euclidean Fog Distance

Instead of interpolating a Euclidean distance, uniform fog is more accurate if the vertex program outputs 3D eye-space coordinates that the rasterizer interpolates linearly. The fragment program then computes the true Euclidean distance at every fragment prior to computing the fog exponent and the rest of the fog computation. Although this approach is more accurate, the expense of this technique usually outweighs the quality benefit for reasonably well tessellated scenes.

Encoding the Fog Factor Conversion Function in a Texture

Rather than using the Cg Standard Library's **exp2** (or similar) exponential function, your custom fog implementation can encode the function that converts the fog exponent, or distance, to a fog factor as a 1D, 2D, or 3D texture. Texture accesses are often efficient and give you more control of the fog fall-off. Keep in mind that you will need to scale the fog distance to match the [0, 1] range of the texture image.

9.2 Nonphotorealistic Rendering

Most shader authors try to create continually improving representations of reality with their computer-generated images. In fact, the majority of this book has focused on this objective. We started with simple concepts and gradually added more and more complicated effects—all with the goal of teaching you how to produce more realistic shaders.

Sometimes, however, you want to produce images that *don't* look real. In a computer-aided design (CAD) program, you might want to represent objects in wireframe, or with flat shading, so that their shape is easily discernible. In a physically based rocket simulation, you might color an area of the rocket to represent its temperature instead of its physical appearance. Or perhaps you want to create cartoons.

All these examples fall under an area called *nonphotorealistic rendering*, or NPR. In NPR, the idea is to stylize renderings in a specific way, so that their value comes from something other than representing them as they would look in the "real world."

9.2.1 Toon Shading

A complete survey of the NPR world is beyond the scope of this book, but we will look at a common and useful NPR technique called *toon shading*. Toon shading is a rendering technique that shades objects with constant, sharply delineated colors—as if they were cartoons instead of real-world objects.

Figure 9-3 gives you an idea of the results you can achieve with toon shading. The left side of the figure shows a ray gun with ordinary diffuse and specular lighting; the right side shows an equivalent toon-shaded version. The surfaces on the toon-shaded ray gun are shaded with just three tones: one for bright diffuse regions, another for dark diffuse regions, and a third for specular highlights. Also, note that the toon-shaded ray gun is outlined in black.

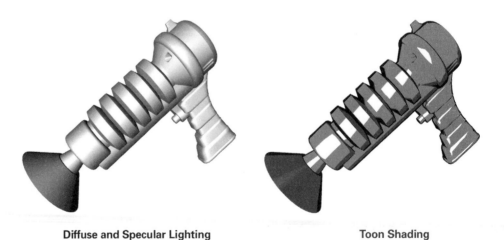

Diffuse and Specular Lighting   **Toon Shading**

Figure 9-3. Toon Shading

A very useful aspect of toon shading is that you don't have to change how you represent your characters and objects. Instead of drawing everything as two-dimensional images (or *sprites*), you continue to draw them as three-dimensional meshes. The trick is in shading them. By replacing a conventional lighting shader with a new kind of shader, you can make these renderings look like cartoons.

9.2.2   Implementing Toon Shading

Most of the time, lighting is used to give an object a realistic, shaded appearance. For toon shading, however, the goal is to reduce the variation in shading.

Your toon shader has three main components:

1. The diffuse shading needs to be represented by just two values: one for bright regions, and another for dark regions.

2. Specular highlights need to be identified and represented as a single color where their intensity is sufficiently high.

3. Objects need to be outlined to complete the cartoon look.

Diffuse Shading

A toon shader needs to convert diffuse lighting from many shades of color into just a few. Think of a monochromatic example with diffuse lighting, where every pixel has a color that ranges from 0.0 to 1.0. Because of the diffuse lighting, the values in the pixels usually vary gradually from 0.0 (in unlit regions) to 1.0 (in fully lit regions).

One way to create a toon shader would be to divide this continuous range into two distinct ranges. For example, you could take pixels with values from 0.0 to 0.5 and represent those with 0.2, and take pixels with values from 0.5 to 1.0 and represent those with 1.0. The result would be a two-toned image with a more cartoon-like appearance.

Mathematically speaking, the conversion rule we just discussed is called a *step function*. Unlike most functions, which have a continuous range of values, step functions have just two distinct values. Figure 9-4 illustrates an ordinary function and a two-valued step function. Step functions are useful for toon shading because they tell you how to map a large range of colors to just two. You can also use functions with more steps, if you prefer.

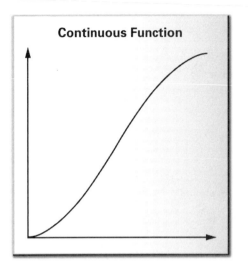 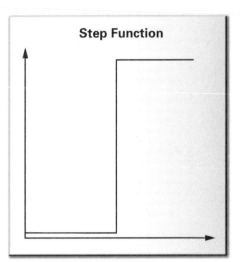

Figure 9-4. A Continuous Function vs. a Step Function

Based on this principle, the diffuse part of a toon shader takes the N dot L part of the diffuse lighting calculation and classifies it as "bright" or "dark." You can choose the thresholds that you prefer, to get a "look" that you like.

To map N dot L values from a continuous range to a step function, use a texture lookup. Similar to the way you used a normalization cube map to encode a "normalize" function in Chapter 8, you can use a 1D texture to apply a step function. In this case, a 1D texture suffices because N dot L is a scalar. Figure 9-5 shows an example of a 1D texture that is two texels wide, along with the step function that it represents.

Assuming that the application passes a texture called **diffuseRamp** to your toon shader, it's easy to apply a step function to the diffuse lighting:

```
diffuseLighting = tex1D(diffuseRamp, diffuseLighting);
```

The old diffuse lighting value is replaced with the corresponding value from the step function. (Assume for now that no filtering is performed on the 1D texture. This ensures that the queried texture has only two distinct values, producing the sharp step function.)

Chapter 9: Advanced Topics

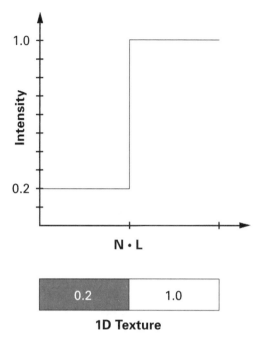

Figure 9-5. Encoding a Step Function in a 1D Texture

Specular Highlights

Handling the specular component is similar to handling the diffuse component. The idea is to apply a step function to the specular highlights, so that instead of having a gradual variation in strength, each highlight either exists or does not. This time, an application-specified texture called **specularRamp** provides the step function:

```
specularLighting = tex1D(specularRamp,
                         specularLighting);
```

Silhouette Outlining

Finally, you need to outline the objects. To do this, you need to find pixels that lie on the objects' silhouettes and color them with the outline color (normally black).

An easy way to find the silhouettes of objects is to use N dot V as a measuring stick. Just as N dot L measures how much light a surface receives, N dot V measures how much surface is visible from the current viewpoint. Recall that when you were calculating lighting for a point, the point was lit when N dot L was positive, and it was shadowed when N dot L was negative.

Similarly, a point is visible when N dot V is positive, and hidden when N dot V is negative. Points at which N dot V is close to zero represent transitions from visible to hidden—these are the points on or close to an object's silhouette. Once again, a 1D texture applies the step function:

```
// Calculate edge color
float edge = max(dot(N, V), 0);
edge = tex1D(edgeRamp, edge);
```

Addressing Aliasing

The approach that we just described does create a toon-shaded effect, but it is prone to flickering artifacts (caused by aliasing) during animation. Why? Because the diffuse, specular, and edge tests are too strict: their results tend to fluctuate considerably as the object moves. This is a natural consequence of using a step function, whose value jumps abruptly when the function value changes.

To address this problem, you can create a larger 1D texture (for each test) that encodes a smoother transition. For example, you might use a texture that is 16 texels wide, and encode additional in-between steps in the middle 4 texels. Then, you can turn on bilinear texture filtering, which will smooth the transition automatically. The example in the accompanying software framework produces more visually pleasing results by using this approach.

9.2.3 Putting It All Together

Examples 9-3 and 9-4 show the complete programs and put the preceding discussion into a concrete form.

9.2.4 Problems with This Technique

The method we've described for toon shading is simple to implement, but it has a significant drawback: it works well only for curved objects. This is because the program relies on a gradual fall-off of N dot V to find silhouette edges. When objects have sharp edges, N dot V suddenly changes at the boundary, immediately causing the outline to turn completely black.

A common way to get around this problem is to use a two-pass approach. First, draw a version of the model that is slightly expanded along its normals. Draw this geometry

```
void C9E3v_toonShading(float4 position : POSITION,
                       float3 normal   : NORMAL,

                   out float4 oPosition     : POSITION,
                   out float  diffuseLight  : TEXCOORD0,
                   out float  specularLight : TEXCOORD1,
                   out float  edge          : TEXCOORD2,

               uniform float3 lightPosition,
               uniform float3 eyePosition,
               uniform float  shininess,
               uniform float4x4 modelViewProj)
{
    oPosition = mul(modelViewProj, position);

  // Calculate diffuse lighting
  float3 N = normalize(normal);
  float3 L = normalize(lightPosition - position.xyz);
  diffuseLight = max(dot(N, L), 0);

  // Calculate specular lighting
  float3 V = normalize(eyePosition - position.xyz);
  float3 H = normalize(L + V);
  specularLight = pow(max(dot(N, H), 0), shininess);
  if (diffuseLight <= 0) specularLight = 0;

  // Perform edge detection
  edge = max(dot(N, V), 0);
}
```

Example 9-3. The `C9E3v_toonShading` Vertex Program

in black (or whatever color you want for the outline). Next, draw the remaining geometry as usual, using the toon shader but omitting the outline calculation. The result will be a rendering that has a toon-shaded appearance internally and a clear shell that defines each object's outline. Unfortunately, this approach only addresses silhouette edges, not internal edges.

Another solution is to perform edge detection in image space. This approach lets you find internal edges and ensure uniform edge widths. However, adding this analysis increases the cost of the shader.

```
void C9E4f_toonShading(float diffuseLight  : TEXCOORD0,
                       float specularLight: TEXCOORD1,
                       float edge          : TEXCOORD2,

                 out float4 color : COLOR,

             uniform float4 Kd,
             uniform float4 Ks,
             uniform sampler1D diffuseRamp,
             uniform sampler1D specularRamp,
             uniform sampler1D edgeRamp)
{
  // Apply step functions
  diffuseLight = tex1D(diffuseRamp, diffuseLight).x;
  specularLight = tex1D(specularRamp, specularLight).x;
  edge = tex1D(edgeRamp, edge).x;

  // Compute the final color
  color = edge * (Kd * diffuseLight +
                  Ks * specularLight);
}
```

Example 9-4. The **C9E4f_toonShading** Fragment Program

9.3 Projective Texturing

When people refer to "texturing," they're usually talking about explicitly assigning texture coordinates to apply a texture onto a surface. However, this isn't the only way to use textures. In this section, you'll learn how textures can be projected onto surfaces, as if from a slide projector. Naturally, this technique is called *projective texturing*.

Figure 9-6 shows an example of projective texturing. The scene consists of a plane, along with two objects—a box and a sphere—floating above it. The projector is almost directly above the objects, and is projecting the image of a demon down onto the scene. Notice that there is no notion of objects "blocking" light. For example, the demon's eye and nose appear on both the sphere and on the plane beneath it. Similarly, the demon's teeth appear on the box and on the plane. In its basic form, projective texturing does not account for the shadowing relationships between objects. The reasons for this will be clearer when you learn how projective texturing works. (The exercises at the end of this chapter explore one solution to this problem.)

Figure 9-6. Projective Texturing

9.3.1 How Projective Texturing Works

So how does projective texturing work? A projective texture is just like an ordinary texture—the only difference is in how the texture is applied to geometry. Like regular texturing, projective texturing requires every triangle in your scene to have the appropriate texture coordinates. If you get the texture coordinates right, you'll end up with the correct part of the light's texture on each triangle. The trick is assigning the correct coordinates to the various polygons.

Remember the discussion in Chapter 4, where we went through the various transformations in the graphics pipeline? Many of these concepts apply to projective texturing.

We started with object-space coordinates for each triangle and applied a series of transformations to map the vertices into a sequence of coordinate systems. The transformations projected the object-space vertices into window space, so that the triangles could be rasterized and displayed in the viewport. If you think of the viewport as a texture, it's evident that you ended up mapping each vertex to a texel on the texture.

Projective texturing works in much the same way. By applying a sequence of transformations, you map object-space coordinates into a 2D space (a texture), and you find out where each vertex maps to on the texture. Then you assign this position as the texture coordinate for the vertex, and apply the appropriate piece of the texture to each triangle as it is rendered.

Comparing Transformations

Figure 9-7 illustrates the parallel between transformations in a conventional pipeline and those in projective texturing.

On the left is the sequence of transformations in the conventional pipeline (for a typical "camera"), and on the right is the sequence of transformations for projective texturing. Notice that on the right side, the texture coordinates remain in homogeneous space. If you're wondering what "homogeneous space" means for texture coordinates, don't worry. That's what you're about to learn.

Homogeneous Texture Coordinates

When texture coordinates are used, they're usually two-dimensional and nonprojective. Conventional 2D textures are accessed using a pair of texture coordinates: the s and t texture coordinates. Sometimes, when a 3D texture is applied, the r texture co-

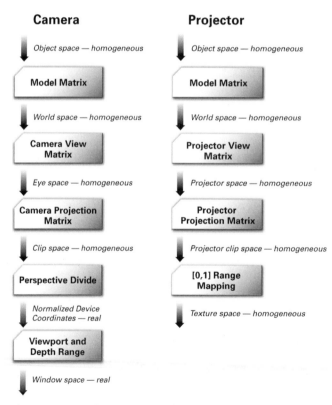

Figure 9-7. Transformations for a Conventional Camera vs. Those for a Projector

ordinate is used to index the texture's third dimension. You can think of the s, t, and r texture coordinates in the same way that you think of x, y, and z when you're dealing with homogeneous positions.

Just as homogeneous positions have a fourth component called w, homogeneous texture coordinates also have a fourth component, called q. This component allows you to express projections, rotations, translations, and scales in texture space, all with convenient 4×4 matrix multiplications.

When it's time to perform a projective texture lookup, the hardware takes the original texture coordinate set (s, t, r, q) and divides each component by q, giving (s/q, t/q, r/q, 1). This is analogous to the perspective division that takes place after the vertex program runs. After this division, the coordinates index correctly into a 2D or 3D texture.

It should be clear by now that the theory for projective texturing is very similar to that of the basic graphics pipeline. For example, when you specify just s and t texture coordinates, q is assumed to be 1. This is just like specifying a position directly in clip space (with w equal to 1), as you did in Chapter 2. The only difference is that projections are almost always used when dealing with positions, but projective texturing is used sparingly when dealing with texture coordinates.

9.3.2 Implementing Projective Texturing

Now it's time to put the theory into practice. If you understand the concepts, you'll find that you don't have to do much at all in Cg to make projective texturing work.

There are two operations that you have to take care of: calculating projective texture coordinates in the vertex program, and performing the projective texture lookup in the fragment program.

Calculating Texture Coordinates in the Vertex Program

In some of our previous vertex programs, you dealt with nonprojective texturing and simply passed the application's texture coordinates to the fragment program.

For projective texturing, you don't use explicitly specified per-vertex texture coordinates from the application. Rather, you use a vertex program to compute texture coordinates from the object-space per-vertex positions automatically. In fixed-function vertex processing, this computation occurs when automatic texture generation (commonly called "texgen") is enabled. The great thing about implementing texture generation in the vertex program is that you know exactly what's going on.

Equation 9-2 shows the sequence of transformations that you have to implement in the vertex program for projective texturing. Remember, it's the same sequence you would use if the eye were at the light's position, but with one extra matrix tacked on. This matrix scales and biases the results into the [0, 1] range that is used to access textures. For efficiency, you'll probably want to concatenate the matrices into a single matrix. We will call this concatenated matrix the *texture matrix*.

$$
\begin{bmatrix} s \\ t \\ r \\ q \end{bmatrix} =
\begin{bmatrix} \frac{1}{2} & & & \frac{1}{2} \\ & \frac{1}{2} & & \frac{1}{2} \\ & & \frac{1}{2} & \frac{1}{2} \\ & & & 1 \end{bmatrix}
\begin{bmatrix} Light \\ Frustum \\ (projection) \\ Matrix \end{bmatrix}
\begin{bmatrix} Light \\ View \\ (look\ at) \\ Matrix \end{bmatrix}
\begin{bmatrix} Modeling \\ Matrix \end{bmatrix}
\begin{bmatrix} x_0 \\ y_0 \\ z_0 \\ w_0 \end{bmatrix}
$$

Equation 9-2. The Sequence of Transformations for Projective Texturing

Let's go through the transformations, to clarify what's going on. The vertices start in object coordinates.

1. **Multiply by the modeling matrix.** This applies any necessary modeling transformations to the vertices. The modeling matrix needs to be applied regardless of whether or not you're using projective texturing.

2. **Multiply by the light's viewing matrix.** This rotates and translates the vertices so that they are in the light's frame of reference.

3. **Multiply by the light's projection matrix.** This defines the light's frustum, including its field of view and aspect ratio.

4. **Scale and bias the results.** Following steps 1 to 3, the transformed vertex values range from –1 to 1. However, textures are indexed from 0 to 1, so the results have to be mapped to this range. This is done by multiplying the x, y, and z components of the results by ½ and then adding ½. A single matrix multiplication accomplishes this mapping.

Now you need to come up with the matrices, which is easy. You already have the modeling matrix, because it was used to create the modelview matrix in Chapter 4. The light's viewing and projection matrices are what you would use if you were to render a scene from the light's point of view. And the scale-and-bias matrix is simply a collection of constants.

The Code for Projective Texturing

Once you've made sure that your application is passing the correct texture matrix to the vertex program, you need to add only one line to the vertex and fragment programs.

In the vertex program, you have to calculate the projective texture coordinates from the object-space positions:

```
float4 texCoordProj = mul(textureMatrix, position);
```

The fragment program receives the interpolated four-component texture coordinate set. Prior to using the texture coordinate set to access a 2D texture, the **tex2Dproj** Standard Library routine first divides the *s* and *t* texture coordinates (the first and second components) by the *q* texture coordinate (the fourth component):

```
float4 textureColor = tex2Dproj(projTexture,
                                texCoordProj);
```

Notice that the complete four-component texture coordinates are passed to **tex2Dproj**, with the *q* component as the fourth component.

The Vertex Program

Example 9-5 shows the complete vertex program for projective texturing.

The Fragment Program

Example 9-6 shows the corresponding fragment program.

Notable Issues

Projective texturing has two issues that you should be aware of. First, there are no occlusion checks. This means that the intuitive notion of triangles shadowing one another as with a real slide projector does not exist—the projective texture is applied to every triangle that is within the light's frustum. This behavior shouldn't come as a surprise, considering that the hardware simply transforms vertices according to the matrices that it's given, and uses the transformed locations to query a texture. As the hardware transforms each triangle, it has no knowledge of the triangle's relationship to any others.

```
void C9E5v_projTex(float4 position : POSITION,
                   float3 normal    : NORMAL,

              out float4 oPosition        : POSITION,
              out float4 texCoordProj     : TEXCOORD0,
              out float4 diffuseLighting : COLOR,

          uniform float Kd,
          uniform float4x4 modelViewProj,
          uniform float3   lightPosition,
          uniform float4x4 textureMatrix)
{
  oPosition = mul(modelViewProj, position);

  // Compute texture coordinates for
  // querying the projective texture
  texCoordProj = mul(textureMatrix, position);

  // Compute diffuse lighting
  float3 N = normalize(normal);
  float3 L = normalize(lightPosition - position.xyz);
  diffuseLighting = Kd * max(dot(N, L), 0);
}
```

Example 9-5. The `C9E5v_projTex` Vertex Program

```
void C9E6f_projTex(float4 texCoordProj     : TEXCOORD0,
                   float4 diffuseLighting : COLOR,

              out float4 color : COLOR,

          uniform sampler2D projectiveMap)
{
  // Fetch color from the projective texture
  float4 textureColor = tex2Dproj(projectiveMap,
                                  texCoordProj);

  color = textureColor * diffuseLighting;
}
```

Example 9-6. The `C9E6f_projTex` Fragment Program

The second issue is that back-projection artifacts can appear when the q coordinate is negative. *Back-projection* refers to the texture being projected on surfaces that are behind the light source (or projector). On many older GPUs, the texture interpolators produce undefined results in this case.

There are several ways to avoid artifacts when q is negative:

- Use culling to draw only geometry that is in front of the light source.
- Use clip planes to remove geometry that is behind the light source.
- Fold the back-projection factor into a 3D attenuation texture.
- Use a fragment program to check when q is negative.

The first two solutions are tedious to implement; the fragment program solution is simple and efficient but requires an advanced fragment profile. Just check the value of the q coordinate. If q is negative, you can ignore the projective texture computation and output black. In this case, you can rewrite the texture lookup in **C9E6f_projTex** to read:

```
float4 textureColor = texCoordProj.w < 0 ?  // is q less than 0?
                      0 :                    // then zero
                  tex2Dproj(projTexture, texCoordProj);
                      // otherwise sample the texture
```

9.4 Shadow Mapping

If you've used OpenGL or Direct3D, you know that lights in these APIs do not automatically cast shadows. There are lots of ways to compute shadows, but we're going to look at only one of the popular methods, called *shadow mapping*. Figure 9-8 shows the effect of adding shadows to a simple scene. The shadows help to establish the relative locations of the sphere and the cube.

We cover shadow mapping for two reasons. First, it's based on the projective texturing concept that we just introduced. And second, the fragment programming capabilities of recent graphics hardware let you control shadow mapping more precisely than ever before.

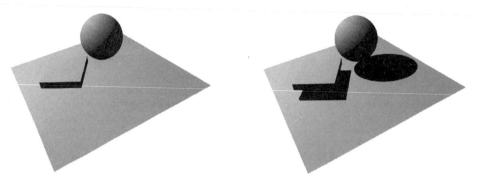

Figure 9-8. Using Shadow Mapping to Add Shadows to a Scene

Shadow mapping is a two-pass technique:

1. First, the scene is rendered from the light's point of view. The depth at each pixel of the resulting image is recorded in a "depth texture." (This texture is often called the *shadow map*.)

2. Next, the scene is rendered from the eye position, but with the shadow map projected down from the light onto the scene using standard projective texturing. At each pixel, the depth sample (from the projected shadow map texture) is compared with the fragment's distance from the light. If the latter is greater, the pixel is not the closest surface to the light source. This means that the fragment is shadowed, and that it should not receive light during shading.

Figure 9-9 illustrates the shadow mapping comparison. On the left panel of the figure, the point P that is being shaded is in shadow, because the point's depth (z_B) is greater than the depth that is recorded in the shadow map (z_A). In contrast, the right panel of the figure shows a case where the point P has the same depth as the recorded value in the shadow map. This means that there isn't any object between P and the light source, so P is not in shadow.

Shadow mapping uses the same setup that projective texturing uses, so the shadow map is indexed using (s/q, t/q). Because the light source is the center of projection for the shadow map, r/q holds the distance from the light. Therefore, by comparing the shadow map texel depth at (s/q, t/q) with r/q, you can determine if the current pixel is lit or in shadow.

When you do a projective texture lookup on a shadow map, the hardware automatically takes care of the comparison for you: the **tex2Dproj** function returns a value that represents how "lit" the current pixel would be. That is, the **tex2Dproj** function

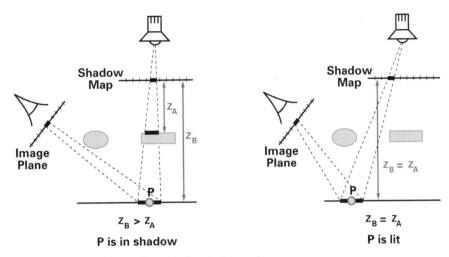

Figure 9-9. The Shadow Mapping Depth Comparison

returns a four-component vector of the form (c, c, c, 1), where c is 0 if the pixel is in shadow, and 1 if the pixel is lit. You can then treat this vector as a color. If bilinear texture filtering is enabled, c will range from 0 to 1 instead of being restricted to just the two values. Filtering is useful along the shadow boundaries, where the transition between being fully occluded to fully lit takes place. In these situations, the filtering helps make the shadow look softer, and reduces edge aliasing (jaggedness).

The following code sample shows how you would use a shadow map in a fragment program. In the example, the diffuse lighting is modulated by the result of the shadow map query:

```
// Calculate diffuseLighting as usual

// Fetch depth value from the shadow map
float4 shadowCoeff;    // 0 means "in shadow",
                       // 1 means "not in shadow"
shadowCoeff = tex2Dproj(shadowMap,
                        texCoordProj);


float4 shadowedColor = shadowCoeff *
                       diffuseLighting;
```

Notice that the code for the shadow map query is virtually identical to the code for the projective texture lookup in Example 9-6. To a Cg programmer, shadow maps are like other projective textures, except that instead of returning a texture color,

tex2Dproj returns a value representing shadow coverage. The underlying hardware implementation automatically recognizes when a texture is a depth texture (instead of a color texture) and performs the shadow map comparison instead of an ordinary texture fetch.

Extensions

Conventional shadow mapping with the fixed-function pipeline automatically handles the shadow map comparison for you. But with fragment programs, you can take full control of this operation and apply it to create new effects.

Shadow generation is a very difficult topic, and it has been the subject of many research papers and projects. The "Further Reading" section at the end of this chapter lists several sources that you can use to learn more about shadow mapping and other ways of generating shadows. As you experiment, you're likely to find new techniques that you can incorporate into your own projects to give them a unique look.

9.5   Compositing

The same fragment-processing power available for high-level shading of 3D surfaces can be usefully employed in 2D imaging as well. Applications such as painting programs and digital photo readers already make use of complex 2D processes. And most motion-picture uses of computer graphics now rely heavily on the ability to composite multiple images, sometimes from widely different sources, into a single final frame. Even games can benefit from fast, high-quality imaging effects, applied as a postprocess to their original 3D outputs.

Simple compositing has been around for many years, using the technique of alpha blending; this capability is present in both Direct3D and OpenGL. The technique is mostly used when rendering individual 3D polygons to a partially filled frame buffer, but it can also be used for 2D image processing. But the precision of alpha blending is limited to fixed-point math, and this limitation can sometimes lead to serious errors in the compositing process.

Recent GPUs have introduced floating-point offscreen buffers, permitting extremely complex compositing effects while essentially removing concerns about loss of precision. Floating-point buffers do not use hardware alpha blending, but instead depend on the fragment-shading pipeline. Floating-point buffers are brought back into the fragment pipeline as floating-point textures. Thus, we can combine images using fragment program operations, and then write out the final processed result to the frame buffer. Fragment programs permit us to perform not only all of the many combinations previously available in alpha blending, but also any fragment-oriented processes we can imagine.

 The CineFX architecture provides four-component floating-point math operations and frame buffer formats. Each component is processed and stored as an industry-standard (IEEE) 32-bit floating-point value.

9.5.1 Mapping Input to Output Pixels

When using fragment programs to perform 2D image processing, we are actually still doing 3D imaging! We render polygons directly aligned with the screen, and covering the screen. We apply our 2D fragment programs directly to this surface.

The typical way to cover the screen is with a simple screen-aligned rectangle (two triangles). If we define a 3D unit-sized square, ranging from –0.5 to 0.5 in x and y and with $z = 0$ for all points, then the Cg vertex program in Example 9-7 will align it with the screen.

Note that depending on the graphics API that you use, you may have to add offsets to align images correctly. For instance, in Example 9-7, **0.5/imgWidth** and **0.5/imgHeight** are tiny offsets that align images for Direct3D. This is necessary because in Direct3D, texture coordinates address the center of each texel, not one corner. The slight shift is seldom visible to the naked eye, but it can create numerous problems if you attempt to combine the results of multiple imaging passes. Each pass, if misaligned, will be offset a half-texel, which can create some cool effects of its own, but is generally undesirable if unintended!

9.5.2 Basic Compositing Operations

Once we have aligned a screen-shaped surface and placed texture coordinates onto it, we can combine any input images we like.

To copy an image directly to the screen (potentially rescaling it as you go), use a very simple fragment program shown in Example 9-8 (which includes a tint color, just for fun).

```
void C9E7v_screenAlign(float3 position : POSITION,
                       float4 texCoord : TEXCOORD0,

                   out float4 oPosition : POSITION,
                   out float4 oTexCoord : TEXCOORD0,

              uniform float imgWidth,
              uniform float imgHeight)
{
  float4 screen = float4(position.x, position.y,
                         2.0, 2.0);
  oPosition = screen;
  oTexCoord = float4(0.5 * (1.0 + screen.x/screen.w) +
                     (0.5/imgWidth),
                     0.5 * (1.0 + screen.y/screen.w) +
                     (0.5/imgHeight),
                     0.0,
                     1.0);
}
```

Example 9-7. The `C9E7v_screenAlign` Vertex Program

```
void C9E8f_tint(float3 position : POSITION,
                float2 texCoord : TEXCOORD0,

            out float4 result   : COLOR,

        uniform sampler2D colorMap,
        uniform float4 tintColor)
{
  result = tintColor * tex2D(colorMap, texCoord);
}
```

Example 9-8. The `C9E8f_tint` Fragment Program

Example 9-9 adds a second image to open up the realm of compositing.

Note that Example 9-9 and the other compositing examples that follow work only on advanced profiles, though you can easily rewrite them for basic profiles by replicating the texture coordinate set. Then, you would access each sampler with its own texture coordinate set (even though the two sets of texture coordinates would in fact be identical), which is allowed in basic profiles.

```
void C9E9f_a_over_b(float3 position  : POSITION,
                    float2 texCoord  : TEXCOORD0,

               out float4 result      : COLOR,

            uniform sampler2D imageA,
            uniform sampler2D imageB)
{
  float4 aPixel = tex2D(imageA, texCoord);
  float4 bPixel = tex2D(imageB, texCoord);
  result = (aPixel.w * aPixel) +
           ((1.0 - aPixel.w) * bPixel);
}
```

Example 9-9. The **C9E9f_a_over_b** Fragment Program

This fragment program implements a typical compositing "over" operator, based on input values that are not premultiplied (sometimes called "nonpremultiplied"). In other words, the RGB portion of **imageA**'s pixels isn't already integrated with the alpha. Sometimes, particularly when dealing with images that have been antialiased, the alpha and RGB components have already been scaled, or premultiplied. If **imageA** had been premultiplied by alpha, we would change the equation slightly:

```
float4 result = aPixel + ((1.0 - aPixel.w) * bPixel);
```

Note that since we've ignored the alpha for **imageB** in this case, it doesn't matter if **imageB** is premultiplied or postmultiplied—unless you plan to use the result of the operation in further compositing passes. Beware of mixing premultiplied and nonpremultiplied images!

Using only slight variations, you can create other standard compositing operations, such as the following:

- **In:** Show **imageA** only when it overlaps with **imageB**, as shown in Example 9-10.
- **Out:** Show **imageA** only when it's *not* overlapping **imageB**, as shown in Example 9-11.
- **Dissolve:** Blend the two images (also called "additive blend" or just "mix" in compositing circles), as shown in Example 9-12.

Combining these simple pixel-to-pixel operations can create a near-infinite variety of effects. For example, you may want to overlay **imageB** with **imageA** but apply a dissolve-like **lerp** to **imageA**'s alpha channel. You can use channel swizzles to create

```
void C9E10f_a_in_b(float3 position : POSITION,
                   float2 texCoord : TEXCOORD0,

             out float4 result    : COLOR,

          uniform sampler2D imageA,
          uniform sampler2D imageB)
{
  float4 aPixel = tex2D(imageA, texCoord);
  float4 bPixel = tex2D(imageB, texCoord);
  result = bPixel.w * aPixel;
}
```

Example 9-10. The **C9E10f_a_in_b** Fragment Program

```
void C9E11f_a_out_b(float3 position : POSITION,
                    float2 texCoord : TEXCOORD0,

              out float4 result    : COLOR,

           uniform sampler2D imageA,
           uniform sampler2D imageB)
{
  float4 aPixel = tex2D(imageA, texCoord);
  float4 bPixel = tex2D(imageB, texCoord);
  result = (1.0 - bPixel.w) * aPixel;
}
```

Example 9-11. The **C9E11f_a_out_b** Fragment Program

```
void C9E12f_a_dissolve_b(float3 position : POSITION,
                         float2 texCoord : TEXCOORD0,

                    out float4 result    : COLOR,

               uniform sampler2D imageA,
               uniform sampler2D imageB,
               uniform float dissolve)
{
  float4 aPixel = tex2D(imageA, texCoord);
  float4 bPixel = tex2D(imageB, texCoord);
  result = lerp(aPixel, bPixel, dissolve);
}
```

Example 9-12. The **C9E12f_a_dissolve_b** Fragment Program

new "chroma-key" values for alpha on the fly. You can also perform useful alterations to the color and look of your input images before and after direct compositing. Color alterations of the input and final images can give you access to a wide range of image effects, applied in 2D, without having to change your underlying 3D models and rendering pipeline.

9.6   Exercises

1. **Try this yourself:** Depth cueing is a nonphotorealistic technique that is similar to fog. Both techniques attenuate apparent color with distance from the viewer. Unlike uniform fog, which uses an exponential function, depth cueing uses a simpler linear attenuation. Depth cueing helps a CAD designer viewing complex wireframe models to tell which lines are closer and which are farther away. Change the **C9E1f_fog** and **C9E2v_fog** examples to implement depth cueing. *Hint:* For example, OpenGL supports depth cueing through its **GL_LINEAR** fog mode. In this mode, the *f* in Equation 9-1 is computed this way, with no exponential:

$$f = \max\left[0, \min\left(1, \frac{e - Z}{e - s}\right)\right]$$

where *s* is the location where the fog starts in eye space (**GL_FOG_START** in OpenGL) and *e* is where the fog ends (**GL_FOG_END** in OpenGL).

2. **Answer this:** Describe a uniform fog situation where computing the distance per-vertex with the Euclidean distance function **length** would create artifacts. *Hint:* Think about a situation where two vertices could have the same distance from the eye but be far apart from each other.

3. **Try this yourself:** Modify the **C9E4f_toonShading** example so that, rather than using two 1D textures—one for diffuse and one for specular—the program uses a single 2D texture index with the diffuse contribution for *s* and the specular contribution for *t*. You will have to create an appropriate 2D texture.

4. **Try this yourself:** Use projective texturing to create a spotlight pattern in the shape of a blurred five-point star. Combine the spotlight attenuation term from projective texturing with a diffuse and specular lighting model from Chapter 5.

5. **Try this yourself:** Try combining shadow mapping with the results from Exercise 4.

6. **Try this yourself:** You saw in Section 9.5.1 that remapping an image to match exactly the output screen can be performed by a very small vertex program to define *s-t* texture coordinates. Extend such a vertex program to include standard 2D affine transformations to the 2D image, such as scaling, translation, and rotation.

9.7   Further Reading

To learn more about fog, read the "Atmospheric Models" chapter by Ken Musgrave, Larry Gritz, and Steven Worley in *Texturing and Modeling: A Procedural Approach, Second Edition* (Academic Press, 1998), edited by David S. Ebert. The classic computer graphics topic on atmospheric effects is Victor Klassen's "Modeling the Effect of the Atmosphere on Light," which appeared in a 1987 issue of *ACM Transactions on Graphics*.

Fog is more interesting when you relax the restriction of having uniform fog color and density. Justin Legakis presented a technical sketch at SIGGRAPH 1998, called "Fast Multi-Layer Fog" (ACM Press), in which he assumed that fog density varies with elevation.

Tomoyuki Nishita and his collaborators published a host of papers on natural phenomena, particularly atmospheric effects such as shafts of light. Much of their work could be easily adapted for use in Cg programs. His Web site is **http://nis-lab.is.s. u-tokyo.ac.jp/~nis.**

In 2001, Amy and Bruce Gooch wrote *Non-Photorealistic Rendering* (A. K. Peters), which describes cartoon rendering in more detail, along with many other nonphotorealistic rendering techniques. Thomas Strothotte and Stefan Schlechtweg wrote *Non-Photorealistic Computer Graphics: Modeling, Rendering and Animation* (Morgan Kaufmann, 2002).

Mark Segal, Carl Korobkin, Rolf van Widenfelt, Jim Foran, and Paul Haeberli introduced projective texturing for graphics hardware in their SIGGRAPH 1992 paper "Fast Shadows and Lighting Effects Using Texture Mapping" (ACM Press). This paper also describes hardware texture mapping as an extension of projective texturing.

Lance Williams first described shadow mapping in his classic SIGGRAPH 1978 paper "Casting Curved Shadows on Curved Surfaces" (ACM Press). William Reeves, David Salesin, and Robert Cook described their work on shadow maps at Pixar in their SIG-

GRAPH 1987 paper "Rendering Antialiased Shadows with Depth Maps" (ACM Press).

OpenGL 1.4 standardized shadow mapping for graphics hardware in 2002. Cass Everitt, Ashu Rege, and Cem Cebenoyan published "Hardware Shadow Mapping" for OpenGL and Direct3D in 2002. The white paper is available on NVIDIA's Developer Web site (**developer.nvidia.com**).

"A Survey of Shadow Algorithms," by Andrew Woo, Pierre Poulin, and Alain Fournier, is an excellent paper to learn more about shadows and shadow algorithms. The paper appeared in *IEEE Computer Graphics and Applications* in 1990.

Thomas Porter and Tom Duff published "Compositing Digital Images" (ACM Press) at SIGGRAPH 1984 and introduced compositing to the graphics community. More recently, Ron Brinkmann published *The Art and Science of Digital Compositing* (Morgan Kaufmann, 1999).

Chapter 10

Profiles and Performance

This chapter provides additional information about the profiles supported by your Cg compiler and offers advice on how to write high-performance Cg programs. This chapter has the following two sections:

- **"Profile Descriptions"** describes the capabilities and limitations of the OpenGL and Direct3D profiles supported by Cg.
- **"Performance"** gives practical advice about improving the performance of your Cg programs.

10.1　Profile Descriptions

This section describes the profiles that are available in Cg at the time of writing, along with brief summaries of their capabilities and limitations. More detailed information is available in the *Cg Toolkit User's Manual: A Developer's Guide to Programmable Graphics,* which is available online at NVIDIA's Developer Web site, **developer.nvidia.com.**

10.1.1　The Vertex Shader Profile for DirectX 8

The DirectX 8 vertex shader profile compiles Cg source code to DirectX 8 vertex shaders. The profile's identifier is **vs_1_1**. The profile restricts Cg to matching the capabilities of DirectX 8 vertex shaders. To understand the capabilities of DirectX 8 vertex shaders and the code produced by the compiler, refer to the "Vertex Shader Reference" section of the *DirectX 8.1 SDK* documentation.

The following list describes some important details about the **vs_1_1** profile:

- 128-instruction limit.
- There are a maximum of 96 four-component uniform parameters and constants per program. The Cg compiler does its best to pack constants efficiently.
- **if** statements and the **?:** operator are treated as conditional assignments.
- **while**, **do**, and **for** statements are allowed only if the loops they define can be unrolled by the compiler (that is, if the compiler can determine the number of iterations in the loop).
- This profile treats all continuous data types (such as **float**) as 32-bit floating-point values.
- This profile allows variable indexing of arrays as long as the array is a uniform constant. This profile does not support writing to arrays with variable indexing.
- No sampling of textures.
- Arbitrary swizzling and negation have no performance penalty.

10.1.2 The Basic NVIDIA Vertex Program Profile for OpenGL

The NVIDIA vertex program profile compiles Cg source code to vertex programs that are compatible with the **NV_vertex_program** OpenGL extension supported by NVIDIA and Mesa. The profile's identifier is **vp20**. The profile restricts Cg to matching the capabilities of the **NV_vertex_program** OpenGL extension. To understand the capabilities of NVIDIA vertex programs, refer to the extension's specification online.

This profile is functionally comparable to the **vs_1_1** profile discussed previously. The details pertaining to the **vs_1_1** profile apply to the **vp20** profile as well.

For **vp20** programs to operate correctly, constants in a **vp20** profile must be loaded into the appropriate program parameter registers. Be sure to use the Cg runtime to ensure that the proper constants are loaded.

This profile, unlike the **vs_1_1** profile, provides output semantics for both a front-facing and a back-facing primary and secondary color to support two-sided lighting.

10.1.3 The ARB Vertex Program Profile for OpenGL

The OpenGL Architecture Review Board (ARB) vertex program profile compiles Cg source code to vertex programs that are compatible with the **ARB_vertex_program** multivendor OpenGL extension. The profile's identifier is **arbvp1**. The profile restricts Cg to matching the capabilities of the **ARB_vertex_program** OpenGL extension. To understand the capabilities of ARB vertex programs, refer to the extension's specification online.

Like the **vp20** profile, this profile is functionally comparable to the **vs_1_1** profile discussed previously. The details pertaining to the **vs_1_1** profile apply to the **arbvp1** profile as well. Like **vp20**, the **arbvp1** supports outputting front-facing and back-facing colors.

Unlike the **vp20** profile, the **arbvp1** profile allows Cg programs to refer to the OpenGL state directly. However, if you want to write Cg programs that are compatible with **vp20** and **vs_1_1** profiles, you should use the alternate mechanism of setting uniform variables with the necessary state using the Cg runtime. Additionally, referring to OpenGL state directly results in a slight driver validation penalty when binding to **arbvp1** programs.

10.1.4 The Vertex Shader Profiles for DirectX 9

The DirectX 9 vertex shader profiles compile Cg source code to DirectX 9 vertex shaders. The profile identifiers are either **vs_2_0** or **vs_2_x**. These profiles restrict Cg to matching the capabilities of DirectX 9 vertex shaders. The **vs_2_x** profile is an extended version of the **vs_2_0** profile; the main enhancement is support for dynamic branching. To understand the capabilities of DirectX 9 vertex shaders and the code produced by the compiler, refer to the "Vertex Shader Reference" section of the *DirectX 9 SDK* documentation.

These profiles support more instructions and temporaries than the **vs_1_1** profile does. The **vs_2_x** profile also supports generalized looping and conditionals.

10.1.5 The Advanced NVIDIA Vertex Program Profile for OpenGL

The advanced NVIDIA vertex program profile compiles Cg source code to vertex programs compatible with the **NV_vertex_program2** OpenGL extension supported by NVIDIA's CineFX architecture. The profile identifier is **vp30**. This profile restricts Cg to matching the capabilities of the **NV_vertex_program2** OpenGL extension.

This profile is a superset of the **vp20** profile. Any program that compiles for the **vp20** profile should also compile for the **vp30** profile. Like the **vs_2_x** profile, the **vp30** profile supports more instructions and temporaries than the **vp20** profile does. The **vp30** profile also supports generalized looping and conditionals.

10.1.6 The Pixel Shader Profiles for DirectX 8

The DirectX 8 pixel shader profiles compile Cg source code to DirectX 8.1 pixel shaders. Cg provides profiles for pixel shader versions 1.1, 1.2, and 1.3. The profile identifiers are **ps_1_1**, **ps_1_2**, and **ps_1_3**, respectively. Each profile restricts Cg to matching the capabilities of the respective version of DirectX 8 pixel shaders. To understand the capabilities of DirectX 8 pixel shaders and the code produced by the compiler, refer to the "Pixel Shader Reference" section of the *DirectX 8.1 SDK* documentation.

The following list describes some important details about the **ps_1_1**, **ps_1_2**, and **ps_1_3** profiles:

- No more than four texture operations.
- No more than eight arithmetic operations.
- Texture access operations must precede arithmetic operations.
- **while**, **do**, and **for** statements are allowed only if the loops they define can be unrolled by the compiler.
- This profile represents all continuous data types (such as **float**) as signed values clamped to the range [-1, 1], [-2, 2], or [-8, 8] (depending on the underlying GPU and Direct3D capabilities).
- Limited swizzling capabilities:
    - **.x/.r**, **.y/.g**, **.z/.b**, **.w/.a**
    - **.xy/.rg**, **.xyz/.rgb**, and **.xyzw/.rgba**
    - **.xxx/.rrr**, **.yyy/.ggg**, **.zzz/.bbb**, **.www/.aaa**
    - **.xxxx/.rrrr**, **.yyyy/.gggg**, **.zzzz/.bbbb**, **.wwww/.aaaa**
- Only limited versions of the Cg Standard Library functions are supported.

- Only a few arithmetic operations are allowed:
  - Modifiers (see the *DirectX 8.1 SDK* documentation)
  - Binary operators (**+**, **-**, and *****)
  - Built-in functions (**dot**, **lerp**, **saturate**)
- This profile does not support arrays with variable indices.

10.1.7   The Basic NVIDIA Fragment Program Profile for OpenGL

The basic NVIDIA fragment program profile for OpenGL compiles Cg source code into textual register combiners and texture shader configurations supported by the **NV_register_combiners2** and **NV_texture_shader** OpenGL extensions. The profile's identifier is **fp20**. To understand the capabilities of this profile, refer to the **NV_register_combiners**, **NV_register_combiners2**, **NV_texture_shader**, **NV_texture_shader2**, and **NV_texture_shader3** OpenGL extension specifications. The code generated by the compiler for this profile conforms to NVIDIA's **nvparse** format.

The capabilities of this profile are slightly superior to those of the **ps_1_3** profile.

This profile supports the **samplerRECT** data type to access non-power-of-two dimensioned textures exposed by the multivendor **NV_texture_rectangle** OpenGL extension.

10.1.8   The DirectX 9 Pixel Shader Profiles

The DirectX 9 pixel shader profiles compile Cg source code to DirectX 9 pixel shaders. The profile identifiers are either **ps_2_0** and **ps_2_x**. These profiles restrict Cg to matching the capabilities of DirectX 9 vertex shaders. The **ps_2_x** profile is an extended version of the **ps_2_0** profile; the main enhancement is support for many more instructions and texture accesses. To understand the capabilities of DirectX 9 vertex shaders and the code produced by the compiler, refer to the "Pixel Shader Reference" section of the *DirectX 9 SDK* documentation.

The key capabilities and limitations of the **ps_2_0** or **ps_2_x** profiles are as follows:

- Floating-point per-fragment operations.
- Up to 16 texture units and, for **ps_2_x**, no limit on the number of texture fetch instructions.

- For **ps_2_0**, up to four levels of dependent texture accesses. For **ps_2_x**, there is no limit on dependent texture accesses.

- Arbitrary swizzles and negation.

- General comparison and boolean operations.

- Optional access to gradient instructions.

- Variable indexing of arrays is not allowed (use textures instead).

- Bitwise operators such as **&**, **|**, and **^** are not supported.

10.1.9 The ARB Fragment Program Profile for OpenGL

The ARB fragment program profile compiles Cg source code to vertex programs compatible with the **ARB_fragment_program** multivendor OpenGL extension. The profile's identifier is **arbfp1**. The profile restricts Cg to matching the capabilities of the **ARB_fragment_program** OpenGL extension. To understand the capabilities of ARB fragment programs, refer to the extension's specification online.

This profile is functionally comparable to the **ps_2_x** profile discussed previously. The details pertaining to the **ps_2_x** profile apply to the **arbfp1** profile as well.

10.1.10 The Advanced NVIDIA Fragment Program Profile for OpenGL

The advanced NVIDIA fragment program profile compiles Cg source code to vertex programs that are compatible with the **NV_fragment_program** OpenGL extension supported by NVIDIA's CineFX architecture. The profile identifier is **fp30**. This profile restricts Cg to matching the capabilities of the **NV_fragment_program** OpenGL extension.

This profile is the most functional fragment-level profile at the time of this book's writing. It is a superset of the **ps_2_x** profile.

In addition to all the functionality mentioned in the section describing the **ps_2_x** profile, the **fp30** profile also provides:

- Support for the **samplerRECT** data type for sampling non-power-of-two textures.

- Support for the **fixed** data type with a range of [-2,+2].

- Support for the **half** data type for half-precision floating-point.

- Support for additional instructions exposed by the **NV_fragment_program** extension.

10.2 Performance

The flexibility offered by modern and future GPUs, combined with the ease-of-use that Cg provides, makes it easy to write lengthy fragment programs. A practical problem arises, though: as your programs get longer, they execute more slowly. In the majority of cases, the Cg compiler will take care of optimizations for you. But it cannot choose high-level algorithms for you. Therefore, this section presents some concepts and techniques that will help you obtain optimal performance from your programs. A few of these have already been presented in some form or another earlier in the book, but we've put them all together here with additional explanation, for easier reference.

10.2.1 Use the Cg Standard Library

As you've worked through the examples in this book, you've probably found Cg's Standard Library functions quite convenient. But the Standard Library is about more than convenience—it's also about performance. The Standard Library functions are defined to allow the Cg compiler to convert them into highly optimized assembly code. In many cases, Standard Library functions compile to single assembly instructions that run in just one GPU clock cycle! Examples of such functions are **sin**, **cos**, **lit**, **dot**, and **exp**. In addition, using the Standard Library provides some amount of future-proofing. New versions of the Standard Library will be available with future versions of Cg, and these versions will be optimized for future GPUs.

Despite all these advantages, there may be occasions when you won't want to use the Standard Library functions. If you require a simpler version of a function, or if you can write an especially fast but simplified version of a function that suits your particular needs, you may be better off not using the Standard Library. One example of this, from Chapter 8, is using normalization cube maps rather than the Standard Library's **normalize** routine for normalizing vectors in fragment programs.

10.2.2 Take Advantage of Uniform Parameters

Always be wary of what you're passing to your vertex and fragment programs as uniform parameters. For example, if you're passing a **time** variable to the fragment program, and the program ends up using **sin(time)** instead, you're better off computing **sin(time)** once in your application, and passing that as the uniform parameter to your fragment program. This is far more efficient than computing **sin(time)** needlessly for each fragment that's generated! Even if your program needed **time** and **sin(time)**, it's more efficient to pass in these values as two uniform parameters than to pass just **time** and to compute **sin(time)** in your program.

10.2.3 Using Vertex Programs vs. Fragment Programs

Earlier in this book, you saw how fragment programs often can produce more accurate images than vertex programs can. If your scene is poorly tessellated, vertex programs often produce faceted and coarse images. But per-fragment shading doesn't come for free. A fragment program executes for each fragment that is generated, so fragment programs typically run several million times per frame. On the other hand, vertex programs normally run only tens of thousands of times per frame (assuming that your models are not heavily tessellated). In addition, fragment programs have more limited looping and branching capabilities than do vertex programs, though their capabilities will improve over time. In particular, fragment programs for third-generation and earlier GPUs are rather limited.

Each time you write a Cg program, you have to decide how you're going to distribute the program's workload between the vertex and fragment programs. A simple rule of thumb is to use the vertex program to perform basic transformations and texture coordinate manipulations, and rely on the fragment program for the remaining calculations. In general, this approach is a good one, because it lets you move the more expensive mathematical operations to the vertex program. By balancing the workload between the GPU's vertex and fragment processors, you prevent either one from becoming an overwhelming bottleneck.

In some situations, you might want to trade image quality for performance. For these circumstances, it might make sense to move more of your computations to the vertex program, if doing so balances the program workload by reducing the fragment program's length. The drop in image quality might be smaller than you'd expect, because interpolated values often work quite well. If the quantity that you're interpolating varies linearly, you won't see any drop in image quality at all when using a vertex program instead of a fragment program.

Another way to decide when to use a vertex program or a fragment program is to think about how often your program parameters vary. If the parameters vary slowly (for example, in diffuse lighting), it is probably adequate to make your calculations in the vertex program. However, if rapidly changing parameters are involved (for example, in specular lighting), you'll want a fragment program to get accurate results.

10.2.4 Data Types and Their Impact on Performance

A number of Cg's profiles support a variety of data types. To achieve optimal performance, you should use the smallest data type that is appropriate for any particular computation.

The **fixed** type is useful for low-precision computations, such as color calculations. In the **fp30** and **ps_2_x** fragment program profiles, fixed values range from -2 to +2 and provide 12 bits of fixed-point precision. What **fixed** gives up in precision it gets back in performance: calculations using the **fixed** data type often run at several times the speed of their **half** or **float** counterparts on the CineFX architecture.

The **half** type is helpful when you want high precision and more range, and you don't require the highest possible precision. In the **fp30** profile, **half** provides 16 bits of floating-point precision (1 bit of sign, 10 bits of mantissa, and 5 bits of exponent), which is well suited for many graphics-related quantities such as colors and normals. Particularly when you are dealing with color calculations, the **half** type is usually sufficient. On the CineFX architecture, programs that minimize their temporary storage by using **half** for intermediate values run faster than if all values were stored as **float** values.

Use the **float** type when you need the highest possible range and precision. For example, at the fragment level, you should use **float** when dealing with extreme texture coordinates and derivatives.

10.2.5 Take Advantage of Vectorization

It's a lot more efficient to perform computations with vector types than with individual scalars. For most operations, it takes the same amount of time to apply them to a vector as it takes to apply them to a scalar! This means that you can speed up some sequences of instructions by up to four times by using vectors prudently. Cg's swizzling and write-masking features make it easy to insert and extract scalars from vectors, so it makes good sense to pack your computations into vectors whenever possible.

For example, recall the particle system from Chapter 6. In the vertex program, you calculated the particle positions using the following vectorized code:

```
float4 pFinal = pInitial +
                vInitial * t +
                0.5 * acceleration * t * t;
```

This terse approach could be four times faster than calculating each component of the position individually:

```
float4 pFinal;
pFinal.x = pInitial.x + vInitial.x*t + 0.5*acceleration.x*t*t;
pFinal.y = pInitial.y + vInitial.y*t + 0.5*acceleration.y*t*t;
pFinal.z = pInitial.z + vInitial.z*t + 0.5*acceleration.z*t*t;
pFinal.w = pInitial.w + vInitial.w*t + 0.5*acceleration.w*t*t;
```

In a simple case like this, the compiler might actually be able to vectorize the code for you, but in general, it's more natural to think in terms of vectors rather than individual component calculations. Take advantage of the convenient vector types that Cg offers. In addition to being more efficient, vectorized code is often clearer and more concise than nonvectorized code.

10.2.6   Use Textures to Encode Functions

One way to speed up your fragment programs is to evaluate functions by looking up textures instead of performing arithmetic operations. Consider a function that takes one floating-point value as input and returns a floating-point value as its result. If the input value ranges from 0 to 1, you can use the input value as the texture coordinate for a 1D texture. The result of the query is a texel color, which is the function's result.

This technique isn't limited to just 1D textures. You can use a 2D texture to encode a function of two variables, or you can use a cube map to look up a 3D function. A good example is the normalization cube map you used in Chapter 8. Also, don't forget that RGBA textures allow you to encode values in each of the four components! Keep this in mind and you'll often find opportunities to make your programs more efficient by encoding useful information (that may have nothing to do with color) in each channel.

Using textures to encode functions has many advantages. First, no arithmetic operations are required, which means that valuable GPU cycles are saved. Second, texture lookups take advantage of the GPU's specialized texture-filtering hardware, which can automatically smooth out your function (if you want it to). That is, you can represent your function using a small texture, and allow the hardware to interpolate between the texels. Third, textures give you the flexibility to encode any arbitrary function, because they don't necessarily have to be created using a specific formula or pattern. You could even have an artist paint a function into a texture, giving the artist a higher level of aesthetic control.

10.2.7 Use Swizzling and Negation Freely

Vertex programs on NVIDIA GPUs provide swizzling and negation of variables without any performance penalty. Use this capability to your advantage.

 CineFX GPUs have these same free negation and swizzling capabilities at the fragment level.

CineFX GPUs also compute saturation (clamping to the [0, 1] range) and absolute values for free at the fragment level. Use the **saturate** Standard Library routine for saturation and the **abs** Standard Library routine for absolute values.

10.2.8 Shade Only the Pixels That You Must

For complex programs, the fragment program tends to be the bottleneck in your application. In these cases, it's judicious to make sure you don't waste valuable GPU cycles on parts of the scene that aren't visible. A good way to ensure this is to draw the scene once without shading, but with depth testing enabled. We call this "laying down z first." After this first pass, each pixel of the frame buffer contains only the closest surface that is visible at that pixel. For subsequent passes, configure the depth test to draw only those fragments whose depths match the depth values in the frame buffer. In this way, the fragment program executes only for visible fragments, instead of for all potentially visible fragments.

If you're familiar with OpenGL or Direct3D, you're probably wondering how this helps, since depth testing conventionally takes place at the end of the pipeline, after the fragment program has already executed. Fortunately, most modern graphics processors have special hardware that performs depth testing before the fragment program runs, making it possible to avoid running the fragment program when it's not necessary.

10.2.9 Shorter Assembly Is Not Necessarily Faster

When the Cg compiler creates assembly code from your Cg source code, it tries to produce code that will run most efficiently on the specified target profile or GPU. Modern GPUs are complex, and may require instructions to be scheduled in specific ways to achieve optimal performance. In some cases, the compiler may generate extra instructions that make its assembly code output longer than the assembly code generated by DirectX 9's **fxc** compiler, for example. In these situations, the extra assembly instructions run faster because they can be executed in parallel, or because they don't have dependencies that would cause the GPU's shader pipeline to stall.

The lesson to take from this discussion is that you shouldn't judge the performance of a compiler by the length of the assembly code that it outputs. However, it still is often true that the shorter the compiled code, the faster the program runs. In the end, the best way to evaluate a program's performance is to measure the frame rate that you get using the program. This lets you put all theory aside and quantify concrete, real-world performance.

10.3 Exercises

1. **Try this yourself:** Rewrite earlier fragment program examples in this book to take advantage of the **fixed** data type when compiled for the **fp30** and **ps_2_x** profiles.

2. **Answer this:** As graphics hardware continues to advance, you can expect more powerful and general profiles. Research the latest available Cg profiles supported by your compiler.

10.4   Further Reading

Specifications for the OpenGL extensions mentioned in this chapter can be found online at **http://oss.sgi.com/projects/ogl-sample/registry.** NVIDIA also publishes *NVIDIA OpenGL Extension Specifications,* which collects all the OpenGL specifications implemented by NVIDIA OpenGL drivers. Documentation found on the NVIDIA Developer Web site (**developer.nvidia.com**) explains the **nvparse** textural representation output by the **fp20** profile.

Microsoft documents DirectX 8 and DirectX 9 vertex and pixel shaders at **http://msdn.microsoft.com/library**, under "Graphics and Multimedia" in its DirectX SDK documentation.

Appendix A

Getting Started with Cg

A.1 Getting This Book's Accompanying Software

The examples and hands-on software that accompany this book are freely available for download from the book's Web site:

http://developer.nvidia.com/CgTutorial

The site will also list any changes, additions, or corrections to the book and the software. Any supplementary material that we make available will also be posted on the site.

A.2 Getting the Cg Toolkit

Although the book's accompanying software is self-contained, you should download the latest version of the NVIDIA Cg Toolkit when you're ready to add Cg to your own projects. You can get the toolkit from the NVIDIA Cg Web site:

http://developer.nvidia.com/Cg

Refer to this site often to keep up with the latest changes and additions to the Cg language. Information on how to report any bugs you may find in the release is also available on this site.

Appendix B

The Cg Runtime

B.1 What Is the Cg Runtime?

Cg programs supply programs for GPUs, but they need the support of an application to render images. To interface Cg programs with an application, you must do two things:

1. **Compile the programs for the appropriate profile.** This step translates your Cg program into a form that is compatible with the 3D programming interface used by the application and the underlying hardware.

2. **Link the programs to the application program.** This step allows the application to configure the program for execution, and to feed it varying and uniform parameters.

You can choose when you want to perform these operations. You can perform them at *compile time*, when the application program is compiled into an executable, or you can perform them at *runtime*, when the application is actually executed. The Cg runtime is a set of application programming interfaces (APIs) that allows an application to compile and link Cg programs at runtime.

B.2 Why Use the Cg Runtime?

B.2.1 Future-Proofing

Most applications need to run on a variety of GPUs with various levels of functionality, so these applications need to run on a variety of profiles. If an application precompiles its Cg programs (at compile time), it must store a precompiled version of each program for each profile. Although possible, the precompiled approach is cumbersome for an application that uses many Cg programs. What's worse, the Cg programs become frozen in time. By precompiling Cg programs, an application sacrifices the optimizations that future compilers could offer.

In contrast, Cg programs compiled by applications at runtime benefit from future compiler optimizations for existing profiles. And these programs can run on future profiles corresponding to new hardware and 3D API functionality that did not exist when the application's Cg programs were written.

B.2.2   No Dependency Issues

If you link a compiled Cg program to an application, the application becomes tied to the result of the compilation, particularly with respect to how the compiler allocates parameters. The application program would have to refer to the Cg program input parameters by using the hardware register names that the Cg compiler outputs. This approach causes two significant problems:

1. Register names cannot be easily matched to the corresponding meaningful names in the Cg program without looking at the compiler output.

2. Register allocations can change each time the Cg program, the Cg compiler, or the compilation profile changes. This means you would have to update the application each time as well, which would be inconvenient.

In contrast, linking a Cg program to the application program at runtime removes the dependency on the Cg compiler. With the Cg runtime, you only need to alter the application code when you add, delete, or rename Cg input parameters.

B.2.3   Input Parameter Management

The Cg runtime also offers facilities to manage the input parameters of the Cg program. In particular, it makes data types such as arrays and matrices easier to deal with.

These additional functions also encompass the necessary 3D API calls to minimize code length and reduce programmer errors.

B.3   How Does the Cg Runtime Work?

Figure B-1 shows the three libraries that make up the Cg runtime API.

- A core set of functions and structures encapsulating the 3D API–independent functionality of the runtime.

- An OpenGL-specific set of functions built on top of the core set.

- A Direct3D-specific set of functions built on top of the core set.

To make it easier for application writers, the OpenGL and Direct3D libraries each adopt the philosophy and data structure style of their respective APIs. You need only link with the 3D API–specific Cg runtime library for the 3D API your application uses. Therefore, most applications use either the OpenGL or Direct3D Cg runtime library.

The rest of this appendix provides code fragments, written in C, for using the Cg runtime in the framework of an application. Each step includes source code for OpenGL and Direct3D programming.

Functions that involve only pure Cg resource management belong to the core runtime and have a **cg** prefix. In these cases, the same code is used for OpenGL and Direct3D.

When functions from the OpenGL or Direct3D Cg runtime libraries are used, notice that the API name is indicated by the function name. Functions belonging to the OpenGL Cg runtime library have a **cgGL** prefix, and functions in the Direct3D Cg runtime library have a **cgD3D8** or **cgD3D9** prefix, for DirectX 8 and DirectX 9, respectively. In the examples that follow, we show the DirectX 9 versions of the examples. Replacing "**D3D9**" with "**D3D8**" will produce the DirectX 8 versions of the same examples. Note that the functions we list here take the same parameters in DirectX 8 and DirectX 9. In general, this is not always the case.

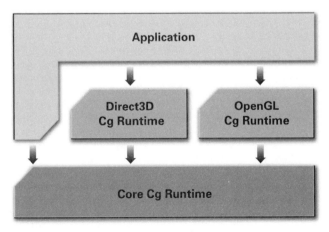

Figure B-1. The Parts of the Cg Runtime API

B.3 How Does the Cg Runtime Work?

B.3.1 Header Files

Here's how to include the core Cg runtime API into your C or C++ program:

```
#include <Cg/cg.h>
```

Here's how to include the OpenGL-specific Cg runtime API:

```
#include <Cg/cgGL.h>
```

Here's how to include the DirectX 8–specific Cg runtime API:

```
#include <Cg/cgD3D8.h>
```

Here's how to include the DirectX 9–specific Cg runtime API:

```
#include <Cg/cgD3D9.h>
```

B.3.2 Creating a Context

A context is a container for Cg programs. It holds the Cg programs you load, as well as their shared data.

Here's how to create a context:

```
CGcontext context = cgCreateContext();
```

B.3.3 Compiling a Program

Compile a Cg program by adding it to a context, using the **cgCreateProgram** function:

```
CGprogram program =
cgCreateProgram(context,              // from cgCreateContext
                CG_SOURCE,            // type: source or object
                programString,        // program text/data
                profile,              // profile
                "main",               // entry function name
                args);                // compiler options
```

The **CG_SOURCE** parameter indicates that the following string argument, **programString**, is an array of bytes containing Cg source code, not precompiled code. The Cg runtime does let you create a program from compiled code (called object code) by using the **CG_OBJECT** rather than **CG_SOURCE** parameter, if you want to.

profile specifies the profile for which the program will be compiled—for example, **CG_PROFILE_ARBVP1** for OpenGL applications, or **CG_PROFILE_VS_2_0** for Direct3D applications. The **main** string parameter gives the name of the function to use as the entry function for your program. Finally, **args** is a list of strings that supplies options to the compiler.

B.3.4   Loading a Program

After you compile a program, you need to pass the resulting object code to the 3D API that you are using. For this, you need to invoke the Cg runtime's 3D API–specific functions.

In OpenGL, you load a program like this:

```
cgGLLoadProgram(program);
```

The Direct3D-specific functions require the Direct3D device structure in order to make the necessary Direct3D calls. The application passes it to the runtime using the following call:

```
cgD3D9SetDevice(device);
```

You must do this every time a new Direct3D device is created, typically only at the beginning of the application.

You can then load a Cg program this way in Direct3D 9:

```
cgD3D9LoadProgram(program,       // CGprogram
                  false,         // Parameter shadowing
                  0);            // Assembly flags
```

or this way in Direct3D 8:

```
cgD3D8LoadProgram(program,              // CGprogram
                  false,                // Parameter shadowing
                  0,                    // Assembly flags
                  0,                    // Vertex shader usage
                  vertexDeclaration);   // Vertex declaration
```

vertexDeclaration is the Direct3D vertex declaration array that describes where to find the necessary vertex attributes in the vertex streams.

B.3.5   Modifying the Program Parameters

The runtime lets you modify the values of your program parameters. The first step is to get a handle to the parameter:

```
CGparameter myParameter = cgGetNamedParameter(program,
                                             "myParameter");
```

myParameter is the name of the parameter as it appears in the program source code.

The second step is to set the parameter value. The function used depends on the parameter type.

Here is an example in OpenGL:

```
cgGLSetParameter4fv(myParameter, value);
```

Here is the same example in Direct3D:

```
cgD3D9SetUniform(myParameter, value);
```

These function calls assign the four floating-point values contained in the array **value** to the parameter **myParameter** (assumed to be of type **float4**).

In both APIs, there are variants of these calls to set matrices, arrays, textures, and texture states.

B.3.6   Executing a Program

Before you can execute a program in OpenGL, you must enable its corresponding profile. For example:

```
cgGLEnableProfile(CG_PROFILE_ARBVP1);
```

In Direct3D, nothing special needs to be done to enable a specific profile.

Next, you bind the program to the current 3D API state. This means that it will execute, in the subsequent drawing calls, for every vertex (in the case of a vertex program) and for every fragment (in the case of a fragment program).

Here's how to bind a program in OpenGL:

```
cgGLBindProgram(program);
```

Here's how to bind a program in Direct3D:

```
cgD3D9BindProgram(program);
```

You can bind only one vertex and one fragment program at a time for a particular profile. Therefore, the same vertex program is executed as long as no other vertex program is bound. Similarly, the same fragment program is executed as long as no other fragment program is bound.

In OpenGL, disable profiles with the following call:

```
cgGLDisableProfile(CG_PROFILE_ARBVP1);
```

Disabling a profile issues commands, based on the profile, to return OpenGL to its fixed-function mode.

B.3.7 Releasing Resources

If your application no longer needs a Cg program, it is good programming practice to free the resources maintained for the program by the Cg runtime. Because the Direct3D runtime keeps an internal reference to the Direct3D device, you must tell it to release this reference when you finish using the Direct3D runtime. This is done with the following call:

```
cgD3D9SetDevice(0);
```

To free resources allocated for a single program, use this function call:

```
cgDestroyProgram(program);
```

To free all the resources allocated for a context, use this function call:

```
cgDestroyContext(context);
```

Note that destroying a context destroys all the programs it contains as well.

B.3.8 Handling Errors

The core Cg runtime reports an error by setting a global variable that contains the error code. You can query it, as well as the corresponding error string, in the following way:

```
CGerror error = cgGetError();
const char* errorString = cgGetErrorString(error);
```

Each time an error occurs, the core library also calls a callback function optionally provided by the application. This callback function would usually call **cgGetError**:

```
void MyErrorCallback(void)
{
  const char* errorString = cgGetErrorString(cgGetError());
  printf(logfile, "Cg error: %s", errorString);
}

cgSetErrorCallback(MyErrorCallback);
```

Calls to 3D API–specific Cg runtime functions can also generate API-specific errors. For the OpenGL Cg runtime library, they are checked using **glGetError**. Most of the Direct3D Cg runtime library functions also return a Direct3D error code (**HRESULT**). Similar to the Direct3D runtime, the Direct3D Cg runtime library can be run in a debug mode, provided you use the debug version of the Direct3D Cg DLL. This mode is enabled by the following call:

```
cgD3D9EnableDebugTracing(true);
```

In this mode, many helpful messages and traces will be output to the debug output console.

B.4 More Details

The latest information and documentation about the Cg runtime is available at the NVIDIA Cg Web site:

http://developer.nvidia.com/Cg

Appendix C

The CgFX File Format

C.1   What Is CgFX?

CgFX is a powerful and versatile shader specification and interchange format. As a file format, it is identical to Microsoft's .fx Effect format for DirectX 9. However, the CgFX runtime, like Cg, supports OpenGL as well as DirectX 8 and DirectX 9. For artists and developers of real-time graphics, this format provides several key benefits:

- Cross-API, cross-platform compatibility and portability.
- Encapsulation of multiple techniques, enabling fallbacks for level-of-detail, functionality, or performance.
- Support for Cg, assembly language, and fixed-function shaders.
- Editable parameters and GUI descriptions embedded in the file.
- Multipass shaders.
- Render state and texture state specification.

In practical terms, by wrapping both Cg vertex programs and Cg fragment programs together with render state, texture state, and pass information, developers can describe a complete rendering effect in a CgFX file. Although individual Cg programs may contain the core rendering algorithms necessary for an effect, only when combined with this additional environmental information does the shader become complete and self-contained. The addition of artist-friendly GUI descriptions and fallbacks enables CgFX files to integrate well with the production workflow used by artists and programmers.

C.2   Format Overview

The Cg language lets you easily express how an object should be rendered. Although current Cg profiles describe only a single rendering pass, many shading techniques, such as shadow volumes or shadow maps, require more than one rendering pass.

Many applications need to target a wide range of graphics hardware functionality and performance. Thus, versions of shaders that run on older hardware, and versions that aid performance for distant objects, are important.

Each Cg program typically targets a single profile, and doesn't specify how to fall back to other profiles, to assembly-language shaders, or to fixed-function vertex or fragment processing.

To generate images with Cg programs, some information about their environment is needed. For instance, some programs might require alpha blending to be turned on and depth writes to be disabled. Others may need a certain texture format to work correctly. This information is not present in standard Cg source files.

CgFX addresses these kinds of issues through a text-based file containing Cg, assembly, and fixed-function shaders, along with the render states and environment information needed to render the effect. As we've mentioned, this text file syntax matches that of the Microsoft .fx 2.0 format (the DirectX 9.0 Effect format).

CgFX encapsulates, in a single text file, everything needed to apply a rendering effect. This feature lets a third-party tool or another 3D application use a CgFX text file as is, with no external information other than the necessary geometry and texture data. In this sense, CgFX acts as an interchange format. CgFX allows shaders to be exchanged without the associated C++ code that is normally necessary to make a Cg program work with OpenGL or Direct3D.

C.2.1   Techniques

Each CgFX file usually presents a certain effect that the shader author is trying to achieve—such as bump mapping, environment mapping, or anisotropic lighting. The CgFX file contains one or more *techniques*, each of which describes a way to achieve the effect. Each technique usually targets a certain level of GPU functionality, so a CgFX file may contain one technique for an advanced GPU with powerful fragment programmability, and another technique for older graphics hardware supporting fixed-function texture blending. CgFX techniques can also be used for functionality, level-of-detail, or performance fallbacks. For example:

```
effect myEffectName
{
  technique PixelShaderVersion
  {…};

  technique FixedFunctionVersion
  {…};

  technique LowDetailVersion
  {…};
};
```

C.2.2   Passes

Each technique contains one or more *passes*. Each pass represents a set of render states and shaders to apply for a single rendering pass within a technique. For instance, pass 0 might lay down depth only, so that passes 1 and 2 can apply an additive alpha-blending technique without requiring polygon sorting.

Each pass may contain a vertex program, a fragment program, or both, and each pass may use fixed-function vertex or pixel processing, or both. For example, pass 0 might use fixed-function pixel processing to output the ambient color. Pass 1 could use a **ps_1_1** fragment program, and pass 2 might use a **ps_2_0** fragment program. In practice, all passes within a technique typically use fixed-function processing, or all use Cg or assembly programs. This method prevents depth-fighting artifacts that can occur when the fixed-function and programmable parts of some GPUs process the same data in different ways.

C.2.3   Render States

Each pass also contains render states such as alpha blending, depth writes, and texture filtering modes, to name a few. For example:

```
pass firstPass
{
    DepthWriteEnable = true;
    AlphaBlendEnable = false;
    MinFilter[ 0 ] = Linear;
    MagFilter[ 0 ] = Linear;
    MipFilter[ 0 ] = Linear;

    // Pixel shader written in assembly
    PixelShader = asm
    {
        ps.1.1
        tex t0;
        mov r0, t0;
    };
};
```

Notice that CgFX, in addition to embedding Cg programs, allows you to encode assembly-language vertex and fragment programs with the **asm** keyword.

C.2.4   Variables and Semantics

Finally, the CgFX file contains global and per-technique Cg-style variables. These variables are usually passed as uniform parameters to Cg functions, or as the value for a render or texture state setting. For instance, a **bool** variable might be used as a uniform parameter to a Cg function, or as a value enabling or disabling the alpha blend render state:

```
bool AlphaBlending = false;
float bumpHeight = 0.5f;
```

These variables can contain a user-defined semantic, which helps applications provide the correct data to the shader without having to decipher the variable names:

```
float4x4 myViewMatrix : ViewMatrix;
texture2D someTexture : DiffuseMap;
```

A CgFX-enabled application can then query the CgFX file for its variables and their semantics.

C.2.5 Annotations

Additionally, each variable can have an optional *annotation*. The annotation is a per-variable-instance structure that contains data that the effect author wants to communicate to a CgFX-aware application, such as an artist tool. The application can then allow the variable to be manipulated, based on a GUI element that is appropriate for the type of annotation.

An annotation can be used to describe a user interface element for manipulating uniform variables, or to describe the type of render target a rendering pass is expecting.

```
float bumpHeight
<
    string gui   = "slider";
    float  uimin = 0.0f;
    float  uimax = 1.0f;
    float  uistep = 0.1f;
> = 0.5f;
```

The annotation appears after the optional semantic, and before variable initialization. Applications can query for annotations, and use them to expose certain parameters to artists in a CgFX-aware tool, such as Discreet's 3ds max 5 or Alias|Wavefront's Maya 4.5.

C.2.6 A Sample CgFX File

Example C-1 shows a sample CgFX file that calculates basic diffuse and specular lighting.

```
struct VS_INPUT
{
        float4 vPosition  : POSITION;
        float4 vNormal    : NORMAL;
        float4 vTexCoords : TEXCOORD0;
};

struct VS_OUTPUT
{
        float4 vTexCoord0 : TEXCOORD0;
        float4 vDiffuse   : COLOR0;
        float4 vPosition  : POSITION;
        float4 vSpecular  : COLOR1;
};
```

Example C-1. A Sample CgFX File

```
VS_OUTPUT myvs(uniform float4x4 ModelViewProj,
               uniform float4x4 ModelView,
               uniform float4x4 ModelViewIT,
               uniform float4x4 ViewIT,
               uniform float4x4 View,
               const VS_INPUT vin,
               uniform float4 lightPos,
               uniform float4 diffuse,
               uniform float4 specular,
               uniform float4 ambient)
{
  VS_OUTPUT vout;
  float4 position = mul(ModelView, vin.vPosition);
  float4 normal =   mul(ModelViewIT, vin.vNormal);

  float4 viewLightPos = mul(View, lightPos);
  float4 lightvec = normalize(viewLightPos - position);
  float4 eyevec =   normalize(ViewIT[3]);
  float self_shadow = max(dot(normal, lightvec), 0);

  float4 halfangle = normalize(lightvec + eyevec);
  float spec_term =  max(dot(normal, halfangle), 0);

  float4 diff_term = ambient + diffuse * self_shadow +
                     self_shadow * spec_term * specular;
  vout.vDiffuse = diff_term;
  vout.vPosition = mul(ModelViewProj, vin.vPosition);
  return vout;
}


float4x4 vit      : ViewIT;
float4x4 viewmat  : View;
float4x4 mv       : WorldView;
float4x4 mvit     : WorldViewIT;
float4x4 mvp      : WorldViewProjection;
float4 diffuse    : DIFFUSE = { 0.1f, 0.1f, 0.5f, 1.0f };
float4 specular   : SPECULAR = { 1.0f, 1.0f, 1.0f, 1.0f };
float4 ambient    : AMBIENT = { 0.1f, 0.1f, 0.1f, 1.0f };
```

Example C-1 (*continued*). A Sample CgFX File

```
float4 lightPos : Position
<
     string Object = "PointLight";
     string Space = "World";
> = { 100.0f, 100.0f, 100.0f, 0.0f };


technique t0
{
  pass p0
  {
    Zenable = true;
    ZWriteEnable = true;
    CullMode = None;
    VertexShader = compile vs_1_1 myvs( mvp, mv, mvit, vit,
                                        viewmat, lightPos,
                                        diffuse, specular,
                                        ambient);

  }
}
```

Example C-1 (*continued*). A Sample CgFX File

C.3   Cg Plug-Ins Supporting the CgFX Format

At the time of publication, Cg plug-ins are available for major digital content creation (DCC) applications, such as Alias|Wavefront's Maya 4.5 and Discreet's 3ds max 5, which directly support the CgFX format.

The *Cg Plug-in for 3ds max* allows an artist to view and adjust the editable parameters of a CgFX shader right from within 3ds max. All changes made to the shader settings are displayed in real time in the native 3ds max viewports while running max under DirectX. This affords the artist more direct control of real-time 3D shaders.

The *Cg Plug-in for Maya* also allows an artist to view and adjust the editable parameters of a Cg shader "live," right within Maya's shading editor windows (such as the attribute editor and animation graph windows). Again, changes made to the shader settings are displayed in real time in Maya's OpenGL viewports.

C.4   Learning More About CgFX

CgFX-related software is available from the NVIDIA Cg Web site:

http://developer.nvidia.com/Cg

Refer to this site often to keep up with the latest applications, plug-ins, and other software that leverages the CgFX file format. Information on how to report any bugs you may find in the release is also available on this site. Also, see the *DirectX 9.0* effect reference documentation for additional specification details and examples.

Appendix D

Cg Keywords

D.1   Cg Keyword List

Following is the list of Cg reserved words. Words marked with an asterisk are case-insensitive.

In addition to the words on this list, any identifier with two underscores as a prefix (for example, __newType) is reserved. Note that matrix and vector types (such as half2x3 or float4) are not on this list because they can be used as identifiers. Still, we recommend that you treat the matrix and vector types as reserved words, thereby avoiding confusion.

asm*	explicit	pixelfragment*	template
asm_fragment	extern	pixelshader*	texture*
auto	FALSE	private	texture1D
bool	fixed	protected	texture2D
break	float*	public	texture3D
case	for	register	textureCUBE
catch	friend	reinterpret_cast	textureRECT
char	get	return	this
class	goto	row_major	throw
column_major	half	sampler	TRUE
compile	if	sampler_state	try
const	in	sampler1D	typedef
const_cast	inline	sampler2D	typeid
continue	inout	sampler3D	typename
decl*	int	samplerCUBE	uniform
default	interface	shared	union
delete	long	short	unsigned
discard	matrix*	signed	using
do	mutable	sizeof	vector*
double	namespace	static	vertexfragment*
dword*	new	static_cast	vertexshader*
dynamic_cast	operator	string*	virtual
else	out	struct	void
emit	packed	switch	volatile
enum	pass*	technique*	while

Appendix E

Cg Standard Library Functions

Cg provides a set of built-in functions and predefined structures with binding semantics to simplify GPU programming. These functions are similar in spirit to the C standard library, offering a convenient set of common functions. In many cases, the functions map to a single native GPU instruction, so they are executed very quickly. Of the functions that map to multiple native GPU instructions, you may expect the most useful to become more efficient in the near future.

Although you can write your own versions of specific functions for performance or precision reasons, it is generally wiser to use the Cg Standard Library functions when possible. The Standard Library functions will continue to be optimized for future GPUs; a program written today using these functions will automatically be optimized for the latest architectures at compile time. Additionally, the Standard Library provides a convenient unified interface for both vertex and fragment programs.

This appendix describes the contents of the Cg Standard Library, and is divided into the following five sections:

- "Mathematical Functions"
- "Geometric Functions"
- "Texture Map Functions"
- "Derivative Functions"
- "Debugging Function"

Where appropriate, functions are overloaded to support scalar and vector variants when the input and output types are the same.

E.1   Mathematical Functions

Table E-1 lists the mathematical functions that the Cg Standard Library provides. The table includes functions useful for trigonometry, exponentiation, rounding, and vector and matrix manipulations, among others. All functions work on scalars and vectors of all sizes, except where noted.

Table E-1. Mathematical Functions

Function	Description
`abs(x)`	Absolute value of x.
`acos(x)`	Arccosine of x in range $[0, \pi]$, x in $[-1, 1]$.
`all(x)`	Returns **true** if every component of x is not equal to 0. Returns **false** otherwise.
`any(x)`	Returns **true** if any component of x is not equal to 0. Returns **false** otherwise.
`asin(x)`	Arcsine of x in range $[-\pi/2, \pi/2]$; x should be in $[-1, 1]$.
`atan(x)`	Arctangent of x in range $[-\pi/2, \pi/2]$.
`atan2(y, x)`	Arctangent of y/x in range $[-\pi, \pi]$.
`ceil(x)`	Smallest integer not less than x.
`clamp(x, a, b)`	x clamped to the range $[a, b]$ as follows: • Returns a if x is less than a. • Returns b if x is greater than b. • Returns x otherwise.
`cos(x)`	Cosine of x.
`cosh(x)`	Hyperbolic cosine of x.
`cross(A, B)`	Cross product of vectors A and B; A and B must be three-component vectors.

Table E-1 *(continued).* Mathematical Functions

Function	Description
`degrees(x)`	Radian-to-degree conversion.
`determinant(M)`	Determinant of matrix **M**.
`dot(A, B)`	Dot product of vectors **A** and **B**.
`exp(x)`	Exponential function e^x.
`exp2(x)`	Exponential function 2^x.
`floor(x)`	Largest integer not greater than **x**.
`fmod(x, y)`	Remainder of **x**/**y**, with the same sign as **x**. If **y** is 0, the result is implementation-defined.
`frac(x)`	Fractional part of **x**.
`frexp(x, out exp)`	Splits **x** into a normalized fraction in the interval [½, 1), which is returned, and a power of 2, which is stored in **exp**. If **x** is 0, both parts of the result are 0.
`isfinite(x)`	Returns **true** if **x** is finite.
`isinf(x)`	Returns **true** if **x** is infinite.
`isnan(x)`	Returns **true** if **x** is NaN (Not a Number).
`ldexp(x, n)`	$\mathbf{x} \times 2^n$.
`lerp(a, b, f)`	Linear interpolation: `(1 - f)*a + b*f` where **a** and **b** are matching vector or scalar types. **f** can be either a scalar or a vector of the same type as **a** and **b**.

Table E-1 *(continued).* Mathematical Functions

Function	Description
`lit(NdotL, NdotH, m)`	Computes lighting coefficients for ambient, diffuse, and specular light contributions.

Expects the **NdotL** parameter to contain $N \cdot L$ and the **NdotH** parameter to contain $N \cdot H$.

Returns a four-component vector as follows:
- The **x** component of the result vector contains the ambient coefficient, which is always 1.0.
- The **y** component contains the diffuse coefficient, which is 0 if $(N \cdot L) < 0$; otherwise $(N \cdot L)$.
- The **z** component contains the specular coefficient, which is 0 if either $(N \cdot L) < 0$ or $(N \cdot H) < 0$; $(N \cdot H)^m$ otherwise.
- The **w** component is 1.0.

There is no vectorized version of this function.

Function	Description
`log(x)`	Natural logarithm $\ln(x)$; **x** must be greater than 0.
`log2(x)`	Base 2 logarithm of **x**; **x** must be greater than 0.
`log10(x)`	Base 10 logarithm of **x**; **x** must be greater than 0.
`max(a, b)`	Maximum of **a** and **b**.
`min(a, b)`	Minimum of **a** and **b**.
`modf(x, out ip)`	Splits **x** into integral and fractional parts, each with the same sign as **x**. Stores the integral part in **ip** and returns the fractional part.
`mul(M, N)`	Matrix product of matrix **M** and matrix **N**, as shown below:

$$\text{mul}(M, N) = \begin{bmatrix} M_{11} & M_{21} & M_{31} & M_{41} \\ M_{12} & M_{22} & M_{32} & M_{42} \\ M_{13} & M_{23} & M_{33} & M_{43} \\ M_{14} & M_{24} & M_{34} & M_{44} \end{bmatrix} \begin{bmatrix} N_{11} & N_{21} & N_{31} & N_{41} \\ N_{12} & N_{22} & N_{32} & N_{42} \\ N_{13} & N_{23} & N_{33} & N_{43} \\ N_{14} & N_{24} & N_{34} & N_{44} \end{bmatrix}$$

If **M** has size $\mathbf{A} \times \mathbf{B}$, and **N** has size $\mathbf{B} \times \mathbf{C}$, returns a matrix of size $\mathbf{A} \times \mathbf{C}$.

Table E-1 *(continued)*. Mathematical Functions

Function	Description
`mul(M, v)`	Product of matrix **M** and column vector **v**, as shown below:

$$\texttt{mul}(M,\ v) = \begin{bmatrix} M_{11} & M_{21} & M_{31} & M_{41} \\ M_{12} & M_{22} & M_{32} & M_{42} \\ M_{13} & M_{23} & M_{33} & M_{43} \\ M_{14} & M_{24} & M_{34} & M_{44} \end{bmatrix} \begin{bmatrix} v_1 \\ v_2 \\ v_3 \\ v_4 \end{bmatrix}$$

If **M** is an **A** × **B** matrix and **v** is a **B** × **1** vector, returns an **A** × **1** vector.

`mul(v, M)` — Product of row vector **v** and matrix **M**, as shown below:

$$\texttt{mul}(v,\ M) = \begin{bmatrix} v_1 & v_2 & v_3 & v_4 \end{bmatrix} \begin{bmatrix} M_{11} & M_{21} & M_{31} & M_{41} \\ M_{12} & M_{22} & M_{32} & M_{42} \\ M_{13} & M_{23} & M_{33} & M_{43} \\ M_{14} & M_{24} & M_{34} & M_{44} \end{bmatrix}$$

If **v** is a **1** × **A** vector and **M** is an **A** × **B** matrix, returns a **1** × **B** vector.

`noise(x)` — Either a one-, two-, or three-dimensional noise function, depending on the type of its argument. The returned value is between 0 and 1, and is always the same for a given input value.

`pow(x, y)` — x^y.

`radians(x)` — Degree-to-radian conversion.

`round(x)` — Closest integer to **x**.

`rsqrt(x)` — Reciprocal square root of **x**; **x** must be greater than 0.

`saturate(x)` — Clamps **x** to the [0, 1] range.

`sign(x)` — 1 if **x** > 0; −1 if **x** < 0; 0 otherwise.

`sin(x)` — Sine of **x**.

Table E-1 (continued). Mathematical Functions

Function	Description
`sincos(float x, out s, out c)`	**s** is set to the sine of **x**, and **c** is set to the cosine of **x**. If both `sin(x)` and `cos(x)` are needed, this function is more efficient than calculating each individually.
`sinh(x)`	Hyperbolic sine of **x**.
`smoothstep(min, max, x)`	For values of **x** between **min** and **max**, returns a smoothly varying value that ranges from 0 at **x = min** to 1 at **x = max**. **x** is clamped to the range [**min, max**] and then the interpolation formula is evaluated: $-2*((x - min)/(max - min))^3 + 3*((x - min)/(max - min))^2$
`step(a, x)`	0 if **x** < **a**; 1 if **x** >= **a**.
`sqrt(x)`	Square root of **x**; **x** must be greater than 0.
`tan(x)`	Tangent of **x**.
`tanh(x)`	Hyperbolic tangent of **x**.
`transpose(M)`	Matrix transpose of matrix **M**. If **M** is an **A** × **B** matrix, the transpose of **M** is a **B** × **A** matrix whose first column is the first row of **M**, whose second column is the second row of **M**, whose third column is the third row of **M**, and so on.

E.2   Geometric Functions

Table E-2 presents the geometric functions that are provided in the Cg Standard Library.

Table E-2. Geometric Functions

Function	Description
distance(*pt1*, *pt2*)	Euclidean distance between points *pt1* and *pt2*.
faceforward(*N*, *I*, *Ng*)	*N* if dot(*Ng*, *I*) < 0; −*N* otherwise.
length(*v*)	Euclidean length of a vector.
normalize(*v*)	Returns a vector of length 1 that points in the same direction as vector *v*.
reflect(*I*, *N*)	Computes reflection vector from entering ray direction *I* and surface normal *N*. Valid only for three-component vectors.
refract(*I*, *N*, *eta*)	Given entering ray direction *I*, surface normal *N*, and relative index of refraction *eta*, computes refraction vector. If the angle between *I* and *N* is too large for a given *eta*, returns (0, 0, 0). Valid only for three-component vectors.

E.3   Texture Map Functions

Table E-3 presents the texture map functions that are provided in the Cg Standard Library. Currently, these texture functions are fully supported by the **ps_2_0**, **ps_2_x**, **arbfp1**, and **fp30** profiles (though only OpenGL profiles support the **samplerRECT** functions). They will also be supported by all future advanced fragment profiles with texture-mapping capabilities. All of the functions listed in Table E-3 return a **float4** value.

Because of the limited pixel programmability of older hardware, the **ps_1_1**, **ps_1_2**, **ps_1_3**, and **fp20** profiles have restrictions on the use of texture-mapping functions. See the documentation for these profiles for more information.

Table E-3. Texture Map Functions

Function	Description
`tex1D(sampler1D tex, float s)`	1D nonprojective texture query
`tex1D(sampler1D tex, float s,` `      float dsdx, float dsdy)`	1D nonprojective texture query with derivatives
`tex1D(sampler1D tex, float2 sz)`	1D nonprojective depth compare texture query
`tex1D(sampler1D tex, float2 sz,` `      float dsdx, float dsdy)`	1D nonprojective depth compare texture query with derivatives
`tex1Dproj(sampler1D tex, float2 sq)`	1D projective texture query
`tex1Dproj(sampler1D tex, float3 szq)`	1D projective depth compare texture query
`tex2D(sampler2D tex, float2 s)`	2D nonprojective texture query
`tex2D(sampler2D tex, float2 s,` `      float2 dsdx, float2 dsdy)`	2D nonprojective texture query with derivatives
`tex2D(sampler2D tex, float3 sz)`	2D nonprojective depth compare texture query
`tex2D(sampler2D tex, float3 sz,` `      float2 dsdx, float2 dsdy)`	2D nonprojective depth compare texture query with derivatives
`tex2Dproj(sampler2D tex, float3 sq)`	2D projective texture query
`tex2Dproj(sampler2D tex, float4 szq)`	2D projective depth compare texture query
`texRECT(samplerRECT tex, float2 s)`	2D nonprojective texture rectangle texture query (OpenGL only)
`texRECT(samplerRECT tex, float2 s,` `       float2 dsdx, float2 dsdy)`	2D nonprojective texture rectangle texture query with derivatives (OpenGL only)
`texRECT(samplerRECT tex, float3 sz)`	2D nonprojective texture rectangle depth compare texture query (OpenGL only)
`texRECT(samplerRECT tex, float3 sz,` `       float2 dsdx, float2 dsdy)`	2D nonprojective depth compare texture query with derivatives (OpenGL only)

Function	Description
`texRECTproj(samplerRECT tex, float3 sq)`	2D texture rectangle projective texture query (OpenGL only)
`texRECTproj(samplerRECT tex, float3 szq)`	2D texture rectangle projective depth compare texture query (OpenGL only)
`tex3D(sampler3D tex, float3 s)`	3D nonprojective texture query
`tex3D(sampler3D tex, float3 s, float3 dsdx, float3 dsdy)`	3D nonprojective texture query with derivatives
`tex3Dproj(sampler3D tex, float4 sq)`	3D projective texture query
`texCUBE(samplerCUBE tex, float3 s)`	Cube map nonprojective texture query
`texCUBE(samplerCUBE tex, float3 s, float3 dsdx, float3 dsdy)`	Cube map nonprojective texture query with derivatives
`texCUBEproj(samplerCUBE tex, float4 sq)`	Cube map projective texture query (ignores q)

In the table, the name of the second argument to each function indicates how its values are used when performing the texture lookup:

- s indicates a one-, two-, or three-component texture coordinate.
- z indicates a depth comparison value for shadow map lookups.
- q indicates a perspective value, and is used to divide the texture coordinate (s) before the texture lookup is performed.

When you use the texture functions that allow specifying a depth comparison value, the associated texture unit must be configured for depth-compare texturing. Otherwise, no depth comparison will actually be performed.

E.4   Derivative Functions

Table E-4 presents the derivative functions that are supported by the Cg Standard Library. Vertex profiles do not support these functions.

Table E-4. Derivative Functions

Function	Description
ddx(a)	Approximate partial derivative of **a** with respect to screen-space **x** coordinate
ddy(a)	Approximate partial derivative of **a** with respect to screen-space **y** coordinate

E.5   Debugging Function

Table E-5 presents the debugging function that is supported by the Cg Standard Library. Vertex profiles are not required to support this function.

The intent of the **debug** function is to allow a program to be compiled twice—once with the **DEBUG** option and once without. By executing both programs, it is possible to obtain one frame buffer containing the final output of the program and another frame buffer containing an intermediate value to be examined for debugging purposes.

Table E-5. Debugging Function

Function	Description
void debug(float4 x)	If the compiler's **DEBUG** option is enabled, calling this function causes the value **x** to be copied to the **COLOR** output of the program, and execution of the program is terminated. If the compiler's **DEBUG** option is not enabled, this function does nothing.

Index

2D geometry, 37-46, 77, 79-82
    (equation), 81
3D geometry, 4
3dfx company, 10
3ds max (Discreet company), 32, Plate 3, Plate 4

+ operator, 71
, operator, 72
{ }, 40
/ operator, 71, 72
. operator, 46, 72, 113, 129
* operator, 71, 72
- operator, 71
?: operator, 72, 119
( ) operator, 72
[ ] operator, 72
% operator, 72
<< operator, 72
>> operator, 72
< operator, 72
<= operator, 72
>= operator, 72
> operator, 72
== operator, 72
^ operator, 72
| operator, 72
|| operator, 72
&& operator, 72
= operator, 72
+= operator, 72
-= operator, 72
*= operator, 72
/= operator, 72
! unary operator, 72

++ unary operator, 72
- unary operator, 72
+ unary operator, 72
* unary operator, 72
& unary operator, 72

A

abs function, 76, 77, 277
absolute value function, 76
absorption
    fog, mathematics of, 236
abstract execution model (Cg), 3
acceleration
    graphics, pre-GPU history, 10
accessing
    decal textures, 69
    matrix rows, 115
    structure members, 46, 129
addition (+) operator, 71
affine modeling transform, 178
Airey, John, 232
Akenine-Möller, Tomas, 35
Alias|Wavefront company, 32, Plate 1
aliasing
    in nonphotorealistic rendering, handling issues of, 246
    as shadow mapping issue, 257
alignment issues in compositing, 259
alpha
    blending, compositing use, 258
    in RGBA, transparency encoding with, 46
    testing, 16

alphanumeric characters
   not supported by current GPUs, 73
ambient lighting term, 104, 116, Plate 7
   (equation), 105
amplitude controls
   adding to pulsating objects program, 147
Angel, Edward, 98
animation, 167
   calculating displacement, 146-149
   (chapter), 143-168
   controls, 147
   rate, 4
   (term description), 143
anisotropic lighting model, 102, 142, Plate 29
annotations, 31, 297
API (application programming interface)
   See Direct3D programming interface; DirectX
      programming interface; OpenGL 3D pro-
      gramming interface
appearance(s)
   CgFX file format use, 30-34
   of objects, 2
application(s)
   Cg runtime relationship to, 29, 30
   CgFX relationship with, 33
   data, needed for graphics pipeline, 112
   user interface hooks, CgFX toolkit manipulation,
      31
ARB_fragment_program OpenGL extension, 55,
   272
ARB (OpenGL Architecture Review Board), 26
ARB_vertex_program OpenGL **extension**, 11,
   47, 269
arbfp1 fragment profile, 55, 74, 272
arbvp1 vertex profile, 47, 69, 75, 269
architecture
   See ARB (OpenGL Architecture Review Board);
      CineFX architecture (NVIDIA company);
      PixelFlow architecture
arithmetic operators, 72
array reference operator ([]), 72
arrays, 129-130
   Cg support for, 6
   packed

matrix data type use, 42
   using, (advanced), 41
   passing, 130
assembly language
   code example, 6
   efficiency issues, 278
   GPU, Cg relationship to, 5
   graphics hardware, Cg as high-level language
      replacement, 1
assignment operators, 72
associativity of math operators, 72
ATI company, 10, 11
atmospheric effects
   See fog
attenuation
   3D attenuation texture, 255
   C5E10_spotAttenLighting internal func-
      tion, 139
   C5E6_attenuation internal function, 134
   C5E7_attenuate internal function, 135
   distance, 133
   (equation), 133
   not in Basic lighting model, 110
authors
   bibliographic references, *See under specific author
      names*

B

back-projection artifacts, 255
Banks, David, 142
Basic lighting model
   (equation), 103
   extending, 132-140
   fragment program, 120
   per-vertex, 103-120
      concepts, 103-110
      implementation, 110-120
bit masks
   not supported by current GPUs, 73
blending/blend
   alpha, compositing use, 258
   during graphics hardware pipeline raster opera-
      tions stage, 16

processor (*continued*)
  programmable vertex
    capabilities, 18-19
    flow chart, 18
    operations, 51
profile(s), 78, 267-273
  bibliography, 279
  data types supported by, 75
  -dependent errors, 49-50
  -dependent numeric data types, 73-75
  fragment, 54-56, 69
  hardware, 7
  independence, 48, 78
  multiple, 48
  performance and, 267-279
  vertex, 47, 47-48, 48
program(s)
  fragment, downloading and configuring, 51-53
  termination, Cg vs. C and C++, 51
  vertex, downloading and configuring, 51-53
programmable
  fragment processor
    capabilities, 19-20
    flow chart, 10
    operations, 52
  graphics hardware, Cg relationship to, 5
  graphics pipeline, 17-20, 17
  vertex processor
    capabilities, 18-19
    flow chart, 18
    operations, 51
programming
  in Cg, simple programs, (chapter), 37-60
  interface
    See Also Direct3D programming interface
    See Also DirectX programming interface
    See Also OpenGL 3D programming interface
    vertex profile selection relationship to, 47
projective/projection
  3D texture lookup function, description and profile support, 77
  back-projection artifacts, projective texturing issue, 255
  matrix, 95

effect of, 96
texturing, 248-255, 249
  calculating projective coordinates for, 251
  implementation, 251
transform, 95-96
transformations, homogeneous position advantages, 91
Proudfoot, Kekoa, 25, 35
ps_1_1 fragment profile, 55, 69, 74, 75, 270
ps_1_2 fragment profile, 55, 75, 270
ps_1_3 fragment profile, 55, 75, 270
ps_2_0 fragment profile, 55, 75, 271
ps_2_x fragment profile, 55, 69, 75, 271
PSIZE semantic, 153
pulsating
  alien, 145
  objects, 144-149

Q

quadratic interpolation, 158
querying
  See Also accessing
  textures, 68

R

Radeon 7500 GPU (ATI company), 10
Radeon 8500 GPU (ATI company), 11
Radeon 9700 GPU (ATI company), 11, 123
radians function, 76
Rage (ATI company), 10
raster operations
  graphics hardware pipeline stage, 15
  OpenGL and Direct3D operations pipeline, 16
rasterization, 14
rational polynomials, 91
real-time
  3D applications, performance requirements, 4
  shading language, Cg characterized as, 4
Real-Time Shading Language (Stanford University), 22
Reality Lab (RenderMorphics company), 22
reciprocal function, 77

runtime (*continued*)

Cg (*continued*)

applications relationship to, 30

loading and compiling Cg programs with, 47

generation of Cg programs, 51

S

S3 company, 10

Salesin, David, 264

sampler1D type qualifier, 68

sampler2D type qualifier, 68

sampler3D type qualifier, 68

samplerCUBE type qualifier, 68

samplerRECT type qualifier, 68, 271, 272

samplers/sampling

objects, 67-68

textures, 67-70, 69

types, 68

saturate function, 210, 277

Savage3D (S3 company), 10

scalar/vector relationships, 71

scaling, 92

scattering

diffuse light, 106

fog, mathematics of, 236

in specular lighting, 107

Schlechtweg, Stefan, 264

scissor testing, 16

Segal, Mark, 264

Seidel, Hans-Peter, 142

semantics, 42-43

in Cg structures, 39

COLOR semantic, 42, 54, 66

errors, 49

initializing varying parameters with, 65

input, 44, 44-45, 45

not used with internal functions, 44

output, input vs., 44-45

POSITION semantic, 42, 44, 49, 65

PSIZE semantic, 153

of return values, handling of, 46

specification of variable values with, 63

(term description), 42

TEXCOORD0 semantic, 66

SGI (Silicon Graphics Inc.), 10, 22, 25

shade trees, 24, 35

concept and history of, 23-24

shaders/shading

algorithms, Cg translation of, 21

annotations to, 31

diffuse, toon shading use, 243

fragment profiles

ps_1_1, 55, 270

ps_1_2, 55, 270

ps_1_3, 55, 270

ps_2_0, 55, 271

ps_2_x, 55, 271

Gooch, Plate 30

Gouraud, 121

languages, 22

Cg relationship to, 2

hardware-amenable, 25

noninteractive, 23-25

RenderMan, 24

in Maya 4.5, Plate 1

multiple instancing of, 31

performance issues, 277

Phong, 122

skin, Plate 15

toon, 242-246, 242

implementing, 243

vertex profiles

vs_1_1, 47, 267-268

vs_2_0, 47, 269

vs_2_x, 47, 269

shadow mapping, 264

shadows/shadowing

adding to a scene, 255-258

mapping, 255-258

stencil-based, 16

shift operations, 72

shininess exponents, 108

Shreiner, Dave, 35, 141

side effects, 7

silhouette outlining, 245

Silicon Graphics

See SGI (Silicon Graphics Inc.)

structure(s) (*continued*)
    output (*continued*)
        out parameters vs., 84
        (term description), 39, 45
subtraction (-) operator, 71
surface(s)
    complex , 199
    curved, 91
    hidden, removal, 15
    -local coordinate systems, torus, 220
    tangent, binormal, and normal on, (equation),
        222
switch
    as unsupported reserved keyword, 132
swizzling, 113-115
    compositing use, 261
    smearing in, 114
    (term description), 19

T

tangent-space bump mapping
    See texture(s)/texturing, space, bump mapping
termination of program, 51
tessellation
    effects on lighting quality, 121
    vertex programs, importance of, 82
tex2D function, 69, 77
tex3Dproj function, 77
TEXCOORD0 semantic, 66
texCUBE function, 69, 77, 181
texels
    See Also texture(s)/texturing
    height field relationship to, 202
    storing data in, 201
texgen, 252
textures/texturing
    1D, encoding a step function in, 245
    accesses, vertex, errors, 49
    bump mapping, textured polygonal meshes, 224-
        229
    bump mapping use for representation of complex
        surfaces, 199
    coordinates

calculating, for projective texturing, 251
    sending, while sampling a texture, 69
cube map, 170-171
    images, 170
    lookup function, description and profile sup-
        port, 77
    lookup function, for chromatic dispersion, 195
decal
    accessing, 69
    blending reflections with, 175
    direction independence, 228
    lookups, 181
    (term description), 68
    uniform fog creation use, 239
double vision effects, 83-87
    results, 84
dynamic diffusion, Plate 22
encoding
    fog factor in, 241
    reflectivity in, 181
encoding functions as, performance advantages,
    276
expressions, and parameters, (chapter), 61-99
filtering specification, 31
homogeneous coordinates, 250
mapping, Plate 23
    functions, (appendix), 309
matrix, (term description), 252
normal map, storing bump maps as, 201
programmable fragment processor support, 19
projective, 248-255, 249
    calculating projective coordinates for, 251
    implementation, 251
querying, 68
sampling, 67-70
    lookup use, 69
    sending coordinates while, 69
space
    bump mapping, 213
    negative-area triangles caveats, 227
    orthogonality of object space caveats, 227
    per-vertex, 218
    zero-area triangles caveats, 227
type qualifiers for, 68

Addison-Wesley Warranty on the CD-ROM

Addison-Wesley warrants the enclosed disc to be free of defects in materials and faulty workmanship under normal use for a period of ninety days after purchase. If a defect is discovered in the disc during this warranty period, a replacement disc can be obtained at no charge by sending the defective disc, postage prepaid, with proof of purchase to:

> Editorial Department
> Addison-Wesley Professional
> Pearson Technology Group
> 75 Arlington Street, Suite 300
> Boston, MA 02116
> Email: AWPro@awl.com

Addison-Wesley makes no warranty or representation, either expressed or implied, with respect to this software, its quality, performance, merchantability, or fitness for a particular purpose. In no event will Addison-Wesley, its distributors, or dealers be liable for direct, indirect, special, incidental, or consequential damages arising out of the use or inability to use the software. The exclusion of implied warranties is not permitted in some states. Therefore, the above exclusion may not apply to you. This warranty provides you with specific legal rights. There may be other rights that you may have that vary from state to state. The contents of this CD-ROM are intended for personal use only, unless otherwise addressed under a separate license.

NVIDIA Statement on the Software

The source code provided is freely distributable, so long as the NVIDIA header remains unaltered and user modifications are detailed.

NO WARRANTY

THE SOFTWARE AND ANY OTHER MATERIALS PROVIDED BY NVIDIA ON THE ENCLOSED CD-ROM ARE PROVIDED "AS IS." NVIDIA DISCLAIMS ALL WARRANTIES, EXPRESS, IMPLIED OR STATUTORY, INCLUDING, WITHOUT LIMITATION, THE IMPLIED WARRANTIES OF TITLE, MERCHANTABILITY, FITNESS FOR A PARTICULAR PURPOSE AND NONINFRINGEMENT.

LIMITATION OF LIABILITY

NVIDIA SHALL NOT BE LIABLE TO ANY USER, DEVELOPER, DEVELOPER'S CUSTOMERS, OR ANY OTHER PERSON OR ENTITY CLAIMING THROUGH OR UNDER DEVELOPER FOR ANY LOSS OF PROFITS, INCOME, SAVINGS, OR ANY OTHER CONSEQUENTIAL, INCIDENTAL, SPECIAL, PUNITIVE, DIRECT OR INDIRECT DAMAGES (WHETHER IN AN ACTION IN CONTRACT, TORT OR BASED ON A WARRANTY), EVEN IF NVIDIA HAS BEEN ADVISED OF THE POSSIBILITY OF SUCH DAMAGES. THESE LIMITATIONS SHALL APPLY NOTWITHSTANDING ANY FAILURE OF THE ESSENTIAL PURPOSE OF ANY LIMITED REMEDY. IN NO EVENT SHALL NVIDIA'S AGGREGATE LIABILITY TO DEVELOPER OR ANY OTHER PERSON OR ENTITY CLAIMING THROUGH OR UNDER DEVELOPER EXCEED THE AMOUNT OF MONEY ACTUALLY PAID BY DEVELOPER TO NVIDIA FOR THE SOFTWARE OR ANY OTHER MATERIALS.

More information and updates are available at:
http://developer.nvidia.com
http://www.awprofessional.com/

Versions for other operating systems will be available at:
http://developer.nvidia.com/CgTutorial